Contents

Preface   xiii
Acknowledgments   xv

Part I Introduction and Strategic Landscape   *1*
  Big Data   1

Chapter 1 The Business Analytics Revolution   **3**
  Information Technology and Business Analytics   4
  The Need for a Business Analytics Strategy   5
  The Complete Business Analytics Team   6
  Section 1.1 Best Statistical Practice = Meatball Surgery   8
    Bad News and Good News   9
  Section 1.2 The Shape of Things to Come—Chapter
    Summaries   11
    PART I The Strategic Landscape—Chapters 1 to 6   11
    PART II Statistical QDR: Three Pillars for Best
      Statistical Practice—Chapters 7 to 9   13
    PART III Data CSM: Three Building Blocks for
      Supporting Analytics—Chapters 10 to 12   14
  Notes   15

Chapter 2 Inside the Corporation   **17**
  Section 2.1 Analytics in the Traditional Hierarchical
    Management Offense   18
    Leadership and Analytics   19
    Specialization   23
    Delegating Decisions   24
    Incentives   26
  Section 2.2 Corporate Analytics Failures—Shakespearean
    Comedy of Statistical Errors   27
    The Financial Meltdown of 2007–2008: Failures in Analytics   *27*

Fannie Mae: Next to the Bomb Blast   29
The Great Pharmaceutical Sales-Force Arms Race
   by Tom "T.J." Scott   35
Inside the Statistical Underground—Adjustment Factors
   for the Pharmaceutical Arms Race by Brian Wynne   37
Section 2.3 Triumphs of the Nerds   40
Proving Grounds—Model Review at The Associates/Citigroup   41
Predicting Fraud in Accounting: What Analytics-Based
   Accounting Has Brought to "Bare" by Hakan Gogtas, Ph.D.   43
Notes   46

Chapter 3 Decisions, Decisions   **49**
Section 3.1 Fact-Based Decision Making   **50**
Combining Industry Knowledge and Business Analytics   52
Critical Thinking   55
Section 3.2 Analytics-Based Decision Making: Four Acts in a
Greek Tragedy   **55**
Act I: Framing the Business Problem   56
Act II: Executing the Data Analysis   57
Act III: Interpreting the Results   58
Act IV: Making Analytics-Based Decisions   58
Consequences (of Tragedy)   58
Act V: Reviewing and Preparing for Future Decisions   59
Section 3.3 Decision Impairments: Pitfalls, Syndromes,
and Plagues in Act IV   **59**
Plague: Information and Disinformation Overload   59
Pitfall: Overanalysis   60
Pitfall: Oversimplification   61
Syndrome: Deterministic Thinking   61
Syndrome: Overdependence on Industry Knowledge   62
Pitfall: Tunnel Thinking   62
Syndrome: Overconfident Fool Syndrome   63
Pitfall: Unpiloted Big Bang Launches   63
Notes   64

Chapter 4 Analytics-Driven Culture   **67**
Left Brain–Right Brain Cultural Clash—Enter the Scientific Method   68
Denying the Serendipity of Statistics   70
Denying the Source—Plagiarism   70

Section 4.1 The Fertile Crescent: Striking It Rich   70
   Catalysts and Change   71
   Two-Trick Pony   73
Section 4.2 The Blend: Mixing Industry Knowledge and
  Advanced Analytics   74
   Cultural Imbalance   76
   The Gemini Myths   78
Notes   79

Chapter 5 Organization: The People Side of the Equation   83

Section 5.1 Analytics Resources   84
   Business Quants—Denizens of the Deep   88
   Analytics Power Users   89
   Business Analysts   89
   Knowledge Workers   89
Section 5.2 Structure of Analytics Practitioners   90
   Integration Synergies   91
   Technical Connectivity   91
   Specialization   91
   Teamwork   93
   Technical Compatibility   94
Section 5.3 Building Advanced Analytics Leadership   95
   Leadership and Management Skills   95
   Business Savvy   97
   Communication Skills   97
   Training and Experience   98
    On-Topic Leadership by Charlotte Sibley   *98*
   Expert Leaders (ELs)—Corporate Trump Cards   100
   The Blood-Brain Barrier   101
   Advantages of On-Topic Business Analytics Leaders 102
    Management Types by David Young   *103*
Section 5.4 Location, Location, Location of Analytics Practitioners 106
   Outsourcing Analytics   107
   Dispersed or Local Groups   108
   Central or Enterprise-Wide Groups   109
   Hybrid: Outside + Local + Enterprise-Wide   112
Notes   112

Chapter 6 Developing Competitive Advantage   115

    Approach for Identifying Gaps in Analytics   116
    Strategy   116
    Protecting Intellectual Property   116
   Section 6.1 Triage: Assessing Business Needs   **117**
    Process Mapping of Analytics Needs   117
    Innovation: Identifying New Killer Apps   120
    Scrutinizing the Inventory   121
    Assigning Rigor and Deducing Resources   123
   Section 6.2 Evaluating Analytics Prowess: The White-Glove Treatment   **126**
    Leading and Organizing   126
    Progress in Acculturating Analytics   127
    Evaluating Decision-Making Capabilities   127
    Evaluating Technical Coverage   127
    Executing Best Statistical Practice   128
    Constructing Effective Building Blocks   130
    Business Analytics Maturity Model   131
   Section 6.3 Innovation and Change from a Producer on the Edge   **131**
    Emphasis on Speed   132
    Continual Improvement   132
    Accelerating the Offense—For Those Who Are Struggling   133
   Notes   **135**

Part II The Three Pillars of Best Statistical Practice   137

    Blind Man's Russian Roulette Bluff   138

Chapter 7 Statistical Qualifications   139

   Section 7.1 Leadership and Communications for Analytics Professionals   **140**
    Leadership   140
    Communication   140
    Leadership and Communication Training   141
   Section 7.2 Training for Making Analytics-Based Decisions   **141**
    Statistical "Mythodologies"   143
   Section 7.3 Statistical Training for Performing Advanced Analytics   **144**
    The Benefits of Training   145
    Academic Training   146
    Post-Academic Training—Best Statistical Practice   149
    Training Through Review   149

Section 7.4 Certification for Analytics Professionals   150
   The PSTAT® (ASA) (Professional Statistician)—
     ASA's New Accreditation by Ronald L. Wasserstein, Ph.D.   *151*
   Professionalism   152
Notes   **153**

Chapter 8 Statistical Diagnostics   157
   The Model Overfitting Problem   158
Section 8.1 Overview of Diagnostic Techniques   **158**
   External Numbers   159
   Juxtaposing Results   160
   Data Splitting (Cross-Validation)   162
   Resampling Techniques with Replacement   162
     Standard Errors for Model-Based Group Differences:
     Bootstrapping to the Rescue by James W. Hardin, Ph.D.   *162*
   Simulation/Stress Testing   164
   Tools for Performance Measurement   165
   Tests for Statistical Assumptions   166
   Tests for Business Assumptions   166
   Intervals and Regions   166
   DoS (Design of Samples)   167
   DoE (Design of Experiments)   168
Section 8.2 Juxtaposition by Method   **168**
   Paired Statistical Models   169
Section 8.3 Data Splitting   **169**
   Coping with Hazards   171
   K-Fold Cross-Validation   172
   Sequential Validation (with Three or More Splits)   172
Notes   **174**

Chapter 9 Statistical Review—Act V   177
   Élan   178
   Qualifications and Roles of Reviewers   **179**
     Statistical Malpractice   *179*
Section 9.1 Purpose and Scope of the Review   **181**
   Purpose   182
   Scope   182
   Context   184
Section 9.2 Reviewing Analytics-Based Decision Making—
Acts I to IV   **185**
   Reviewing Qualifications of Analytics Professionals—
   Checking the Q in QDR   185

Restrictions Imposed on the Analysis   186
Appropriate and Reliable Data   186
Analytics Software   187
Reasonableness of Data Analysis Methodology   187
Reasonableness of Data Analysis Implementation   189
Statistical Diagnostics—Checking the D in QDR   190
Interpreting the Results (Transformation Back), Act III   190
Reviewing Analytics-Based Decision Making, Act IV   191
Closing Considerations—Documentation, Maintenance,
    Recommendations, and Rejoinder   191
Notes   **192**

Part III Building Blocks for Supporting Analytics   195

Chapter 10 Data Collection   197
Randomization   202
Interval and Point Estimation   202
Return on Data Investment   204
Measuring Information   204
Measurement Error   205
Section 10.1 Observational and Censual Data (No Design)   **206**
Section 10.2 Methodology for Anecdotal Sampling   **206**
Expert Choice   207
Quota Samples   208
    Dewey Defeats Truman   *208*
Focus Groups   208
Section 10.3 DoS (Design of Samples)   **209**
Sample Design   211
Simple Random Sampling   211
Systematic Sampling   212
Advanced Sample Designs   212
The Nonresponse Problem   212
Post-Stratifying on Nonresponse   214
Panels, Not to Be Confused with Focus Groups   215
Section 10.4 DoE (Design of Experiments)   **215**
Experimental Design   217
Completely Randomized Design   219
Randomized Block Design   219
Advanced Experimental Designs   220
Experimental Platforms   220
Notes   **220**

Chapter 11 Data Software **223**

Section 11.1 Criteria 228

Functional and Technical Capabilities 229

Maintenance 230

Governance and Misapplication 230

Fidelity 231

Efficiency and Flexibility 232

Section 11.2 Automation 233

Data Management 233

Data Analysis 233

Presenting Findings 233

Monitoring Results 234

Decision Making 234

Notes 234

Chapter 12 Data Management **237**

Information Strategy 238

Data Sources 238

Security 239

Section 12.1 Customer-Centric Data Management 239

Customer Needs 240

Data Quality—That "Garbage In, Garbage Out" Thing 240

Inspection 240

Data Repair 241

Section 12.2 Database Enhancements 242

Database Encyclopedia 243

Data Dictionaries 243

Variable Organization 245

Notes 247

Concluding Remarks **249**

Appendix: Exalted Contributors: Analytics Professionals **251**

References **253**

Index **257**

Preface

"… true learning must often be preceded by unlearning…"
—Warren Bennis

A Practitioner's Guide to Business Analytics is a how-to book for all those involved in business analytics—analytics-based decision makers, senior leadership advocating analytics, and those leading and providing data analysis. The book is written for this broad audience of analytics professionals and includes discussions on how to plan, organize, execute, and rethink the business. This is certainly not a "stat book" and, hence, will not talk about performing statistical analysis.

The book's objective is to help others build a corporate infrastructure to better support analytics-based decisions. It is hard to judge a book by its cover. To get a feel for the book, look at Figure 6.1 on p. 117, which shows types of business analytics that can support decision making. Table 6.2 on p. 118 provides a glimpse of how to organize business analytics projects. Figure 6.4 on p. 123 depicts how to assess the relative technical difficulties of a set of business problems. Do these items complement how you think about your business?

There is a tremendous opportunity to improve analytics-based decision making. This book is designed to help those who believe in business analytics to better organize and focus their efforts. We will discuss practical considerations in how to better facilitate analytics. This will include a blend of the big-picture strategy and specifics of how to better execute the tactics. Many of these topics are not discussed elsewhere. This journey will require continually updating the corporate infrastructure. At the center of these enhancements is placing the right personnel in the right roles.

This book serves to enrich the conversation as the reference book you can take into planning sessions. It is usually difficult to find a reference that addresses the specifics of what to do. This is largely because one size does not fit all. The first part of the book provides insights into how we can update our infrastructure; the second part provides three pillars for measuring the quality of analytics and analytics-based decisions; and part three addresses three building blocks for supporting Business Analytics. This book has a great deal of breadth so that professionals, despite not possibly being on the same page, can at least be in the same book.

The recommendations in this book are based upon the cumulative experience of analytics professionals incorporating analytics in numerous corporations—Best Statistical Practice. This book contains 12 sidebars relating experiences from the field and viewpoints on how to best apply analytics to the business. The more you get excited about new ideas, the more you are going to enjoy this insight-intensive book.

Finally, I wish to add that the way companies approach analytics is evolving. Big Data is accelerating this evolution. I fully expect disagreements and respect different opinions,[1] and so should you. To optimize your reading experience, you should retain those ideas that fit into how you think about your business, and leave on the shelf, for now, those ideas that do not complement your approach. Do you want to win? Do you want your company to gain market share? Of course you do. Now is your opportunity to take your game to the next level!

Notes

1. This is a contentious topic and I will not go unscathed.

Acknowledgments

It takes a team effort to write a book by yourself. I am indebted to Isaac "Boom Boom" Abiola, Ph.D.; Jennifer Ashkenazy; Cynthia "Wei" Huang Bartlett, M.D.; Sigvard Bore; Bertrum Carroll; H. T. David, Ph.D.; Karen Fender; Les Frailey; Hakan Gogtas, Ph.D.; James W. Hardin, Ph.D.; Anand Madhaven; Girish Malik; Gaurav Mishra; Robert A. Nisbet, Ph.D.; Sivaramakrishnan Rajagopalan; Douglas A. Samuelson, D.Sc.; Tom "T.J." Scott; Prateek Sharma; Charlotte Sibley; W. Robert Stephenson, Ph.D.; Jennifer Thompson; Ronald L. Wasserstein, Ph.D.; Brian Wynne; and David Young. Their specific contributions are listed in the Appendix. A reviewed book provides a better reading experience.

Part I

Introduction and Strategic Landscape

The ambition of this book is to take up the challenging task of addressing how to adapt the corporation to compete on Business Analytics (BA). We share discoveries on how to transform the corporation to thrive in an analytics environment. We cover the breadth of the topic so that this book may serve as a practical guide for those working to better leverage analytics, to make analytics-based decisions.

Big Data

There has been a great deal of large talk about Big Data. One sensible definition of Big Data is that it comprises high-volume, high-velocity, and/or high-variety (including unstructured) information assets.[1] The threshold beyond which data becomes **Big** is relative to a corporation's capabilities. As we grow our abilities, the challenges of Big Data diminish. The application of the term, Big Data, is evolving to include Business Analytics and the term is overused at the moment, so we will write plainly.

The opportunity stems from the volume, velocity, and variety of the information content. This torrent of information is collected in new ways using new technologies. It can add a different perspective and provide synergy when combined with traditional sources of information. This new information has stimulated fresh ideas and a fresh perspective on (1) how business analytics fits into our business model; and (2) how we can adapt our business model to facilitate better analytics-based decisions.

The first challenge is to wrestle the data into a warehouse. This involves collecting, treating, and storing high-volume, high-velocity, and high-variety data. We address these growing needs by improving our operational efficiencies for handling the data. Although Business Analytics can help in a data-reduction and organizational capacity,[2] this is largely an IT issue and not the subject of this book. IT has introduced exciting new solutions for expanding hardware and software capabilities. Brute force alone, such as continually purchasing hardware, is not a long-term plan for avoiding the Big Data abyss.

The second challenge is to handle the explosion of information extracted from the data. This is largely a business analytics issue and it is addressed by this book. If the volume, velocity, and variety of the data are difficult to manage, then how well are we handling the volume, velocity, and variety of the information? Previous authors have made the case for improving Business Analytics. One implication of Big Data is that we need to accelerate our development of BA.

This book's best practices will facilitate increasing our capabilities for performing Business Analytics and integrating the information into analytics-based decisions. Part I of this book will inform our strategic thinking, enabling us to develop a more effective plan.

1

The Business Analytics Revolution

"All revolutions are impossible till they happen, then they become inevitable."

—Michael Tigar[3]

We are poised to enter a new Information Renaissance that involves making smarter analytics-based decisions. A grove of recent books[4] and articles has made the case for competing based upon *business analytics* (BA). These books reveal a potpourri of success stories illustrating the value proposition.

It took a generation or longer to take full advantage of some past technological revolutions, such as the automobile, electricity, and the computer. Business analytics has been introduced to corporations, yet most lack the infrastructure to fully capitalize on the abundance of high quality decision-making information. This progression requires significant changes. Foremost among these are changes in personnel, organization, and corporate culture. The right infrastructure will facilitate moving from tactical applications hither and yon, to integrating analytics into the corporation.

Recent interest in business analytics has been characterized by a growing awareness of analytics applications, mature IT (Information Technology), ubiquitous electronic data collection devices, increasingly sophisticated decision makers, more data-junkie senior leadership, shorter information shelf life, and "Big Data."[5] We are experiencing such a deluge of data that, in the future, there is the potential for corporations to be buried in it.

Corporate concerns arising from the inefficient use of analytics extend beyond just leaving money on the table because of missed opportunities. Ineffective corporations will not see "it" coming—their demise. They will not know why they suddenly lost their customers one night or why their product is still on the shelves. They will have the data to explain it, yet they will struggle to put the pieces together in time because they will not be prepared. In addition to the need to face Big Data, there is a second layer to the problem. Corporations will continue to be awash in dirty data and filthy information. In a future emergency, they will race to clean the data, filter information from misinformation, and interpret the findings.

In this book, we dispel stubborn myths and provide a perspective for understanding the organization, the planning, and the tools needed for business analytics superstardom. We have seen analytics in the trenches of effective and ineffective corporations. We leverage the perspectives of analytics professionals charged with making it happen—that is, those leading their corporations in how to apply analytics, those basing decisions upon analytics, and those providing data analysis.

Business Intelligence = Information Technology + Business Analytics[6]

Information Technology and Business Analytics

Information technology and business analytics both involve professionals leveraging data to provide business insights, which, in turn, facilitate better decisions. They provide complementary benefits, and we emphasize the synergy of the two.

IT involves data collection, security, integrity, management, and reporting. It begins with gathering data and ends with either constructing a data warehouse or with using the data warehouse

> **Concept Box**
>
> *Information technology—*
> Gathering and managing data to build a data warehouse and providing data pulls, reports, and dashboards. (Bringing the data to the business)
>
> *Business analytics*—Leveraging data analysis and business savvy to make analytics-based business decisions. (Bringing the business questions to the data)

for data pulls, reports, and dashboards. In reporting, IT measures a consistent set of metrics to track business performance and guide planning. IT places a great deal of emphasis on efficiency.

BA is focused upon supporting and making business decisions by connecting business problems to data analysis—analytics. It tends to work from the business need to the available or potentially available data. BA involves reporting, exploratory data analysis, and complex data analysis, and in our definition, we include analytics-based decision making. We want to minimize the distance between the decision and the analytics. BA overlaps with IT with regard to reporting. While IT emphasizes efficiency and reliability in creating standardized reports that address predetermined key performance indicators, BA scrutinizes the reports based upon statistical techniques and business savvy. The BA skill set is valuable for determining and rethinking how these key performance indicators meet the business needs. Additionally, the BA skill set includes statistical tools such as quality control charts and other confidence intervals, techniques that certainly enhance reports for making better decisions.

BA is concerned with scrutinizing the data. To this end, it recognizes nuances or problems with the numbers and traces them back through the data pipeline to discover what these numbers really mean. BA includes complex data collection, such as statistical sampling, designed experiments, and simulations. These endeavors need mathematical, statistical, and algorithmic tools.

We can discern IT and BA by their skills sets; their software; and their respective locations in the corporation. IT has a stronger computer software theme, and BA is about data analysis and analytics-based decision making. IT usually reports to a CIO. BA often resides in or near the same division as business operations, closer to the business decisions. BA and IT provide an important synergy. It is difficult to have BA without IT.

We want to redefine the BA team to make it more inclusive and close the distance between making decisions that are based upon analytics and performing data analysis to support these decisions.

The Need for a Business Analytics Strategy

Running a large corporation can be compared to flying a commercial jet in a storm. Industry knowledge is the equivalent of looking out the windows, while analytics and advanced analytics—tracking, monitoring, and data analysis—comprise the various gauges, monitoring equipment, and warning devices. In some corporations, tracking reports and data analysis cannot withstand the tiniest scrutiny. This means that some portion of the corporation's information is fallacious, and, thus, so are some of the decisions based upon this misinformation. The promise of analytics is to provide better facts and to facilitate better analytics-based decision making.

Our world is becoming more complex at a dramatic rate, and our brains[7] ... not so much. The importance of data analysis has crept up on our corporations over the past decades. Data is now available in abundance, and our analysis needs range from being straightforward to being extremely complex. We want to better integrate business analytics into the decision making process and thus be able to better compete in the marketplace. We want to meet the quickening pace of decision making, the increased business complexity, and the deluge of Big Data. Analytics-based decision making is essential for making the big decisions and thousands of little ones.

A history of business failures underscores the need to master how to compete based upon business analytics. One highly developed application of analytics is in estimating risk and revealing how to manage it. Many of those corporations that fared the best during the 2007–2008 financial meltdown made better analytics-based decisions. First, they validated, reviewed, and refined their risk models. Second, they understood their models well enough to believe them and interpret them in the face of human behavior. To return to our commercial jet example, they understood their instruments well enough to make sense out of them when looking out the window provided the wrong answer. AIG,[8] Fannie Mae, Freddie Mac, Citigroup, Bear Stearns, Lehman Brothers, Merrill Lynch, WAMU, Fitch Ratings, Moody's, and Standard & Poor's were all competing based upon analytics in a prominent manner. At the time, they might not have realized the extent to which their fortunes and their reputations were exposed to their ability to leverage business analytics into their decision making.

The Complete Business Analytics Team

Facing the next phase of the Information Age will require rethinking decision management. The turnaround time allowed for making decisions is decreasing. The amounts of data and the amounts of misinformation are

Table 1.1 Components of the Complete Business Analytics Team

Position	Role
Analytics sponsors(investors)	Business leaders sponsoring analytics, ranging from mid-level to CEO.
Decision makers and Knowledge workers(consumers)	Decision makers ranging from ordinary to those who are more sophisticated in leveraging analytics for their decisions. Knowledge workers who leverage analytics results in their work.
Business analysts and Business quants(practitioners)	Business analysts and business quants leading and performing most of the data analysis.
Directors of analytics(directors)	Managers of those performing data analysis, ranging from ordinary to those with greater analytics sophistication—practice experience.

rising. We need to extend the business analytics team to include senior leaders investing in analytics, those consuming the information, those performing the data analyses, and those directing these practitioners. We must include analytics professionals, who value statistical and mathematical analysis and yet their job might not call upon them to perform data analysis. By including everyone involved, we can foster more cohesion between decision makers, corporate leaders, and those supplying the data analyses. Also, we need to extend the analytics conversation about how we can apply analytics to the business. In Table 1.1, we introduce four basic functional roles.

Our experience has shown that we need sophisticated analytics-based decision makers and directors of analytics with strong quantitative training to meet our business analytics needs. Six Sigma has demonstrated that (1) we must have leadership advocating change, (2) we can change our culture to better leverage analytics in decision making, and (3) it is impracticable to train all of our employees to perform data analysis. Instead, we need to build a specialized group of business analysts and business quants to provide the data analysis. Organizing and expanding the business analytics team will lead to making the other infrastructural changes needed for BA superstardom.

Section 1.1 Best Statistical Practice = Meatball Surgery

"Most people use statistics the way a drunkard uses a lamp post, more for support than illumination."

—Mark Twain

Best Statistical Practice (BSP) is our term for our evolving wisdom acquired from solving business analytics problems in the field. We must perform a data analysis within the context of the business need. This need includes addressing considerations of **Timeliness**, **Client Expectation**, **Accuracy**, **Reliability**, and **Cost**. We perform the data analysis within these constraints using statistics, mathematics, and software algorithms. These tools provide business insights that support analytics-based decision making.[9]

Through experimentation, and some trial and error, we find solutions that are fast, client suitable, accurate, reliable, and affordable enough to meet business needs. We call this ongoing experimentation, **The Great Applied Statistics Simulation**. Hence, the cumulative wisdom of Best Statistical Practice includes our understanding of how to execute techniques quickly, how to meet the client expectation, what information is needed to make the analytics-based decisions, how well techniques perform for certain applications, how to measure the accuracy and reliability of the data analysis, how we can best leverage the serendipity of data analysis, and how we can provide analyses inexpensively.

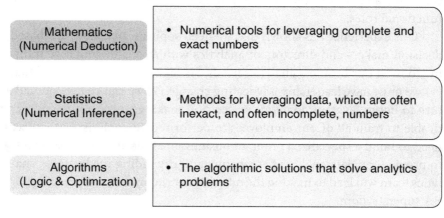

Figure 1.1 Business analytics workbench

Much of our learning comes from performing autopsies (Chapter 9) on failed and on successful analytics-based decisions and data analyses. We infer the best techniques, judge the right amount of rigor, develop our business savvy, and foster the synergism between our training and our experience. We measure the performance of decisions and techniques where possible and extrapolate these findings to where it is impossible to measure performance. For example, a generation of analytics professionals mastered building predictive models on high-quality banking data. Then they applied their refined techniques to other applications and to industries where the data quality was too weak to facilitate mastering the techniques.

Best Statistical Practice consists of know-how built upon this continual learning, which, in turn, facilitates faster, better, and less expensive analytics-based decisions. It protects us from hazards that we can not anticipate.[10] We further develop our BSP by improving our training, our tools, and our understanding of the business problem. This enables us to make great advances in expanding our capabilities. Finally, we need to keep in mind that the three most expensive data analyses continue to be the faulty ones, the absent ones, and the ones nobody uses. The most expensive decisions are those that fail to leverage the available information.

We wish to emphasize that analyzing the data is a technical problem within the business analytics problem. The complete problem includes the broader business needs: Timeliness, Client Expectation, Accuracy, Reliability, and Cost. We must solve the analytics problem within these constraints and work toward an infrastructure that will ease them. Our academic training ignores these business constraints, thus making it imperative that we adapt the theory to practice. BSP, combined with good quantitatively trained leadership, facilitates speed and helps avoid both under-analysis and overanalysis. Quantitatively trained leaders can be relied upon to understand the trade-offs involved in cutting corners to perform the analysis within the broader business constraints.

The last six chapters of this book provide the tools necessary to perform Best Statistical Practice.

Bad News and Good News

First the bad news—all the exciting breakthroughs about leveraging analytics to create space-age nanite technology and revolutionize business are full of embellishments intended to impress us and the shareholders.

Corporations are not as sophisticated or as successful as we might grasp from the sound bytes appearing in conferences, books, and journals. Instead opinion-based decision making, statistical malfeasance, and counterfeit analysis are pandemic. We are swimming in make-believe analytics.

One major part of the problem is that corporations have difficulty measuring the quality of their decisions and the quality of their data analyses. To measure these, we often need a second layer of data analyses. This is one of the most disquieting problems because, just like brain surgery, it takes a second brain surgeon to figure out if the first brain surgeon is working the correct lobe. Even with the best analysis, it is very difficult to measure the quality of some decisions and some data analyses.

At present, there is a rather large gap between obtaining the right data analysis for a decision and actually making the decision. A great deal of good data analysis is misdirected and fails to drive the business. Some of this misdirection suits special interests that want the results to match preset conclusions.[11] Meanwhile, it is difficult for others to recognize when there is a disconnect between the data analysis and the decision.

Now for some good news—this is all one gigantic opportunity and we can easily make substantial progress. Business analytics can build enormous competitive advantages and promote innovation. Analytics simplifies the overwhelming complexity of information[12] and decreases misinformation emissions. Finally, less is more. A tremendous amount of analytics and advanced analytics can be omitted. The trick is to discern what we need from what we want.

The current generation of business analysts and business quants are up to the technical challenges, and they have made incredible breakthroughs. For example, applying predictive models to banking has built more intelligent banks, which is contrasted by the fatal opinion-based decisions and sloppy analyses involved in the financial meltdown of 2007–2008. Also, today's statistical software has evolved in efficiency and capabilities. Finally, for most corporations, IT has matured and can inexpensively provide the data. We have the talent, we have the software, and the data is overflowing.

Section 1.2 The Shape of Things to Come—Chapter Summaries

The corporate pacemaker has quickened and analytics is wanted to speed up and improve decisions. The ambitions of this book are to provide insight into how analytics can be improved within the corporation, and to address the major opportunities for corporations to better leverage analytics.

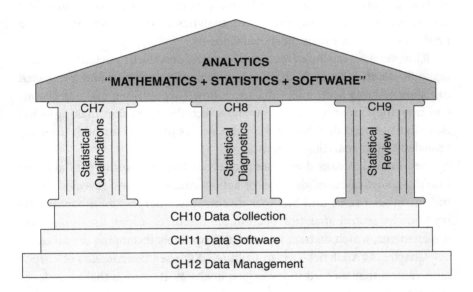

PART I The Strategic Landscape—Chapters 1 to 6

Part I discusses the infrastructure needed to fully leverage analytics in the corporation. We will discuss changes in corporate culture, personnel, organization, leadership, and planning.

Chapter 2, "Inside the Corporation," discusses analytics inside the corporation based upon experience from both successes and failures. Section 2.1 discusses how corporations employ a Hierarchical Management Offense (HMO), which centralizes authority and decision-making. We will discuss how the right calibration of Leadership, Specialization, Delegation, and Incentives can nurture analytics. We outline the typical leaders who support analytics. We note that advanced analytics is a specialization and discuss the implications of this in a corporate environment. We review good delegation practices, pointing out that more authority and decision making must be delegated to those close to the tacit information. Analytics is a team sport, best encouraged in a meritocracy with team incentives in place.

Section 2.2 provides notorious examples of failure due to the sloppy implementation of analytics. We review failures at Fannie Mae, AIG, Moody's, Standard & Poor's, the pharmaceutical industry, among others. Section 2.3 provides examples of triumphs in statistics. These include a success story in reviewing predictive analytics at The Associates/Citi and predicting fraud at PricewaterhouseCoopers.

Chapter 3, "Decisions, Decisions," underscores the importance of leveraging the facts. It notes the schism between opinion-based and fact-based decision making. Section 3.1 discusses how corporations make decisions and how they incorporate data analysis into their decision making—that is, analytics-based decision making. It clarifies the need for both industry knowledge and analytics expertise.

Section 3.2 breaks down the process of integrating the data analysis into the analytics-based decision or action. Autopsies have revealed where the mistakes occur, and we will discuss the interplay between industry knowledge and analytics. Section 3.3 discusses a long list of decision impairments, which distract us from appropriately leveraging the facts.

Chapter 4, "Analytics-Driven Culture," discusses the contents of corporate cultures that succeed in leveraging analytics. It clarifies that analytics is transferrable across all industries.[13] Section 4.1 discusses what is involved in an analytics-driven corporate culture and how such cultures arise. Section 4.2 helps us to better think about blending analytics and industry expertise. It also illustrates that corporations tend to understate analytics in that blend.

Chapter 5, "Organization: The People Side of the Equation," discusses the composition (Section 5.1), structure (Section 5.2), leadership (Section 5.3), and location (Section 5.4) of analytics teams within the corporation. We note the difference between management and leadership as illustrated by Warren Bennis in his book *On Becoming a Leader*.

Chapter 6, "Developing Competitive Advantage," is the lynchpin of this book. It discusses how to assess a corporation's analytics needs (Section 6.1) and evaluate its prowess (Section 6.2). In Section 6.1, we outline how to assess the analytics needs of the corporation and translate that into a strategic analytics plan. This plan will clarify the corporation's needs on an annual basis. Next, in Section 6.2, we lead the reader through evaluating the analytics capabilities of the corporation. The difference between the needs and capabilities is the gap to be addressed. Section 6.3 discusses aggressive measures for pursuing the wanted analytics capabilities.

PART II Statistical QDR: Three Pillars for Best Statistical Practice—Chapters 7 to 9

Part II of this book introduces Statistical QDR—the three pillars for Best Statistical Practice. These pillars—Statistical Qualifications (Chapter 7), Statistical Diagnostics (Chapter 8), and Statistical Review (Chapter 9)— enable the corporation to measure the quality of the analytics-based decisions and the data analyses. This is the methodology behind Best Statistical Practice. These tools create the momentum for continually improving the analytics-based decisions and analytics, and they measure our performance in delivering the same. In short, they allow us to "fly on instruments" in poor visibility.[14] At least one analytics practitioner should be responsible for overseeing and continually improving each of these pillars.

Chapter 7, "Statistical Qualifications," discusses the qualifications necessary to be competent in making analytics-based decisions and performing advanced analytics—including those qualifications needed for reviewers of this work. Section 7.1 reinforces the idea that leadership and communication skills are an essential part of performing analytics. Section 7.2 discusses the needs and training for more sophisticated decision makers and presents the training required for digesting statistical results.

Section 7.3 discusses the advantages of applied statistical training. The delay in certifying statisticians for so many decades has facilitated charlatanism and a credibility problem. Section 7.4 makes the case for certifying those who are qualified to analyze your data.

Chapter 8, "Statistical Diagnostics," discusses the Statistical Diagnostics that business analysts and business quants should apply and decision makers should recognize. Here we list the usual suspects and focus on a few effective techniques. Section 8.1 outlines the various Statistical Diagnostics needed for pursuing success. Section 8.2 discusses applying multiple solutions to solve the same business analytics problem. Section 8.3 discusses the family of Data Splitting techniques, whereby we partition the data into development datasets and validation datasets—the latter are also called control or hold-out datasets.

Chapter 9, "Statistical Review—Act V," discusses what is involved in reviewing analytics-based decisions and data analyses. Section 9.1 discusses the considerations going into the purpose and scope of the review. Section 9.2 discusses the nuances of reviewing the analytics-based decisions and the data analyses.

PART III Data CSM: Three Building Blocks for Supporting Analytics—Chapters 10 to 12

The transition toward an analytics-driven culture requires a number of infrastructural changes. Part III discusses the three usual soft spots that, when poorly managed, hold corporations back. Every analytics professional will recognize the importance of these three building blocks: Data Collection (Chapter 10), Data Software (Chapter 11), and Data Management (Chapter 12)—Data CSM. However, time after time corporations fail to adequately cover these areas. At least one analytics professional should be responsible for overseeing and continually improving each of them. We will clarify what is getting overlooked and dispel the usual myths.

Chapter 10, "Data Collection," discusses "the matter with" data collection. Most corporations have weak data collection abilities. They rely upon the data to find them. We will discuss the application of Design of Samples (DoS); Design of Experiments (DoE); and simulation, and juxtapose the characteristics of these techniques with those of observational, censual, and anecdotal data. Section 10.1 discusses analysis of observational or censual data—the context for data mining, where the data tend to find us. Section 10.2 discusses anecdotal means of collecting information. Section 10.3 discusses the advantages of randomly selecting a representative subset from a population—DoS. Section 10.4 discusses the advantages of randomly assigning treatments (or factors) to a representative subset from a population—DoE.

Chapter 11, "Data Software," communicates the advantages of a complementary suite of data processing and analysis software tools. Section 11.1 discusses the criteria we consider for designing a suite of software tools for manipulating data. It clarifies the importance of software breadth and emphasizes using the right tool to solve the right problem. Section 11.2 discusses the productivity benefits of automated software.

Chapter 12, "Data Management," closes the book with a discussion about what all analytics professionals need to know about organizing and maintaining the data. Datasets are corporate assets and need to be managed to full effect. Section 12.1 discusses the usual data-consumer needs that corporations overlook. Section 12.2 presents a number of database enhancements that will make the data a more valuable asset.

Although these chapters build upon each other, the interested reader might skip ahead to those chapters most relevant to their needs. Chapters 2 – 4 are burdened by providing support for the more impactful later chapters.

Notes

1. "3D Data Management: Controlling Data Volume, Velocity and Variety" by Douglas, Laney. Gartner. Retrieved 6 February 2001, and "The Importance of 'Big Data': A Definition" by Douglas, Laney. Gartner. Retrieved 21 June 2012.
2. In some situations, the winner is the first corporation to learn just enough from the data.
3. "The Trials of Henry Kissinger" (2003).
4. To name a few: *Competing on Analytics* by Harris and Davenport; *Super Crunchers* by Ian Ayres; *Data Driven* by Thomas Redman, and; *The Deciding Factor* by Rosenberger, Nash, and Graham; and *Business Analytics For Managers* by Laursen & Thorlund.
5. Today's "Big Data" was unimaginable ten years ago. We expect tomorrow's datasets to be even more complicated.
6. There are many definitions of Business Intelligence; while less popular, this one is convenient for our purposes.
7. Oh, our Stone-Age brains. Our brains have not evolved a great deal during the last hundreds of thousands of years.
8. See "The Man Who Crashed the World," *Vanity Fair*, August 2009.
9. We will use the term "statistical" slightly more often because we want to keep in mind the uncertainty and the inherent unreliability of data.
10. We do not need to always know exactly how every decision or analysis will fail. In many situations, it is sufficient to know what works and under what circumstances it works.
11. Like in a court case where each side starts with a conclusion and works backward—that being the appropriate direction.
12. When analytics is making things more complex, then we are doing it wrong.
13. In statistician-speak, statistics, mathematics, and algorithmic software are invariate to industry.
14. A side benefit is that these tools expose charlatans, or alternatively, force them to work harder to fool us.

2

Inside the Corporation

"There is one rule for the industrialist and that is: Make the best quality of goods possible at the lowest cost possible, paying the highest wages possible."

—Henry Ford

A corporation is an association of individuals—share holders, embodying their private financial interests, yet possessing distinct powers and liabilities independent of its members. It can be a "legal person"[1] with the right to litigate, hold assets, hire agents, sign contracts, etc. Over the years, corporations have needed to adapt to changing technology. To keep up with the Information Age, their assets have shifted toward intellectual property, company know-how, and more specialized knowledge-based professionals. The promise of business analytics will require greater changes. **We will never fully leverage business analytics without changing the corporate infrastructure—culture, leadership, organization, and planning!**[2]

In this chapter, we address some characteristics of corporations that affect how well they can leverage analytics. We discuss the role of analytics inside the corporation. In the last two sections, we share a number of failures and successes in applying business analytics.

Section 2.1 Analytics in the Traditional Hierarchical Management Offense

"I didn't dictate ever because I really felt that creativity doesn't come from dictation, it comes from emancipation."

—Pen Densham[3]

*"'Politics' comes from the Greek root **poly** meaning many and **ticks** meaning blood sucking parasites."*

—The Smothers Brothers

The Hierarchical Management Offense (HMO) centralizes power and decision making. It is characterized by a vertical reporting structure serving as "ductwork," dispensing directives downward and vacuuming information upward. The speed and accuracy of communications moving up and down depends on the length and quality of the vertical chains of relationships. More hierarchy means that politics can have a greater impact on analytics … and everything else.

Leadership, Specialization, Delegation, and Incentives are pivot points for calibrating the emphasis placed upon analytics. Leadership that embraces analytics-based decision making produces better decisions. Specialization facilitates more efficient and effective analytics. Delegating decisions moves the decision closer to the tacit information and expertise. Aligned Incentive structures encourage the most productive behavior. These pivot points facilitate some immediate adjustments to the corporate culture (see Chapter 4), which can increase the productivity of knowledge-based professionals.

During the progression of the Information Age, we have seen dramatic growth in IT to keep pace. Most corporations have built large, efficient data warehouses. One expectation is that the next phase will focus on better leveraging this information—this investment. This will involve a new Information Renaissance, using business analytics to make smarter analytics-based decisions. The role of analytics inside the corporation will need to be redefined and expanded. It would be easier if corporations could enhance their business analytics capabilities while changing nothing about their current business model. They would prefer to alter analytics so that it will fit their approach. They want analytics to sell in a sales culture, to manufacture in a manufacturing culture, and to build things in an engineering culture. This is reasonable up to a point. However, facilitating analytics requires change; if only because it is intertwined with the decision-making process. Complete rigidity against adapting the corporate structure will dilute the value of analytics.

> *"General, where is your division?"*
>
> —General Nathan Shanks Evans

> *"Dead on the field."*
>
> —General John Bell Hood

Leadership and Analytics

To succeed in applying analytics, leadership must correctly judge the merits of analytics and how to best integrate this information into corporate decision making. There are a number of leadership roles that enhance or retard a corporation's analytical capabilities. We will describe five general leadership roles: Enterprise-Wide Advocates, Mid-Level Advocates, Ordinary Managers of Analytics, Expert Leaders, and On-Topic Business Analytics Leaders.

The first two roles are advocates of analytics; they are investors in the technology. The remaining three roles direct those performing the data analysis. We find that leaders vary dramatically in the degree to which they encourage analytics. Those most enthusiastic are likely to have a history of successfully leveraging analytics—data junkies. Some lead with their own analytics-based decision making. Such a background makes it more likely that they will push the company to the next plateau in applying analytics.

Enterprise-Wide Advocates put forth the corporate vision and find the resources to make it happen. The formal name of the Enterprise-Wide Advocates is up for grabs. The ubiquitous CIOs are in the running. The less common Chief Economists would be appropriate leaders. Also, there are burgeoning new roles, such as Chief Analytics Officer or Chief Statistical Officer. In Section 5.3, we will discuss the leadership of an enterprise-wide analytics group. Enterprise-Wide Advocates are in a position to:

1. Promote examples of applying analytics-based decision-making (Chapter 3)—thus, building an analytics-based or data-driven culture (Chapter 4).
2. Take an interest in the analytics team's organization (Chapter 5).

Table 2.1 Analytics Professionals with Leadership Responsibilities

Talent	Role	Credentials
Investors		
Enterprise-Wide Advocates	Corporate-level business leaders	Corporate-wide authority to influence the business.
Mid-Level Advocates	Unit-level business leaders	Unit-wide authority to influence the business.
Directors		
Ordinary Managers of Analytics	Managers for business analysts and quants	Light training in analytics; discussed in 5.3.
Expert Leaders	Leaders for business analytics projects, for small teams, and for providing leadership during a crisis	Medium to heavy training in analytics; discussed in 5.3.
Expert Leaders	Leaders for Business Analysts & Quants	Medium to heavy training in analytics; discussed in 5.3.

3. Embrace a corporate business analytics plan and make certain that corporate capabilities are evaluated (Chapter 6).

4. Insist that important analyses be performed by professionals with Statistical Qualifications, using Statistical Diagnostics, and with Statistical Review (Chapters 7 to 9).

5. Build and maintain the Data Collection, Data Software, and Data Management infrastructure (Chapters 10 to 12).

6. Remove conflicts of interest and encourage objective analysis, which might or might not fit preconceived conclusions.

7. Select like-minded mid-level managers—shrewdly.

8. "Manage a meritocracy," as mentioned in *Competing on Analytics*.[4]

9. Spread breakthroughs in statistical practice across the entire corporation.

10. Ensure one source of the facts, different corporate units are entitled to their own opinions just not their own facts.

11. Set the tone as to the value of analytics.

Mid-Level Advocates are critical for projecting analytics into the appropriate areas of the business—putting the corporate vision in motion. They can

1. Embrace and advocate analytics-based decision making as the way we do business (Chapter 3)—thus, affirming an analytics-driven culture (Chapter 4).
2. Take an interest in the analytics team's organization (Chapter 5).
3. Embrace a corporate business analytics plan and make certain that corporate capabilities are evaluated (Chapter 6).
4. Insist that important analyses be performed by professionals with Statistical Qualifications, using Statistical Diagnostics, and with Statistical Review (Chapters 7 to 9).
5. Build and maintain the Data Collection, Data Software; and Data Management infrastructure (Chapter 10 to 12).
6. Uphold the meritocracy.
7. Increase the involvement of analytics professionals.
8. Recognize and reward training.
9. Recognize statistical analysis as intellectual property.
10. Quell resistance to analytics.

Typically, when a corporation has an Enterprise-Wide Advocate, it will have or find Mid-Level Advocates. This complete structure does the most to integrate analytics into the business.[5] If a corporation lacks an Enterprise-Wide Advocate but possesses a Mid-Level Advocate, then there will be a pocket of analytics behind them.[6] This pocket will have markedly less impact throughout the company.

Directors of those performing data analysis (business analysts and business quants) fall within a spectrum of management and leadership skills combined with analytics competence (Section 5.3). We will discuss three roles in this book: **Ordinary Managers of Analytics, Expert Leaders**, and **On-Topic Business Analytics Leaders**. We define the Ordinary Managers of Analytics as those with the authority to direct analytics resources, yet who possess less training in business analytics than those who perform it. An Expert Leader is someone with the training and experience to lead analytics, yet less leadership authority. Finally, the On-Topic Business Analytics Leader has the authority, training, and experience—a triple threat.

These three roles are charged with anticipating the information needs of decision makers and building an infrastructure that can meet these needs on a timely basis. Corporations have schedules and must make and remake decisions based upon whatever information is available. The Ordinary Managers of Analytics tend to be less engaged in the analytics. The concerns are that they will think about the business from a perspective that is too light on analytics and that they will miss critical opportunities. These managers must delegate shrewdly in order to be successful in analytics. Most of them will spend a great deal of time managing up[7]—this is probably more comfortable for them. We are concerned that they will not spend enough effort leading the analytics practitioners because they might not be as comfortable with that aspect of the role.

Next, we consider an informal leadership role—the Expert Leader. We define an Expert Leader as someone regarded as knowledgeable of the business, competent in analytics, and possessing leadership skills. This makes this person "bilingual"[8]—quant and business. They comprehend the specialization. They can review an analysis; find mistakes or weak points; and construe its reliability.

A corporation can have several Expert Leaders. They possess business analytics expertise, yet with less formal people management authority. They are sometimes informally "chosen" by the other analytical professionals to boost the leadership and to fill a void as a spokesperson or decision maker. They support the other analytical professionals, and they maintain the integrity of the science.

By granting more formal leadership authority to an Expert Leader, we can derive:

Business Analytics Leader[9] = Expert Leader + Formal Authority

This is a bilingual role with sufficient formal authority and business analytics expertise.

Expert Leaders and Business Analytics Leaders are necessarily trained on the topic of analytics. They can better identify talent and judge results. They understand "best practices" and can skillfully lead a team of practitioners. It is not just about technical ability; it is the way they think. They can think more statistically about the business problem. They have greater appreciation for getting the numbers right and they create less burden on the other analytics professionals on their team. These skilled leaders are usually less politically astute—a trade-off. We will discuss these three roles further in Section 5.3.

Specialization

Specializations facilitate hyper-productivity in the corporation; statistics is a peculiar specialization. Ordinarily the benefits due to analytics are easy to quantify. We can measure an increase in sales, the lift due to a scoring strategy, or a decrease in risk. However, there are situations where the benefits are difficult to measure, difficult to trace, and difficult to claim. It takes analytics ability to measure and trace the benefits, and it takes political sway to claim the credit due. Statistics can produce modest returns for months and then unexpectedly revolutionize the business during a single day—the serendipity of statistics. Many analytics professionals are passionate about pushing the business forward. In addition to producing facts, statistical training facilitates a "scientific" approach to perceiving the business problem. It accelerates the search for solutions, which are yet to be revealed through the trial and error approach that produced the industry knowledge of the past.

Corporations invest in any specialization relative to its perceived value. Estimating the future value of analytics requires foresight integrated with an understanding of analytics. For less analytical corporations, the potential of analytics is often undervalued because of missed opportunities, which have prevented it from providing value.[10] Certification for quants is nonexistent in some countries and is just beginning in others, so corporations struggle to judge qualifications. Hence, it can be a challenge for them to discern the reliability of the results.

The benefits due to analytics are a function of the value of the data, the technical capabilities, the shrewdness of the applications, and the degree to which the analytics team is resourced.[11] In practice, many corporations ring-fence resources (retain resources earmarked for a particular corporate need) based upon their competitors' resourcing and advice from consultants. There is no complicated economic calculation.

> "Analytically based actions usually require a close, trusting relationship between analyst and decision maker ..."
> —Davenport and Harris[12]

> "One important dictum is to make decisions at the lowest level possible."
> —Thomas Redman[13]

Delegating Decisions

Delegation is an important characteristic of HMO. In general, leadership needs to delegate decision making toward those who are in the best position to make the decision. A single corporate-wide decision maker is unlikely to have the most complete knowledge. Furthermore, leadership needs to delegate the execution of analytics to analytics professionals, who have "practiced." Effective delegation requires trusting relationships. There is a burden on the leadership to build strong relationships with their analytics practitioners.

Delegating decision making moves the decision closer to the tacit information and expertise. Most corporations tend to involve too few decision makers.[14] Dispersing the decision-making burden fosters a smarter and less autocratic[15] corporation. Involving more qualified decision makers implies greater engagement and elicits higher quality decisions. Analytics is subject to nuances that cannot be easily explained. Decisions based upon advanced analytics require more sophisticated decision makers and that the decision makers possess greater familiarity with the facts. We need decision makers who are themselves analytics professionals and can (1) trust the analytics, (2) understand analytics, or (3) build relationships with other analytics professionals and recognize analytics qualifications.

Delegating analytics moves the execution closer to the training and experience. This generates dividends by getting things done faster, cheaper, and better. Part of the speed is in avoiding unnecessary or poor analysis. For specialized problems like analytics, the most successful approach for "off-topic leadership"[16] continues to be straightforward:

Delegate analytics to the specialists.

Leadership with on-topic training has serious advantages in delegating to those performing analytics:

1. They can better predict and motivate timeliness and accuracy.
2. They can trust techniques.
3. They are in a position to delegate what they understand to experts, who they can understand and trust.
4. They can better communicate with other analytical professionals. Analytics is a way of thinking.

5. They just do not need as much time to make competent decisions about analytics.
6. They understand that the quants engage in "meatball surgery." The focus is on the critical aspects of the analysis.
7. They recognize that specialists are not interchangeable parts. Analytics does not all look the same to them. Hence, they can match the right task to the right expert's competencies. This enables specialization within specialization—the leap from a vertical organization to a horizontal one (Section 5.2). They do not require that everyone be an interchangeable part in order to simplify their leadership role.
8. It is empowering for the quants to work with analytically enthusiastic leadership.

There are tricks for delegating to all types of specialists. Here are some tips intended to help:

1. All leaders should review and evaluate the results of the assignment. Ordinarily the means used to accomplish the task are less relevant. However, in the case of analytics, the means are an integral part of the results. Managers are responsible for making sure that both the process and the outcome of the delegated task are consistent with the goals.
2. The idea is to retain responsibility while delegating authority and accountability. The analytics professional knows what needs to be done and how to do it, and only needs the opportunity to do it. Delegate the freedom to make decisions and the authority to implement them. Managers should communicate to all individuals affected by the project that it has been delegated and who has the authority to complete the work.
3. Managers should discuss with the analytics professionals what resources they need for a task and then empower them to secure those resources.
4. Good leaders allow employees to participate in the delegation process.
5. If we are concerned that the project will take too long, then include the deadline as part of the problem to be solved. On-topic leaders are better at communicating this point.

6. If we are concerned about over analysis, then we set minimum accuracy targets as part of the problem to be solved. This trick burdens the analytics professionals with stopping unproductive data analysis. We should keep trying to improve solutions yet let the experts discard useless misleading analysis.
7. Even on-topic leaders should avoid the tendency to intervene simply due to style differences.

Corporations with the advanced "power" to delegate have the advantage.[17]

Incentives

Corporations run on their incentives. With the proper incentives, corporations can become highly efficient. Incentives are best when they are aligned with solving the problems. In the U.S., corporate incentive structures have steepened in the past few decades. About 30 years ago, U.S. CEOs received approximately 30 times the average employee's compensation. This multiple has since exceeded 340 times. As individualist incentives steepen, this encourages much more individualism and eventually sociopathic[18] behavior. This tampers with team cohesion and creates horizontal and vertical rifts in the corporation. Analytics, just like innovation, thrives in a meritocracy with team incentives.[19]

Dysfunctional or misaligned incentives will lead a corporation toward destruction. They can make it hazardous to do the right thing for the company. The senior management of Bear Stearns had their bonuses aligned to high-risk behavior.[20] This encouraged their fatal mistake of getting over extended and trapped in a liquidity squeeze.[21]

Incentives for leadership roles need to be long-term, and there should be some team incentives. The concern with excessive individualistic incentives is that they encourage everyone to place their self-interests ahead of the corporation, creating more politics as employees vie for lottery prizes. We think analytics needs more teamwork and that usually individual incentives do little to motivate struggling employees. Those employees who are here for the wrong reasons are difficult to incent.

Complex undertakings, like some analytical projects involving large parts of the corporation, can be more efficient with team incentives. A corporation has an incentive problem when it is hazardous or at least not in an individual's best interests to solve the statistics problem appropriately.

Section 2.2 Corporate Analytics Failures– Shakespearean Comedy of Statistical Errors

"Safety is not a lucky system. It's a system of science, analysis, and facts."
—Mark Rosenker, Chairman, U. S. National
Transportation Safety Board [22]

"Data analysis is an aid to thinking and not a replacement for it."
—Richard Shillington

"It's easy to lie with statistics. But it is easier to lie without them."
—Frederick Mosteller

Statistical malfeasance is one of today's corporate diseases. Several corporations have gone bankrupt, missed breakthrough opportunities, and taken big losses because of statistical mistakes. These mishaps go undiagnosed even after an "autopsy." Sometimes it is difficult to trace business mistakes back to absent or faulty data analysis, just as it is difficult for corporations to measure the quality of the data analysis. The solution to difficult decisions is not riverboat gambling. It is to measure the quality of the information and then interpret the facts. Chapters 7 to 9, Statistical QDR (Qualifications Diagnostics Review), will cover the means by which to measure the quality of the facts, including certification for quants.[23] If we cannot measure analytics quality and we are unable to reasonably confirm that there are no problems with our analytics and our analytics-based decisions, then those are our problems.

For the remainder of this section, we will share accounts of corporate failures due to poor analytics practice.

The Financial Meltdown of 2007–2008: Failures in Analytics

Financial corporations are by necessity the most analytically savvy in the global economy. Part of the banking cycle includes a financial crisis that culls the weakest. The tinderbox that facilitated the financial meltdown of 2007–2008 comprises a web of decisions that were based upon invalid assumptions and faulty analyses. Once the housing bubble reached a certain size, there was no gentle recourse and the bubble was popped by additional mistakes in analytics made by the first victims. Banks, credit rating agencies, and investors struggled to price the risk of subprime assets, which are notorious for destroying banks.[24] Those highly leveraged banks with the worst algebra tended to lose the most.

The subprime melodrama went as follows. First, in 1999 the U.S. Congress repealed the to Glass-Steagall Act of 1933, which protected the economy from banks becoming too big to fail. In time, investment banks were allowed to raise their leverage—the amount they owe versus their cash on hand, to obscene ratios. This increased their ROAs (returns on assets) and made them too soft to experience significant financial stress.

Next, there was a glut of money looking for high-return AAA investments.[25] Investment banks pooled mortgages into MBSs (mortgage-backed securities) and CDOs (credit debt obligations) for sale on this market. They took their CDOs to the rating agencies, who rated the riskiness of these investments. Then the banks sold them to these investors. This generated huge profits for the banks, who demanded more mortgages. Money was cheap. Housing prices rose. As time progressed, the supply of prime mortgages shrank and was outpaced by demand for CDOs. Exotic mortgages appeared to keep the cycle going. This facilitated a growth in subprime mortgage. People who ordinarily could not obtain credit for a single house were buying multiple houses. Real estate investors were also buying a large portion of the new purchases. Housing prices continued to rise at unsustainable rates. It was clear that this was a shift in the economy.

In order to market these CDOs, the banks split them into tranches based upon riskiness. They sold the least risky tranches and tended to retain the highest-risk mortgages. Through magical accounting tricks, they put these off of their balance sheet. In order to cover the risk, most of the investment banks purchased credit default swaps (CDSs) from AIG as an insurance policy against the worst that could happen. This was their "originate to distribute" model, which was supposed to generate fees and distribute all of the risk.

Fitch Ratings, Moody's, and Standard & Poor's

They were the "arbitrators of value" for these CDOs. They received lucrative fees from the investment banks for the service of "objectively" rating these CDOs. An investment bank would solicit multiple ratings prior to selling the financial investments. The companies with the top two ratings would be chosen, and they would be paid. Any other rating agency received nothing. According to *The Big Short,* the rating agencies did not always have their own models or complete granular data. Instead, they relied upon models provided by the investment banks and pooled data for any supporting analysis. Through some strange alchemy, subprime mortgages were turned into AAA-rated investments.

Countrywide Bank, Golden West, and Washington Mutual

To maintain the pace in loan originations, shadow banks dealt in exotic mortgages for consumers lacking the usual credit worthiness. These included "no money down, interest only" loans that would balloon in payments. These loans made sense only in an economy where housing prices would continue to rise. However, the increase in housing prices was unsustainable. Housing prices rose by 124% from 1997 to 2006. The business was so lucrative that these shadow banks failed to heed the mounting warnings from their risk models.

AIG Financial Products

AIG was a AAA-rated corporation with a small Financial Products group that basically insured the risk for large blocks of debt. They unwittingly amassed a vast portfolio of risky CDSs, which essentially were insurance policies on mortgage-related securities. Their experience illustrates *the* classic risk involved in directing analytics with an ordinary off-topic manager of analytics.

Years before the bubble burst, AIG changed its management of the Financial Products group. The incoming manager did not have the on-topic training in mathematics, statistics, and algorithms. This led to a cultural change from vigorous discussions about how well their models were performing toward apathy. **The new head of FP managed up, and for an analytics group, this is mismanagement.** During this time, AIG took on incredible risk without realizing it.[26] At the onset, they were insuring tranches that contained 2% subprime mortgage, and before they realized it, they had grown this proportion to 95%.[27]

Fannie Mae: Next to the Bomb Blast

Although Fannie Mae and Freddie Mac, the two main government-sponsored enterprises (GSEs), continue to haunt the American financial scene, we should remember that they were not the first monoline mortgage companies to fail; they were among the last. Countrywide, Washington Mutual, and a number of others failed first. Golden West, a thrift in California, was so toxic that it killed off its buyer, Wachovia, one of the most widely respected national banks in both commercial and regulatory circles, forcing its sale to Wells Fargo. Of course, non-mortgage businesses, such as the investment banks Lehman Bros. and Bear Stearns, also failed. These banks generated enormous quantities of bad mortgage loans and failed to fully implement their "originate to distribute" model, which would have distributed 100% of their risk.

In order to understand what blew up the mortgage market in 2007–2008 (and the problems continuing to the present day), we have to go back in time. Although I've worked in a number of environments, my perspective is fundamentally based on the years I spent regulating multiple types of risk across a wide variety of banks at the Treasury Department. This experience gave me a strong appreciation for the logic and analytics of risk management, but without the level of intimidation often felt by non-quants around folks with Ph.D.s in things like statistics, economics (econometrics), operations research, and others. These experiences included excoriating whole classes of models that purported to be precise and statistical, but created so-called "reliability" indices with no underlying statistics on their actual reliability—to the delight of users and the chagrin of salespeople. It included catching quants at major institutions faking a model validation. My experience taught me to trust my own doubts, above all, and to always question, with the most humble of attitude, the most lettered of businesspeople. By the time I got to one of the mortgage GSEs, I had lost my youthful arrogance, but also my youthful awe. And I began asking questions—like a financial Colombo.

When the dot-com bubble burst in 2001, the Fed lowered interest rates substantially. This caused a refinancing boom, which, as had happened many times before, drove mortgage banks to greatly expand their staffing to handle the temporary rate-driven increase in volume. As rates hit bottom and stayed there, the "refi boom" consumed most of the traditional borrowers (credit-worthy non-investors) and began to tail off. It was at this point that "exotic" mortgages began to be engineered as a tactic to keep the level of mortgage originations at an artificially elevated level. Many of these exotic mortgages were neg-am (negative amortization), characterized by low down payments and low monthly payments—for a limited time. A large portion were "zero down, interest only" loans. At the same time, corruption blossomed in the real estate industry, and a significant portion of housing purchases were driven by investors who, for "zero money down," could buy a call option on the housing market.

For the most part, these neg-am mortgage products were not actually new; they were simply rediscovered by an industry that had little data covering mortgage performance prior to 1995. Of course, anyone who had been paying attention in the 1990s should have remembered[28] that the neg-am feature, which played a critical role in the new designs, had also contributed to the hole in Citibank's balance sheet in the early 1990s. There were two differences between the 1990s and the 2000s. First, in the 2000s the commercial banks played a trailing, rather than a leading, role. They caught up to the "leaders," namely the mortgage companies and their investment banking partners, only after the latter had seemingly proven the concept, with several years of low losses and high profits. Second, the recession of 1989–1992 shut down the first neg-am experiment before it could grow too large. Whereas in the 2000s, the neg-am experiment was protracted by Wall Street redirecting investment capital from the stock market. This capital came from investors seeking moderate-yield investment-grade bonds. Instead, they would receive new types of sub rosa junk bonds.

Throughout the 1990s and into the early 2000s, there were two major groups in (first) mortgages: (1) conventional and government (i.e., FHA or

VA-insured), and (2) conforming and jumbo (determined by size relative to GSE loan limits). Before the boom in exotics, the GSEs and FHA dominated the smaller loan product market, with the banks and investment banks dominating the rest, albeit at somewhat higher rates and stricter terms.

When exotic mortgages were first introduced in the 2000s, commercial banks did not enthusiastically receive them. They tended to focus on building portfolios of loans and servicing assets, and had relatively strong risk-based federal regulation. It was the mortgage specialists, some non-bank mortgage originators and thrifts, who partnered with investment banks to devise these exotic negatively amortizing loans to save the mostly non-bank mortgage companies from the typical cyclical downturn and mass layoffs following a refi wave. Of course, the investment banks were also eager to bite off as much of the GSE/Govi market as they could—a market that for years they had been complaining was dominated by institutions with an unfair advantage. A confluence of several factors lead to their enthusiasm for this exotic new product, including the following:

1. Lack of publicly available data that would have underscored the poor performance of previous experiments in neg-am mortgages
2. Faith that the "originate-to-distribute" model would really allow the institutions to remove all credit risk from their books
3. A fundamental belief that, because they are backed by real property, mortgages present minimal to no risk
4. A belief that the historical lack of a national fall in home prices since the Depression meant that home prices would never fall nationwide
5. Greed and envy directed toward the sheer scale and profitability of the GSEs and a desire to take a piece of it
6. Demand for new investment classes as the dot-com crash discredited equities generally
7. An overly optimistic faith in the ability of financial engineering to add significant value

So, what likely happened at investment banks is what I witnessed at Fannie Mae, when it belatedly began approving exotic mortgage products for purchase through standard channels in 2005 (it was already buying securitizations). When asked if he had built a model to estimate the credit guarantee-fee for one of these negatively amortizing products, a credit modeler, whom we'll call Jim since he still works there, said to the SVP in charge:

> Yes, I've built a model to calculate the credit guarantee-fee, given the information we have. However, we have no historical data on this product, so we've had to make a lot of very questionable assumptions for the model.[29]

Of course, by the time this discussion occurred, these new mortgages had already reduced the GSE's market share by 50%, and management was concerned with keeping the agencies "relevant" in this "new world."

Jim's final comment was, "Rather than rely on this *very* approximate pricing, what you should ask yourself is, would you want your son to buy a house with this mortgage." This idea was ignored by our senior management, and in their quest to be relevant, they began originating exotics. Although I haven't had the opportunity to analyze the GSEs' actual losses, I believe that they were pushed into failure not by their origination of these questionable loans in competition with the investment banks, or even the purchase of pools of asset-backed securities based on these exotic mortgages. Additionally, it is a well-repudiated myth that the requirement that the GSEs invest a minimum amount in loans for low- and moderate-income borrowers pushed them over the edge. While the GSEs suffered significant losses on their exotics, losses on their required low-mod product suffered minimal losses. Despite what their critics have implied, the GSEs never dominated these high-risk markets but always played catch up to the "more nimble" fully private-sector players. A careful dissection of GSE losses will likely show that the bulk of them were due to the simple fact that home prices declined at double-digit percentage rates nationwide. This decline was due to a bubble that was fueled almost entirely by an out-of-control private sector. What killed the GSEs was nothing that they themselves did, although they were guilty of some lapses in judgment. What killed them was the definition of who they were and the waters in which they sailed.

As the mortgage banking/Wall Street axis pushed down the first-year's monthly payment on mortgages they generated so much additional purchase business that they drove home prices higher—to the point where 10% appreciation per year began to be treated as a new norm. This rate is clearly unsustainable in a world of 3% inflation and 2 to 5% growth, as housing costs would eventually crowd out all other consumption and production. These price increases could only be sustained through a Ponzi "bubble" of neg-am mortgages and house flipping financed by overrated investment vehicles. Underwriters were allowed to calculate qualifying income-to-payment ratios based on the temporarily low payments allowed under these rates—meaning that the ultimate insurance for lenders on the negatively amortizing loan was infinitely rising prices, which could only occur if new, and ever more irrational, buyers were found to pay for increasingly inflated property. Of course, this greater fool was the very same person that the buyers—an enormous number of them motivated by pure speculation—were relying on to protect their minimal investment. It is the collapse of that mechanism that ultimately brought down home prices and with it the GSEs, and severely threatened the financial health of the U.S. and many foreign economies.

At this point I have to refer again to Jim. Over the 2007–2008 period, and perhaps before that, Jim would periodically distribute a very startling graph. It was simply the average nationwide price for homes from 1985 to the present, using Fannie Mae's internal repeat-sales index, in constant dollars (I think it was indexed to 1995). It looked like an artist's rendering of a tsunami—a little wavy line blending into a massive tsunami towering, preparing to crash. I have reproduced it as well as I can by using publicly available information in Figure 2.1 (this chart uses the national FHFA index and the monthly national CPI to deflate it to January 1991 dollars).

Needless to say, the marketing department didn't much care for Jim. In 2007 he attended an enormous marketing department meeting. At one point he asked a senior manager, in this open forum, what we were going to do when the market crashed. The manager retorted, "Jim, you've been saying the market was going to crash for two years. Tell me, when is it going to happen? When?" In less than six months, the overconfident manager's query was answered and a few months after that, the manager retired.

We, in the Economic Capital group, were so taken with Jim's simple analysis that in the fall of 2007, we developed an alternative credit risk stress tool. The tool generated possible future home price stress paths for use in calculating the potential economic damage of a stress to Fannie Mae. We set just a few simple parameters, such as the depth to which prices might fall measured as a percentage below the previous real low, how long it would take to reach the real price nadir, and how long a recovery would

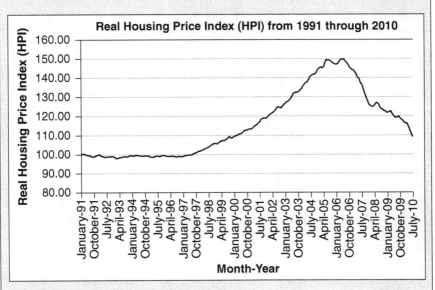

Figure 2.1 Housing Price Index (HPI)

take, as well as the inflation rate that would allow us to translate stress/ mean reversion from the real price space back to nominal. This model did not claim to predict the future. What it did was to create apparently plausible stress scenarios, using simple assumptions and obvious logic, that were far worse than those generated by the Fannie Mae's statistical models at claimed probability levels below 0.1%.

A talented quant on my team built this simple tool, and we wrote up some documentation. We were listened to with politeness in the spring of 2008, but could not get such a stress tool implemented into the corporate credit modeling infrastructure. Of course, since we were taken over that summer, the model would clearly have done us no good. My point is rather the following:

The failure at the GSEs was due to two factors. First, they are mortgage monolines with government charters. They couldn't diversify their risks, and their executives would only maintain their status—and pay—if they continued to be a major force in the market. Second, and equally important, was the fact that these firms were run primarily by people whose job it was to be optimistic and whose imagination only entertained dreams of greater success—never nightmares of doom, no matter how obvious the analytical evidence. Like many successful organizations, they were dominated too much by marketing, in this case with a heavy dose of government relations. Analytics' job was to make fine distinctions in value and risk—not to influence strategy. The GSEs missed the opportunity to integrate analytics into their strategy. The only criticism I ever heard of Jim from other, senior members of the company's analytics community was that he was a "chicken little" who was making no friends. No one ever questioned the relevance or legitimacy of his straightforward analyses.

There are only two ways the GSEs could have possibly saved themselves. The first was to simply stop lending in the mid–2000s. This could have been done by recognizing the bubble and pricing themselves completely out of the market. This would have been incredibly brazen, but because of the GSEs' role in the market, it might well have moved the entire market back to rationality in a way that the federal regulatory authorities did not have the courage to begin until 2007, and might not have been able to accomplish earlier. The second survival path would have been to hedge our credit risk, taking short positions in the relatively illiquid Case–Schiller index, and/or buying credit default swaps on mortgage-backed ABS)—or shorting the ABX index of asset-backed securities. But the faithful don't hedge. They believe in their business, so it was much easier for the pilots to keep running the ship downwind, following the market, then to take a stand and tack into the headwind. I believe that only a senior management with the ability to imagine tragedy as well as triumph, and an appreciation of risk analytics and the courage to follow it wherever it may lead, can be relied upon to safely steer today's leveraged risk-taking institutions.

The Great Pharmaceutical Sales-Force Arms Race by Tom "T. J." Scott

Many senior leaders are not analytically sophisticated. Some lack even a basic understanding of statistics or scientific methods. As a result, these leaders often rely on gut instinct when making decisions. When leaders use gut instinct, they are relying on long-held beliefs and personal experience. There are two obvious problems with this. First, markets are changing rapidly, making many long-held beliefs untrue. Second, relying on one's personal experience is like doing important research with a sample size of one. In this case, ideas outside the experience of our personal sample are considered less reliable.

In big U.S. pharmaceuticals during the last 15 years sales forces grew to an immense and inefficient size, maybe two to six times larger than necessary. This happened for a host of reasons including:

1. Leaders could not let go of their long-held beliefs.
2. Many of the analysts and consultants that supported them were under-qualified and all too happy to provide senior management with results that matched preconceived thinking. This provided unreliable "analysis."

Meanwhile, there were some of us working in a statistical underground with complex contradictory analysis. Unfortunately, we were unsuccessful in convincing our leadership to act on what we had found. Our leaders could not discern that our analysis was more reliable.

It was difficult to convince them, because pharmaceutical leader's long-held beliefs were formed more than 15 years ago, when sales interactions between doctor and sales representatives were critical. At that time, physicians relied on sales representatives to provide efficacy and safety information. Physicians were trained to diagnose; they had very little pharmacology training. Pharmaceutical sales representatives made up for this lack of pharmacology knowledge, and helped physicians stay current with interactions between them and physicians that were valuable and meaningful. At that time a physician might spend 20 minutes discussing clinical trials and mechanisms of action with a sales rep.

Today, however, the typical sales interaction is a 45-second chat about the local sports team while the representative gets a signature for samples. Physicians rely on other sources of information—often managed care providers—to evaluate which drugs are efficacious, cost-effective, and yet covered by insurance companies. One response to the dwindling influence of the sales force was to deny that there was a problem, and the other was to increase the size of the sales force.

The business rules that senior leaders use to determine how to size their sales forces and set activity levels assume that selling interactions today are as valuable and meaningful as they were 15 years ago. Unfortunately, these business rules don't distinguish between a 45-second chat about sports and a 20-minute talk about the latest clinical trial. The business rules assume that all interactions are the same—valuable and meaningful—and assign every sale that occurs to the selling activity preceding it. Even more unfortunate is that most interactions today are not valuable or meaningful, and most aren't even memorable—but the business rules don't know it.

The unreliable analysis grossly exaggerated the benefit that increasing sales calls had on increasing sales. This is because two things changed during the last 15 years that were not always evident, but structured qualitative research eventually showed. **First, when a doctor determined that he or she was going to use a product, the doctor would see that sales representative more often. Second, when a representative found out a doctor was going to write more prescriptions for his or her product, the rep would pretend to make more sales calls on that doctor.** Each year the sales representatives were assigned more visits to the same physician. So each year they recorded more visits that didn't actually occur, and each year they were assigned more to deliver—slow but consistent increases over many years. In time, the data could no longer be interpreted at face value—but it was. This was becoming obvious in both qualitative and quantitative research, but leaders wouldn't or couldn't believe it. And often those supplying numerical execution data and those doing quantitative analytics were not exposed to the contradictory information. Without this, they naively relied upon their leaders to determine if their "analysis" was reliable. What happened then was, if the "analysis" did not match the business expectation, then it was presumed wrong and needed to be adjusted. This wrongly made the results fit the preconceived conclusions of the leaders they were supporting. It became a vicious circle of everyone relying too heavily on the long-held belief of the leaders.

Since the leaders were shown more data that supported their long-held belief that sales interactions were valuable and meaningful, and that sales representatives were making more visits to each physician, they ignored the contradictory data despite obvious signs of change. They followed their guts, even when they knew it was impossible for a representative to make 96 or more valuable sales visits to the same physician in the same year—but stuff like this was being regularly assigned and recorded. Almost all pharmaceutical companies were using the same tactics and the same underpowered analyses, and had leaders that possessed similar experiences and knowledge. So when leaders looking for confirmation viewed competitive companies and saw them engaging in the same behavior—increasing their sales forces—they assumed all was well. From a certain perspective, all *was* well. This was a time of extremely profitable blockbusters, which cloaked the millions of dollars spent on ineffective promotional activities.

Yet all was not really well. Waste and inefficiency were rampant. And not only was the quality of selling interactions that were actually occurring going down, so was the quality of the data being recorded by sales representatives. And this bad data is what was feeding the underpowered analytics.

Findings:

1. Analytics-based decisions need to be delegated to those with the proper training and access to implicit information. (Chapter 3 will discuss fact-based decision making.)
2. Some corporate cultures do not encourage using analytics (Chapter 4).
3. Analytics groups need to report to someone who can challenge other senior leaders' views without fear of reprisal. Those responsible for the "analytics" should report into a separate leader from the decision makers they directly support. (Section 5.3 discusses leading analytics, and Section 5.4 discusses where analytics should reside in the corporation.)
4. There needs to be an independent enterprise-wide analytics team that reviews critical decision support analytics. (Section 5.4 discusses where analytics should reside in the corporation.)
5. Analytics was not integrated into the business (Section 6.1).
6. Companies need to hire quants to do their quant work—instead of programmers or generalists with industry experience. In this case, industry experience was not in short supply. (Chapter 7 discusses qualifications for business analysts and business quants.)
7. Senior management needs greater comfort with analytics results. They were uncomfortable with results that contradicted their beliefs and they could not discern the relative reliability of results. (In Chapters 7 to 9, we discuss tools for discerning the reliability of analytics and analytics-based decisions.)
8. Leaders need more quantitative training, and environments that encourage debate.
9. The quality of the data was poorly understood and needed a quant to challenge beliefs, to ask questions, and to oversee the data collection. The data was not well organized. (Chapters 10 and 12 discuss data collection and management.)

Inside the Statistical Underground—Adjustment Factors for the Pharmaceutical Arms Race by Brian Wynne

There are many business problems where the data available requires additional business assumptions. For example, we survey customers as to whether they will purchase a new product. We assume that their responses are correlated, but not identical to purchasing behavior. Other examples occur when markets change or when we leverage data from one market to support decisions about a similar market. An important aspect of business analytics is deciding to what extent the data available is relevant to the current business problem and how to adjust our results to better support the business decision. One family of tools that we use for adapting results to match changes in the market are "adjustment factors."

In my line of work I am often required to measure the sales resulting from certain types of marketing promotions. My objective is to provide analytics that will support budgeting decisions. Using historical data, the quant applies techniques to isolate the sales driven by a particular promotion and provides a recommendation on the optimal amount to spend on this promotion. Since these promotional events occurred in the past, the challenge is predicting how these activities will fare in the future. Often there are legitimate reasons to adjust results based upon historical data: price changes, the market entry of a new competitor, the promotional strategy has changed, and so on. Analytics providers have significant experience doing these analyses and can use that experience to provide improved accuracy. Unfortunately, these adjustment factors often have a huge impact on the analysis and can provide very misleading results.

In one case, the historical data were adjusted by over 50% based generally upon unsubstantiated assumptions. This raised the estimated effectiveness of the promotion, which in turn increased the recommended

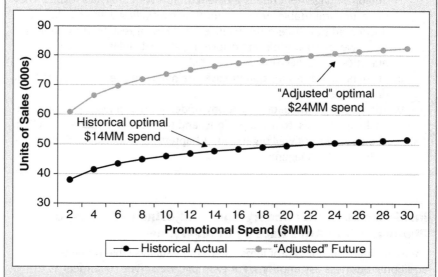

Figure 2.2 Finding optimal promotional spend

promotional spend from $14 million to $24 million. See Figure 2.2, which shows the resulting promotion response curves with estimates of the sales units driven by the promotion dollars, along with the optimal levels of promotion. These curves are developed by analyzing many historical data points over time, and the challenge is projecting this historical data into the future. In this case, there was no evidence of drastically improved promotion in the future, and the marketing strategy hadn't changed significantly, but the general assumption of growth in the future provided enough justification to increase the budget even though the data didn't support that same conclusion.

In some cases these adjustments dwarf the information contributed by the real data. For one survey we asked customers how much more product they would purchase after seeing a particular piece of information. Based on experience, the consulting company discounted the result by 90%, saying that historically these customers overestimate their purchasing by 10 times in these types of surveys. How sure is the consulting company that 90% is the correct value for this particular situation? If it used 80%, this would double the sales impact—does the client really know if 80% or 90% is more accurate? In these situations, small changes in the adjustment factors can have a disproportionate impact on the conclusion. However, the final presentation doesn't note this lack of stability. The decision makers need this piece of information to determine how much weight to give to this one input when reviewing all the data in order to make the final decision.

Another challenge to adjusting raw data results occurs when changes are made based on unsubstantiated marketing assumptions. In order to justify increased budgets, the client may request to increase the historical impact because "promotions will be more impactful in the future." Usually this client is a new marketing team, which points out flaws in the previous strategy. Rarely is there strong quantitative market research to back up these adjustments. Consulting companies will often comply, having no evidence to the contrary, and wanting to avoid calling their client's claims into question. In my experience, the same type of promotion to the same people does not become significantly more impactful over time, but this is a claim marketing teams make year after year.

Also, I have seen consulting companies proactively offer marketing assumptions to flatter ineffective promotions, or to justify a higher promotional budget. Since the paying client is often the developer of the promotion and owner of the promotional budget, the consulting company will want to avoid presenting unflattering results. The presentation usually follows the pattern of a "here's what happened" slide that shows poor results followed by "here is what we think will happen in the future" slide that offers up a rosy picture. In the past I have had consultants offer to adjust the results higher (resulting in a larger budget) if the marketing team deems it necessary for "strategic considerations"—a vague enough opportunity that few could resist. There is hope that these adjustments are prominently noted in the analysis; however, with limited presentation time these details are often merely footnoted.

The proper technical approach is to either obtain accurate adjustment factors through rigorous techniques, perform sensitivity analysis on how the adjustment factors affect the results, leverage more sophisticated decision makers, or apply an econometric approach to the decision-making process. Presenting the raw results along with the assumptions provides much needed transparency into the process. Strong quantitative market research should be required for any adjustments, with the null hypothesis being that promotional impact will not change over time. In the example where the budget was changed from $14 million to $24 million, the underlying assumption is that the new promotion would be over 50% more effective than the previous promotion—no leader would accept that claim on face value without strong market research evidence.

In the end, senior leadership never gets to see the detailed steps, just the final results—and may not make the proper budgetary decision for the company. The key is to understand the blend between actual historical data and theoretical assumptions about the future. Only business investments with the best data showing historical results along with solid quantitative analysis showing improved marketing techniques should merit funding. It is important to ask the question "What does the raw data tell us?" A strong consultant should be able to separate the objective facts from subjective assumptions and provide an explanation of the implications.

Section 2.3 Triumphs of the Nerds

"Like Thucydides said, 'I wanted to remember a time when people did this. I did not want that to be forgotten.'"

—Oliver Stone[30]

"In the business world, the rearview mirror is always clearer than the windshield."

—Warren Buffett

In addition to missed opportunities in correctly applying analytics, there have been a number of triumphs.

Proving Grounds—Model Review at The Associates/Citigroup

In the late 1990s, we worked in a modeling group of about 20 to 25 professionals (MSs and Ph.D.s) at The Associates, which later became Citigroup. The group comprised mostly econometricians, a few statisticians, and a sprinkling of other disciplines. The head econometrician, overseeing this and two other groups, insisted that we rigorously reviewed our models—"I want you to knock each other around." This was a watershed experience for all of us.

Technical reviews pushed our predictive models to the next level. We learned a great deal about how the models worked; how to build them faster; how to improve our infrastructure; what training it took for building models; how the right applied training accelerates learning; and so on. An advanced degree in something like statistics, operations research, or economics (econometrics) was a good start, yet our academic training was inadequate to the task. Review was a huge triumph. We needed to continue our unfinished applied training.

There were countless dogfights in our well-attended Arena of Death. On a weekly basis someone presented a model, and 15 to 25 other quants would try to tear him or her apart. This rigorous review process quickly taught us how to adapt our academic training to the real world. We quoted references during the presentations, and we engaged in follow-up e-mails afterwards. We "knew our stuff."

At the beginning of someone's first presentation to the group, the presenter might act like he or she knows everything. Only a fool would repeat that behavior during a second presentation. Such a fool would come out with their all feathers plucked and wearing tar.[31] One of the reviewers would smell the fool's smugness and let the person have it—most likely a pack of veteran reviewers leaving footprints all over "the mark." On a rare occasion, someone with only an off-topic master's degree would step into the arena. If the person showed humility, people would take pity on the person and snicker quietly to themselves. Everyone knew that without adequate training, you were completely out of your league.

I remember one presentation where the speaker was shot down in the first five minutes. Some econometrician said that the speaker misinterpreted some statistical diagnostic. Then this econometrician was shot down by someone saying that the interpretation was correct. This third person was then shot down by someone else, who said that the interpretation was wrong, and this fourth person was subsequently shot down by a fifth person, who was shot down by a sixth—all in rapid succession. It was hard to keep up with who said what. All of them were quoting from conflicting passages and interpretations from various references. This is what it was like.

At the onset of another review, a fresh econometrician started to ask a question of the presenter. Before he could get two words out, some veteran modeler stated that it was not the case and he need not worry about it. The econometrician started to ask a second time, and again the veteran answered his question with a "No" before he could finish his sentence. The econometrician tried a third time to ask about a potential mistake the presenter might have made at the beginning of his or her analysis. The veteran modeler told him no again, and finished the econometrician's sentence before he could finish it, saying that it was not the case that the presenter used that approach for this type of problem. This was the nature of the review experience. Sometimes veterans knew what and how others (the fresh econometrician) were going to think before they thought it, what approach the speaker would have used for that type of problem, and all of this in regards to a predictive model that the veteran had never seen minutes before. Review sharpened the quants to such an extent that they could shoot bull's-eyes behind them by looking through a mirror. All of the off-topic professionals were at a loss to follow our model reviews.

At times the process was too brutal, yet there was no denying the results.

One of our number called our discoveries, Best Statistical Practice. These experiences established three pillars for competing analytically: Statistical Qualifications (Chapter 7), Statistical Diagnostics (Chapter 8), and Statistical Review (Chapter 9). Statistical Review taught us two more things: (1) dogfight style is no way to review your peers and (2) review is *huge*.

The review experience clarified a number of important characteristics for this line of work:

1. Statistical content from advanced (graduate-level) training, whether from an operations research, statistics, economics, or similar department, reigned supreme.
2. Quick impromptu thinking provided agility.
3. Tactics: Run in packs—work as part of a team. before, during and after the presentation.
4. Tactics: Preparation—master the literature and understand what applies and what does not.
5. Tactics: Counter-attack—the weakness is there; you must challenge to find it.
6. Tactics: Follow up the meeting with an e-mail; include references supporting your position and discredit any misquoted references.
7. Tactics: Do not bluff—assume someone will look up your references or get your data and simulate your model performance.
8. Expect people to make stuff up.
9. Do not underestimate anyone. Even someone without on-topic training can catch up if he or she is determined.

> *"Veterans also know that it is not the hard, technical issues that stymie an organization's efforts to better manage and utilize its data and information assets, but rather the soft organizational, political, and social issues."*
>
> —Thomas Redman

Predicting Fraud in Accounting: What Analytics-Based Accounting Has Brought to "Bare" By Hakan Gogtas, Ph.D.

The old auditing paradigm is obsolete in today's "I'll be gone; you'll be gone" environment. In the past, it was understood that the auditor would check the obvious and rely upon all of senior management to be truthful and helpful in finding problems. This approach has been repeatedly discredited.

For years, Enron (Failure in 2001) practiced sophisticated fraud based on complex financial instruments. At the beginning of 2001, Enron was considered to be one of the most innovative companies in the world, with "revenues" over $100 billion and "total asset value" at nearly $60 billion. The Enron scandal is still discussed as a defining example of corporate fraud.

For years, WorldCom (Failure in 2002) employed an unsophisticated scheme of capitalizing several billion dollars in operating expenses. This masked their declining financial condition by falsely professing financial growth and profitability to increase the price of WorldCom's stock.

For years, Satyam Computer Services (Failure in 2009) significantly inflated its earnings and assets. Satyam Computer Services was a leading Indian outsourcing company that served more than a third of the Fortune 500 companies. The company's accounts had been systematically falsified as the company expanded from a handful of employees into a back-office giant with a work force of 53,000 and operations in 66 countries. The company listed $1.04 billion in cash as assets, which did not exist.

After the initial shock of these scandals, some experienced a second shock wave. This was the realization by some that accounting had an incorrect reputation—and still does. We regard accounting as somehow providing a rigorous "investigation" of the numbers. However, it is more of a light "check on work" supported by senior management. Corporate ledgers often contain millions of transactions. Accounting is not "independent" enough to foil conspiracies such as the *huge* Enron conspiracy involving the senior management at Enron and several investment banks. The general public remains unaware of the extent to which accounting is still "loose."

The current auditing approach failed to detect and will continue to fail to detect organized fraud. Meanwhile, advancements in computing have provided criminals with greater opportunities to commit fraud. Traditional forms of fraudulent behaviors such as money laundering, masking suspicious entries, or adding fictional entries are easier to commit and have been joined by new kinds of fraud such as computer intrusion. This only increases the burden on the auditors.

According to *Corporate Fraud Handbook,*[32] there are four types of fraud as described in Table 2.2.

All four types of fraud create patterns. We can build statistical tools to search for suspicious patterns, and examine them more closely.

Even with the customary army of accountants, it is impossible to rigorously review millions of transactions. Enter the era of analytics-based accounting. Data mining and other statistical techniques can help auditors detect fraud, suspicious behaviors, misrepresentations or honest mistakes in companies' general ledgers or financial statements. As companies collect more data, these techniques will be more powerful for identifying suspicious activities.

Table 2.2 Types of Fraud According to Corporate Fraud Handbook

Types	Description	Notable Examples
Fictitious revenues	Fabricating revenue Inadequate provisions for sales and returns Sales with conditions Long-term contracts Channel stuffing	Satyam Computer Services (India)Health South (U.S.) Royal Ahold (Netherlands) Qwest Communications (U.S.) Homestore.com (U.S.) Bristol-Myers Squibb (U.S.) AOL (U.S.)
Timing differences	Early revenue recognition Recording expenses in the wrong period	Merck & Co. (U.S.)
Concealed liabilities and expenses	Liability and/or expense omission Omission of warranty and product liability	Anglo-Irish Bank (Ireland) Halliburton (U.S.)
Improper disclosures	Liability omissions Significant events Management fraud Related-party transactions Changes in accounting policy	Enron (U.S.) WorldCom (U.S.) Lehman Brothers (U.S.) Nortel (Canada)Parmalat (Italy)Tyco International (Bermuda)Merrill Lynch (U.S.) Kmart (U.S.) Xerox (U.S.)

The analysis problem boils down to analyzing millions of transactions that happened in a particular order at a particular time. We can detect and report suspicious numbers to the auditors. In an audit of 39 companies, we demonstrated the potential of advanced analytics by comparing their ledgers to those of six corporations known to have committed fraud. Rather than describe each of these methods, it suffices to note that in the aggregate, these approaches apply simplistic to sophisticated data-analytic techniques that will provide insight into potential fraud.

Figure 2.3 illustrates the ability of one variable (Equities) to discern fraud companies from most audit companies. The median value for the fraud companies was around 1.1, whereas practically all of the audit companies had a value of 1. The three asterisks corresponding to values greater than 1.2 denote audit companies of interest.

These solutions only solve the difficult technical part of the problem. The remaining part of the solution is a team of analytics professionals. We need sophisticated decision makers willing and able to leverage these tools. Also, we need leaders, who either understand or trust analytics enough to invest in them. This might not happen soon, and it is too bad because one of the strengths of an economy is the reliability of the ledgers.

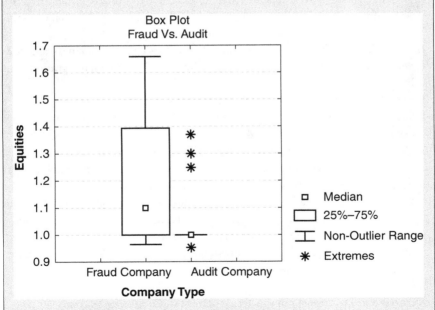

Figure 2.3 Box plot of equities by Fraud versus Audit

> Also note that Lehmann Brothers, Bear Sterns, Fannie Mae, Freddie Mac, AIG, and Merrill Lynch were all rated investment grade just before going bust; this despite off-balance sheet assets and/or extremely high financial leverage. Going forward, analytics-based accounting could provide valuable input into corporate credit risk ratings.
>
> Analytics-based accounting could be the biggest breakthrough in accounting since double-entry book keeping. If today's auditors were supported by advanced analytics tools, then some of the future accounting scandals could be detected in their early stages or discouraged from happening. We have solved the technical aspects of predicting fraud in accounting. We can do it, today.[33] We are waiting for the leadership and the analytics-based decision makers.

Notes

1. For the United States, this was first interpreted by judges under the 14th Amendment, and now the 1st Amendment is being leveraged so that corporations can make larger political contributions.
2. A number of corporations have already tried to leverage business analytics without changing anything, by simply adding it without much integration. This has gone nowhere.
3. Executive producer of *The Outer Limits* television show.
4. See p. 136, paragraph b, in *Competing on Analytics*, Davenport and Harris (2007).
5. One reason to buy their stock: Warren Buffett.
6. This sometimes forms the analytics underground. Our underground is organized in cells of size three. Have you been contacted, yet?
7. By "managing up," we mean managing relationships with our supervisors and other management. Managing up, if done well, can yield the greatest individual dividends. By leadership, we mean leading our team. Helping them to succeed, providing them with the credit and support they earn, and so on. Leadership, if done well, can yield the greatest corporate dividends.
8. Can speak business and analytics.
9. Harris and Davenport put this term forward in *Competing on Analytics*.
10. This can be due to substandard practice or counterfeit analysis.
11. Competent leadership, statistical software, adequate hardware, training, access to the data, and so on.

12. See p. 133, *Competing on Analytics*, Davenport and Harris (2007).
13. *Data Driven: Profiting from Your Most Important Business Asset* (2008).
14. We want "plethora-brain" decision making rather than "few-brain" decision making.
15. Perhaps a way to measure autocracy is the ratio: Decisions/(Decision Makers). Spreading the decision making is the true genius behind a free market economy.
16. Professionals who are not trained in that specialization.
17. Usually these are the same corporations with the ability to identify experts to which to delegate.
18. Or at least sociopathetic.
19. Science has always had a socialist streak.
20. Dysfunctional incentives lit the match that ended it all for Bear Stearns. See *House Of Cards: A Tale of Hubris and Wretched Excess on Wall Street* by William Cohan (2010).
21. Siloing and obsolete infrastructure were additional handicaps for Bear Stearns.
22. See "The Deadliest Plane Crash," *NOVA*.
23. Such as the American Statistical Association's PSTAT® and INFORMS' Certified Analytics Professional (CAP).
24. The subprime business is deceptive, appearing as a "safe" cash cow in the short run and suddenly wrecking companies with a downturn in the economy or by a nest of miscalculations.
25. A similar glut of money drove the dot-com bubble of 1995–2000.
26. There is an old AIG commercial that states, "The greatest risk is not taking one."
27. See "The Man Who Crashed The World" in *Vanity Fair and The Big Short*, both by Michael Lewis.
28. Or, heck, read up on it.
29. The quotes are as close as my memory can take me. Jim still has a career, and if he ever wants to be publicly named, I'm sure he'll let me know—I'm his biggest fan.
30. During an interview about his direction of the film *Platoon*.
31. Tarred and de-feathered.
32. "*Corporate Fraud Handbook: Prevention and Detection*," by Joseph T. Wells (2004).
33. Some auditors might claim that they are leveraging analytics today. They are not referring to the scale or sophistication we are discussing here.

3

Decisions, Decisions

"The chief source of problems is solutions."
　　　　—Eric Sevareid's Law: CBS News, December 29, 1970

"Knowing a great deal is not the same as being smart; intelligence is not information alone but also judgment, the manner in which information is collected and used."
　　　　　　　　　　　　　　　　　　　　　　　　—Carl Sagan

This chapter discusses how corporations use data analysis in their strategic and tactical decision making. We cover the interplay between analytics and industry knowledge, deep-dive into one approach for making analytics-based decisions, and conclude with a discussion of common decision-making impairments.

Analytics supports decision making by supplying facts, which are used to:

1. Provide alternative choices for decision makers.
2. Automate large numbers of "delegated" decisions.
3. Produce business insights to support major decisions.

Analytics accomplishes these goals through data collection and measuring that which is observed or influenced.

> **Concept Box**
>
> *Industry knowledge*—The common sense information particular to an industry. Industry knowledge is vital for competing in the market place. It aids and abets in solving business analytics problems. It frames the business problems. It is acquired quickly and has a similar structure to that of other industries.

Measurement is not the goal, but rather the approach for supplying facts. The objective of data analysis is to provide facts that will support better judgment.

ψ   ψ   ψ

Section 3.1 Fact-Based Decision Making

In the absence of facts, we are forced to depend on opinions, which make us vulnerable to overconfidence and other sources of bias. The challenge is to make smart decisions[1] quickly when the information is complex, copious, and contradictory. Tracking the two, we know that decisions based upon facts are better than ones based upon opinions.[2] The more dynamic the industry, the more valuable fact-based decision making becomes. Additionally, we need to appreciate that fact-based decision making is faster on average because we measure the time it takes to reach a good decision.[3]

The insights from data analysis are only as accurate as the data and the analysis behind them. In practice, ordinary decision makers cannot judge the accuracy and reliability of the analysis. Instead of using numerical forms of validation (as discussed in Chapter 8, "Statistical Diagnostics"), they tend to apply surrogate measures to gauge data analysis quality such as:

1. Source is trusted/historically "demonstrated."
2. Custom—that is, because they always use that type of analysis, so it is assumed to be reliable.
3. Results fit business experience.
4. Results come with depth of explanation.
5. Popular source[4]/well presented source projects confidence.
6. Source has industry experience.

Otherwise, when they cannot measure quality using a surrogate, they look for other considerations, such as price, service, and convenience.

We want to systematically improve decision making to seize competitive advantage. The business strategy needs to encourage fact-based decision making and create an environment where decision makers can sort through the information and quickly obtain most of the reliable facts.

The first component in this environment is selecting a decision maker close enough to the facts[5] and sophisticated enough to interpret them. This may require delegating decisions to those possessing the tacit information and a comprehension of both the business problem and the analytics supplying the facts.[6] Many decision makers today underutilize the available information because it is either not simple enough or arrives in an inconvenient form and hence is not readily usable. We need to ensure that the facts fit the decision makers. Facts are now available in greater abundance. We want decision makers capable of sorting through the chaotic information and disinformation overload, an exercise that can be so overwhelming. Fortunately, we can better measure the accuracy and reliability of various estimates.

Sophisticated decision makers are proactive, have greater breadth of thought, and take responsibility for learning how to interpret analytics. At an advanced level, they can evaluate the reliability of the analytics. At this stage in the Information Age, we need decision makers with enough statistical training to *completely* understand the information. It is their responsibility to know what information they need, when they need it, and from whom to get it. They need to ensure that the information is organized to suit the decision-making process. They need decision agility,[7] decision elasticity,[8] and the ability to prioritize decisions by importance.

The trick is to master the trade-off between timeliness and information quality. In the fast-paced world, we are prone to making rash decisions, some of which could be avoided with proper planning. At the same time, we cannot keep dwelling on decisions. We need to make them and move on. Lastly, we need a passion to make decisions better and not be satisfied with the status quo.

If we cannot find enough sophisticated decision makers to whom we can delegate responsibilities, then we will need to build them. We can train decision makers to better leverage the information and to avoid the decision impairments discussed in Section 3.3. We want them to "unlearn" opinion-based decision making and to incent them to place the corporation's interests first. The "building" process must mandatorily include training around analytics to enable the resources to wield the numbers and to speak "analytics." The ability to speak "analytics" enriches the synergy with other analytics professionals.

Another fast-changing aspect of decision making is strategy. The increasing complexity of business, the abundance of information, and the power of modern computing are directing us to apply analytics to solve more strategic or multi-decision business problems. This point is emphasized by business simulations, which are improving in effectiveness and rapidly gaining in applicability. We are now able to simulate the consequences of a strategy or a set of sequential decisions and we can do this for a number of economic scenarios.

Combining Industry Knowledge and Business Analytics[9]

For a decision maker, the main sources of information are currently held industry knowledge and new business analytics. Data analysis confirms old and creates new industry knowledge.[10] In the past, it was common to assume the data to be wrong when it contradicted strongly held beliefs.[11] We have gained a greater appreciation for the alternative view provided by data. Also, we have learned some humility in that we do not know it all.

Many corporations are lavishly rich in industry knowledge but paupers in analytics capabilities. In solving business analytics problems, it is our understanding of the business problem and the analytics solution that is critical. Furthermore, when we perform data analysis it should be because our industry knowledge is insufficient.

In the case of business analytics, the competitive advantage lies in solving the more challenging business problems, which stymie our competitors. Figure 3.1 illustrates a Business Analytics Capability chart. Quadrant I

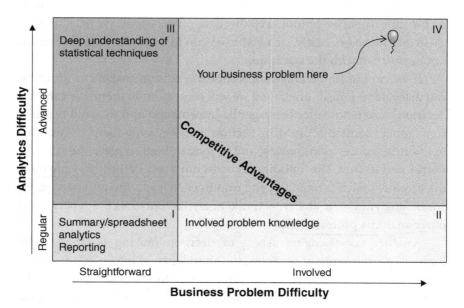

Figure 3.1 Business analytics capability chart

contains BA problems with regular analytics and straightforward business problems. The complexity increases as we move toward Quadrant IV, which contains business problems requiring advanced analytics and involved problem knowledge. Analytics competence is essential for the upper two quadrants. Analytically challenged corporations fail in these quadrants without even realizing it. The same ability to succeed in advanced analytics is needed to measure success or failure.

A successful corporation requires expertise in both dimensions, each of which varies in difficulty. To illustrate the matter, consider the business problem of detecting fraud, which could fall into any of these four quadrants. We might have a clear definition of a specific type of fraud with all of the numbers clearly defined in a data dictionary.[12] If this problem is straightforward in terms of problem difficulty, then it belongs in Quadrants I or III—Quadrant III if the analytics are at the "graduate degree" level and Quadrant I otherwise. Alternatively, we might need to detect any of a number of as yet undefined types of fraud. This might require involved problem knowledge and fall into either Quadrant II or IV. If the analytics for this involved version of the problem is complex, then this problem will fall into Quadrant IV; otherwise, it will fall into Quadrant II. See Figure 3.2.

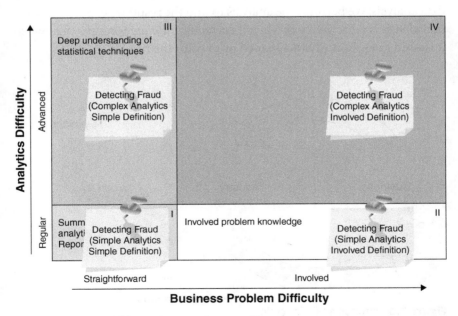

Figure 3.2 The problem of "Detecting Fraud"

The activity in Quadrants II, III, and IV is growing in our knowledge-based economy, and this is where the failures are taking place. Statistically, dysfunctional corporations have unmet needs in Quadrants III and IV, where it is difficult for them to measure ability.

Greater analytics capabilities can do much more than address the top two quadrants. One value-add due to advanced analytics is to find ways to improve our efficiency in Quadrants I and II. Additionally, better statistical prowess means a greater synergism between our current understanding of the business and our understanding of any new discoveries. Business analytics informs and validates industry knowledge, which informs and validates business analytics. We obtain more synergy when we ratchet up the understated emphasis on analytics. Any gaps in the facts are filled in with our opinions as illustrated in Figure 3.3.

One role of industry knowledge is to suggest or hypothesize likely findings before applying data analysis to validate them. In that way analytics can serve to validate new ideas and long-held industry beliefs. If, instead, we anecdotally explain the results once they are known, then the worst case is that industry knowledge will serve to reinforce our tunnel thinking and codependency on opinions, thereby resulting in missed opportunities. Similarly, the preconceptions of industry experience can bleed into the data analysis. We perform the analysis to find the result we expect. Industry knowledge is more virtuous when it correctly anticipates results than when it is used to explain what happened or to color the results.

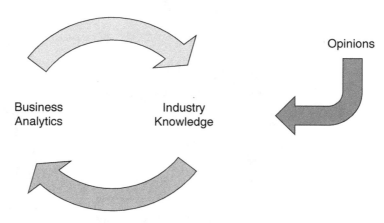

Figure 3.3 Virtuous analytics cycle

Critical Thinking

There is a growing schism between independent critical thought and acting on a fixed set of beliefs.[13] The former forces us to face the complexity and the latter enables fast simple decisions. We strive to place the appropriate amount of thought and specialization toward each decision. Critical decisions like "betting the house" merit critical thinking. We crave enlightened critical thinking and open mindedness over fixed ideology.[14]

Fortunately, excellent decision makers have a talent for reducing the complexity, thinking independently,[15] and delegating to experts. Complexity does not have to necessarily be a bad thing. Delegation[16] can make the complexity go away because experts are often closer to the implicit information. Data analysis should be applied deliberately to simplify the information in order to avoid brain-dead decision making or guessing. Additionally, statistics can wade through pools of information and judge the reliability of the facts, thereby addressing information overload (see Section 3.3, "Disinformation Overload").

Section 3.2 Analytics-Based Decision Making: Four Acts in a Greek Tragedy[17]

> *"...and darkness veiled his eyes."*
>
> —Homer, in *The Iliad*

Act I: Framing the business problem.
Act II: Executing the data analysis.[18]
Act III: Interpreting the results.
Act IV: Making analytics-based decisions.[19]

Analytics supplies many of the facts. In this section, we wish to discuss one paradigm for preparing analytics to support an anticipated decision. The purpose of these four acts is to illustrate a process for analytics-based decision making. This reveals the role of statistical thinking, the interplay between analytics and industry knowledge, and where things go so very wrong. In a real business problem, we may seamlessly move from one act to another, jump back and forth, or follow some other route.

The best "magic sauce" to serve during Acts I, III, and IV consists of a gentle blend of industry knowledge—seldom in short supply, and analytics prowess. These are the "tangled" parts. Act II is defined to describe the part of the process that never involves industry knowledge—pure data analysis. Of these two proficiencies, industry knowledge is either ubiquitous or forthcoming and the involvement of analytics needs to be institutionalized.

The difficulty of the problem knowledge depends on the complexity in Acts I, III, and IV. Involved business problems fall in Quadrants II and IV above. Recall that, when we perform data analysis, it is because our industry knowledge is insufficient. In order to compete on analytics, corporations need to better leverage statistics in all four[20] acts.

The top two quadrants involve advanced, probably graduate-level training in analytics. The analytics challenges can be in any of the four acts. They are most likely in Act II: Executing the Data Analysis. In Act I: Framing the Business Problem, we might need to understand advanced analytics to recognize a viable statistical solution to the business problem. Corporations miss many possible solutions. For Act III, we need to be able to understand advanced analytics so that we can interpret results. For Act IV, decisions might be complicated, requiring us to construct or interpret technically advanced results or utility functions.

In practice, there are business problems where some acts have already been mastered or are otherwise straightforward. For example, there are repeated applications of predictive modeling where Acts I and III have already been clarified. Once we know that the solution is a predictive model and have organized the appropriate data, then there might not be anything more to address in Act I. Similarly, we might already have a developed idea of how to interpret the results of a predictive model in Act III.

By involving competent experts in all four acts, the team is more likely to avoid tragedy. Now we will discuss each act and the causes of tragedy therein—as revealed through autopsy.

Act I: Framing the Business Problem

For Act I, the difficulty is in translating the business problem into an analytics or econometrics problem. The result might be a profit equation, a planned analysis, or a general direction for pursuing data mining. This translation involves understanding what needs to be analyzed to address the business problem. As previously illustrated in the BA capability chart (Figure 3.1), business problems vary from being straightforward to being more involved.

Causes of Death:

A. The necessary qualifications were absent or underutilized in framing the problem.

B. The team did not comprehend all the details and ramifications of the business problem. This can be understandable for some complex problems. The team might have realized from the onset that they did not completely understand the problem or the business problem might have taken a surprising twist.

C. The team did not adequately plan the data analysis or develop an adequate profit equation.

Act II: Executing the Data Analysis

The most important point of this chapter is that Act II is all analytics—by our definition. Any relevant industry knowledge does not belong in Act II. We want to purposely untangle the business problem so that we can better think about it. We can demonstrate that the data analysis in Act II is "invariant to" (does not vary with) industry knowledge.[21] Proof? First, take the data from an analysis performed by a qualified professional in your industry. Translate the data dictionary and the problem statement so as to mask the industry of origin (be diligent with this task). Send the package to a qualified business quant outside your industry and pay them to analyze the data. Finally, compare the findings. We should get valid answers each and every time.[22]

We need to leverage what we know about Acts I and IV to decide on the rigor needed in Act II.

Causes of Death:

D. The necessary qualifications were absent or underutilized in performing the analysis.[23]

E. The business analysts and business quants were insufficiently resourced with analytics software, adequate time, and/or access to appropriate or reliable data.

Act III: Interpreting the Results

For Act III, the involvement of industry knowledge and analytics expertise depends on the nuances. We recommend a generous involvement of the business analysts and business quants in translating the findings back to the business problem. Industry knowledge is ubiquitous; misinterpretations are often unnecessarily due to a lack of statistical involvement. Including the practitioners develops them by removing the blindfold, thus providing them with invaluable insight.

Causes of Death:

F. The necessary qualifications were absent or underutilized in interpreting the results.

G. The team misinterpreted the data analysis.

Act IV: Making Analytics-Based Decisions

Success in Act IV hinges on the decision maker's ability to make objective analytics-based decisions. Many corporations are great at the first three acts, yet they implode because of habitual mistakes in Act IV.

Causes of Death:

H. The necessary qualifications were absent or underutilized in making the decision.

I. The decision makers inadequately or incorrectly incorporated the findings into the decision. This includes not leveraging the findings at all or misinterpreting said findings.

Consequences (of Tragedy)

In Section 2.2, we discussed a few spectacular "big bangs," which can be traced directly to failures in leveraging analytics. These big bangs are unusual events in that (1) the poor decision could be identified; (2) it was traced to a failure to properly apply analytics; and (3) the result was salient. Most failures in leveraging analytics go unnoticed, leaving money on the table or leading the corporation down the wrong path. Mistakes can be slow to manifest themselves; the results can be incremental over time. Unfortunately, it can take analytics to recognize errors and omissions in data analysis and analytics-based decisions.

One common paradigm occurs when a corporation takes the wrong path. For example, Kodak should have pursued its lead in digital technology rather than improving its analog capabilities. The decision makers either misread or failed to collect the proper facts. Clearly, these are difficult decisions to get right. In the case of Kodak, Blockbuster, Sony, and Apple, they had to choose between business as usual and cannibalizing their current income stream! Apple bravely decided that cannibalizing its own business was the right decision. For Kodak, it has turned out that digital cameras were not a fad. For whatever reasons, the decision makers did not get "the picture."

Act V: Reviewing and Preparing for Future Decisions

In Chapter 9, we will discuss how to review data analysis and analytics-based decisions.

ψ   ψ   ψ

Section 3.3 Decision Impairments: Pitfalls, Syndromes, and Plagues in Act IV

Corporate decisions suffer from the same decision impairments as those made outside the corporation. We will discuss the most notorious pitfalls, syndromes, and plagues with a view toward helping decision makers anticipate their foibles.

Plague: Information and Disinformation Overload

The world has gone complex. More information seems like a good idea in the moment. Then when we get the truckload back to the office, it detracts from our focus and our higher brain functions.[24] We need to focus on the critical facts without falling into a familiar pitfall: tunnel thinking. We need to simplify the reliable information.

In this world of information and disinformation overload, part of the challenge is to wade through the information and determine which facts to believe. We should emphasize quality over quantity; trust, but verify; and block sources of disinformation pollution. Disinformation comes from either faulty analytics or a lack of analytics. Analytics professionals should be skeptical of "findings" that are not reviewed or not attributed to a qualified professional. A great deal of "research" is for entertainment, self-promotion, and the like.

Pitfall: Overanalysis

There will always be situations where we need to make a decision without adequate information. We need to strike a balance between prolonging the decision and making a rash under-informed one. We need to master two skills:

1. Making decisions once we have enough information or can not expect any more
2. Framing decisions within the context of other decisions and the time available

We seldom find decision makers who are slow to make decisions once there is adequate information. We are more likely to see them wait for information that is not coming or that is not likely to change the decision.

The solutions to indecision include placing time constraints and choosing a default decision. There is a cost associated with delaying decisions. We need to incorporate that into our thinking. Sometimes decisions have to be based upon guesswork. We should acknowledge, at least to ourselves, that we are guessing and move on. Guessing is not our preferred strategy. It can be a sign of poor planning and a lack of familiarity with what and how information can be collected.

Apple Inc. launches products that are original enough that they create new markets. Their business paradigm challenges the relevance of the usual customer surveys and focus groups. Their approach is to create a solution and then look for a corresponding customer need. They have had mixed results—they launched a product called the Newton and this solution never found a problem. Their experiences are indicative of two things: (1) there are business needs for which we cannot reasonably collect useful information, and (2) acquiring reliable information can be challenging, requiring originality or even genius.

> *"For every complex problem, there is a solution that is simple, neat, and wrong."*
>
> —H. L. Mencken

> *"Seek simplicity, then distrust it."*
>
> —Alfred North Whitehead

Pitfall: Oversimplification

A trend of our times is that burning need to make everything too simple. This problem is pretty well known. One tendency is to oversimplify a complex stochastic problem into a simple deterministic one.

Not all decisions merit the full complement of our analytics arsenal. However, there are decisions that require complex information.

Syndrome: Deterministic Thinking

We want to be careful about inferring causality. Not everything happens for a reason.[25] The human brain evolved to recognize patterns, and we see them even when they are not there. The problem is an overemphasis on causal explanations to the point that even random chance has to have an explanation.[26] We can succumb to pattern hallucination.

If we single out a particular business anecdote, we can invariably "think up" a causal business explanation. Consider the following experiment. Tell half of a group of professionals that the numbers are down and a separate half that the numbers are up. Then pressure both halves for explanations. These explanations are actually untested hypotheses that fit the current "facts" and are not inferences.[27] For every event, the brain can generate an anecdotal explanation, which fits what just happened.[28] What we need are general widely applicable explanations so that we can understand what happened and predict what will occur. We need hypotheses that have been proposed independent of the analysis.

A well-known example of retrospective determinism is called the survivorship bias. This trap can catch us even when we are vigilant. We look at characteristics of those who won big on the stock market (survivors) and we do not see the characteristics of those who lost their shirts. We only observed the survivors. Maybe their characteristics are identical (or at least the noticeable differences could be random). We want to observe both survivors and those not surviving and compare the two.

Deterministic Thinking is great for hypothesis building. The trouble arises when we "bet the house" on an untested hypothesis—management by anecdote.

"Experience by itself teaches nothing."

—W. Edwards Deming

Syndrome: Overdependence on Industry Knowledge

Industry knowledge is needed to optimize the correct business problem. It is vital even though it is plentiful. We are so infatuated with it that it has become a currency within the corporation.

As will be discussed further in Section 4.2, one source of problems arises from skimping on analytics in the face of often ubiquitous industry knowledge. **An overemphasis on industry knowledge crowds out good analytics.** We infer this by observing situations where there is no shortage of industry experience, but we see a surplus of incorrect or absent data analysis.

One symptom of Industry Knowledge Syndrome is the inwardly focused view that "data analysis in our industry is special and distinct from data analysis in all those other industries"[29] (see "The Gemini Myths" in Section 4.2). Statistics should be seen as a cross-industry specialization, and so should accounting, programming, finance, transportation logistics, and others. It is our experience that businesses in other industries have the same analytics problems, just couched in different parlance and occurring in different frequencies. The digits always run from 0 to 9.

Competitors have the same industry knowledge—no competitive advantage. Data analysis provides new information, new insight into the business.

Pitfall: Tunnel Thinking

Opinions can solidify after years of observation. Once we arrive at a conclusion, all subsequent information tends to reinforce it. This force is difficult to deny. The blockage can be from resistance to change—rigidity. We need to make a conscious effort to rethink critical decisions or pass them to fresher minds. *Super Crunchers*[30] makes the case that objective regression models are not subject to past preconceptions.

> *"Firmness in decision is often merely a form of stupidity. It indicates an inability to think the same thing out twice."*
>
> —H. L. Mencken

One interesting paradigm occurs with making an incorrect decision and sticking with it. A corporation sifts through the analytics, which call for a change in strategy, and then remains stuck in last year's decision.[31] To make it more interesting, consider the case where there is an emphasis on making a quick decisive decision, with no time to comprehend the analytics—"decisive leadership." For years the corporation keeps traveling in these wide circles—although they are making quick decisions. The corporation spirals around the abyss of an obsolete strategy at high speed—a Decisive Circle.[32] Such was the problem with the Great Pharmaceutical Arms Race described in Section 2.2. The centripetal force kept corporations from finding the escape opportunity suggested by the numbers. The time it takes to make a decision should be timed by how long it takes to get to a successful solution. We want to get these critical decisions right so that we are not repeating the same mistake. As will be mentioned in the next section, *Super Crunchers* makes the case that preconceptions discourage us from objectively looking at new contradictory information.

Syndrome: Overconfident Fool Syndrome

David Dunning and Justin Kruger[33] state that the least competent people have a deficiency in "self-monitoring skills." "Not only do they reach erroneous conclusions and make unfortunate choices, but their incompetence robs them of the ability to realize it." The danger lies with the huge gap between self-perception and reality.

These overconfident decision makers comprise some of the most hazardous ones. Most of them have some demonstrated ability. People who are less experienced at failure tend to be more overconfident. Their overconfidence is often manifested as Tunnel Thinking, Oversimplification, and Deterministic Thinking. *Super Crunchers* makes the case that experts in every field are overconfident in their ability to predict future events within their domain expertise or industry.

We embrace a humble approach to understanding the facts. We know that we are often wrong (and so is everyone). Thinking statistically[34] can help keep success in perspective. We think our error rate is directly proportional to our overconfidence.

Pitfall: Unpiloted Big Bang Launches

We all want to accomplish important sweeping changes as quickly as possible.

Big Bang launches will always be in vogue as a high-profile approach for getting things done right away.[35] Some of these Big Bangs are best preceded by a pilot study.[36] The pitfall is that some corporations *never* consider a pilot as a tool for planning a sweeping change. This concept is not in their repertoire. However, the planning and the piloting ensure that the "bang" arrives as a crescendo trumpeting success.

Pilots can ensure that a project is performed faster and more successfully. Pilots work out the details and reveal the unknown. When a pilot is warranted, we can test several ideas at once through an experiment.[37] This is faster than iterative trial and error. The pilot serves as the leading antennae. We should use a pilot to launch analytics in a non-analytics corporation.

If our launch repertoire lacks pilot testing capabilities, then this might be a symptom of a larger problem within the organization. Usually, such an organization lacks a culture that is supportive of innovation and experimentation. Omitting the pilot takes the trial out of "trial and error."

Save the corporation, end the unpiloted Big Bang shooting from the hip.

Notes

1. Anyone can just guess or make an opinion-based decision.
2. Ironically, tracking the performance of these two approaches is a fact-based approach to deciding which is better. If we employ an opinion-based approach to measuring these approaches, then we might get a different answer.
3. When we time races, we mark the completion time at the finish line, not when the runner stops running.
4. The salesperson was attractive.
5. Again, "One important dictum is to make decisions at the lowest level possible."—Thomas C. Redman, *Data Driven: Profiting from Your Most Important Business Asset* (2008).
6. Everyone claims to know the former, and a surprising number claim to understand the latter.
7. To make quick, yet not rash, decisions that logically and not arbitrarily leverage the information.
8. The superhuman ability to change one's mind upon encountering new contradictory facts.
9. Industry Knowledge + Business Analytics > Industry Knowledge^2.
10. The pace at which industries continue to redefine themselves is quickening.
11. It was as if we were just checking to see if the data was "right" and not trying to find the right answer. So what was the value add of that data?
12. This is to say that the industry knowledge is baked into the data dictionary.

13. This same schism is present in corporations and society today (see *The Immortal Game: A History of Chess* by David Shenk (2007)).

14. Alan Greenspan adhered to his ideology that banks will self-regulate, and he perceived regulation as very difficult. The former view is an odd perspective for the head of a regulatory body, and it was disastrous for the world economy. Anyone who drives a car knows that self-regulation does not work for many situations. As to his second idea, regulating banks is much easier when employing analytics. Bernie Madoff's Ponzi scheme was detected years earlier using statistics (see "No One Would Listen: A True Financial Thriller" by Harry Markopolos). To his credit, Mr. Greenspan has recognized some of his mistakes—that superhuman ability of decision elasticity.

15. Parts of a corporation are prone to have an environment that encourages conformity and the herd mentality.

16. Just make it someone else's problem; someone qualified.

17. Greek tragedies involve an overly excessively ridiculously harsh punishment for a mistake. Corporate punishments include, yet are not limited to, bankruptcy, garden-variety financial loss, and missed bonanza.

18. We will treat sophisticated data collection as a data analysis—similar tools.

19. For this book, we will treat actions based upon analytics as decisions.

20. For some, the fifth act is to review analytics results and analytics-based decisions (see Chapter 9). By learning from this experience, we prepare for the next business decision. This begets continual improvement.

21. The idea that statistics is invariant is difficult for many to grasp. Many learn statistics within the context of another discipline such as sociology, psychology, biology, physics, engineering, and others.

22. Part of the confusion is that statistics does not generate unique answers.

23. Many corporations have enough talent to address their needs in Act II, yet struggle to employ their talent effectively. This is often a leadership challenge.

24. Well, relatively higher brain functions. Our intelligence is from the Stone Age, and our modern wisdom consists of the arduously accumulated knowledge ever since that first dim bulb lit up—intelligence predates our species.

25. Suppose something happened and it could not possibly have consequences. How could it then have happened for a reason? Unless you have a circular definition that things only happen for a reason if they have consequences. For example, suppose that we flip a coin (by the way, why are we so stuck on flipping coins and rolling dice for these examples?) and never know the outcome. If the unknown outcome was a heads (tails), then this outcome has no consequences because it can never be known.

26. When every event must have an anecdotal explanation, we are not allowed the humility to say "I do not know" and move to more productive endeavors.

27. We deduced when we needed to infer.

28. A senior manager at a large corporation deduced a causal relationship based upon the results of a data analysis. He went around for months with his exciting business insight. Eventually, it was discovered that the data was labeled backward, meaning that his interpretation was also backward (credit my editor with the double entendre here).
29. Statistician parlance is that data analysis is invariant to industry.
30. See *Super Crunchers: Why Thinking-by-Numbers Is the New Way to Be Smart* by Ian Ayres (2007).
31. Sometimes we should just go with the magic eight ball.
32. By this we mean chasing our own tail in long circles. We repeatedly face the same business problem and make the same "decisive" decision as last time. Even though there is new contradictory information that would help us to recognize that we are going in circles and to find the exit door. This scenario is common with decisions that need to be made annually.
33. See *The Journal of Personality and Social Psychology*, Dunning and Kruger, December 1999.
34. By this we mean stochastically, that is, things do not happen for a reason. For every event, there is a probability of it occurring. Events that have occurred did not have a probability of one that they would occur.
35. Just not for getting things done right. Hasty bad decisions consume more time than careful correct decisions.
36. We can hear people bemoaning this already because they want so badly to get things done.
37. This opportunity is routinely missed.

4

Analytics-Driven Culture

"In the final analysis, the root cause of Japan's defeat, not alone in the Battle of Midway but in the entire war, lies deep in the Japanese national character. There is an irrationality and impulsiveness about our people which results in actions that are haphazard and often contradictory."

—Mitsuo Fuchida and Masatake Okumiya[1]

Business Analytics dissolves in an IT culture and in other cultures too. Philosophically, business analysis is in its Romantic Era—an era in which analysis is applied hither and yon in a tactical swashbuckling manner. Corporations aspiring to improve their decision making to become more analytics-based will want to foster a more analytics-driven culture. They should seek a culture that:

1. Rewards analytics-based decision making—as in a meritocracy.
2. Integrates analytics into their strategy.
3. Embraces the pace of dynamic change during this analytics phase of the Information Age.
4. Accepts that understanding data analysis is part of understanding the business.
5. Fosters experimentation and continual learning about the business.

Corporate culture can be defined as "how we do business." An analytics-driven culture necessarily blends analytics and company know-how. We can raise the analytics content of the culture by adjusting the Leadership, Specialization, Delegation, and Incentives (as discussed in Section 2.1).[2]

Analytics-driven cultures have built a legacy of seeking great financial opportunities based upon the numbers. They have learned to accept or tolerate the scientific method, plan for analytics, and enable analytics to drive decision making. They are more deliberate in collecting appropriate data for their decisions. Rather than passively reacting to the data available, their proactive planning includes thinking ahead to seek new types of data that does not yet exist.

Chapters 7 to 12 provide the tools that will help us to reshape the corporate infrastructure to facilitate an analytics-driven culture.

Another crude measure of a corporation's acceptance of analytics is the extent to which Analytics Professionals are spread through the company. If a corporation wants to develop a more analytics-driven culture, then it needs to expose people to business analytics and spread Analytics Professionals throughout the company—growing the culture by spreading the approach.

Left Brain–Right Brain Cultural Clash— Enter the Scientific Method

The explosion of information implies that we need to apply scientific tools and this is not about pottery or poetry. Left-brain purveyors of the scientific method sound like Mr. Spock, or today's modern icons, Dr. Samantha Carter and Dr. Daniel Jackson of *Stargate SG1*. Analytics professionals are trained to accept their ignorance, value humility in presenting results, and qualify their statements. They are often self-made.

At a large bank, a group of predictive modelers was told never to say "I don't know" when answering questions from senior management. Similarly, they were told not to include caveats in their presentations. All these confessions of ignorance, qualified statements, and the 15 footnotes[3] appear like "doubt speak" to the right-brainers. Do you have the answer or not? Captain Kirk, or the sensibly upgraded Dr. Elizabeth Weir of *Stargate Atlantis*, just want the answer so that they can "decide already." Should we put our phasers on stun or close the stargate, and was that so difficult? We can benefit by thinking through these cultural differences.

What you need to know if you are dating a right-brainer: Left-brainers, you need to go to charm school and forget about impressing others with your level of preparedness, intelligence, and impeccable logic.[4] Okay, we get it; analytics is subject to uncertainty. Now start socializing analytics so it is not so threatening.

Making other people feel stupid does not make you appear very smart. Stop qualifying your results. You dwell much too much on the fact that if your analysis is correct, then there is still a chance that the conclusion is wrong—incomplete information being what it is. Finally, if you are in a non-analytics culture, then you need to do more than write a glossary of acronyms and speak the local language. You must walk the walk, too. **You need to behave as much like the right-brainers as you can stand— conform a little, sadly.** When your right-brained peer interrupts you mid-sentence, you interrupt them mid-sentence. When right-brainers go out into the field to see what is really going on, they should find you there taking care of what is going. Just deal with it.

What you need to know if you are dating a left-brainer: Right-brainers, you need to appreciate that the left-brainers have the lonely responsibility for getting the facts right in the face of messed-up incomplete information. Going forward, you need to evolve, to accept more of the communication burden, to think differently. Is this so threatening?[5] You want to embrace or at least accept uncertainty. When reading analysis, you should interpret signs of intellectual humility as signs of intellectual humility and not weakness. If you want the left-brainers to explain things simply, then you can help by reminding them that you realize their work is complex. **Keep asking them the same question until you get it.** Do not give up. However, you cannot expect them to divulge their secret techniques.

If the above was not enough for you, left-brainers will want to share all of the bad news they have discovered. Just deal with it.

What you need to know: In practice, we all have left- and right-brain behaviors and **anyone who thinks that some group of people is homogeneous does not know much about them.** Now that we are in the Information Age, it is no longer wise to run a company with half a brain. Today, our medieval corporate cultures from the Dark Ages place too much of the burden on the left-brainers to get the numbers right, *and* explain it so that right-brainers can understand it.[6] This is unreasonable—or at least not optimal. Instead, we should ask for the caveats and accept the "I don't knows" on our way to cashing in on analytics. In analytics, there can be something suspicious about someone with all of the answers—they are not left-brain. The cultural change we seek is to be both left- and right-brain.

Denying the Serendipity of Statistics

Before purchasing expensive data or executing a sophisticated analysis, you should plan how you are going to use this information or how you are going to analyze a business problem. Having a plan makes sense, just not perfect sense. No one sat down and wrote a detailed plan for the discovery of penicillin. It was a complete accident. Many great discoveries happen by chance. Holding a data request up to the standards of a mathematical proof is a bit much. This is a chronic breakdown point and the site of many a discombobulation. In an analytics-driven culture, it should be sufficient for a plan to entail what you expect and emphasize the economics of the possible exploratory work. We may need to make numerous attempts on our way to success.

Denying the Source—Plagiarism

Finally and foremost, we must resist the temptation of allowing people to present other peoples' analytics work. This delays acclimation and creates a deceptive culture. At a number of corporations, this is the standard. No one below a certain rank is given the privilege of presenting to senior management, and the token few qualified analytics professionals will always be below that rank—whatever it takes. This senior management intends to stay insulated in the "executive management bubble," all right-brain.

Section 4.1 The Fertile Crescent: Striking It Rich

> *"It is from their foes, not their friends, that cities learn the lesson of building high walls."*
>
> —Aristophanes

We wish to discuss characteristics of environments that facilitate a more analytics-driven culture. This will provide insight into how we can alter our environment to encourage analytics. Even with everything we know about the benefits of analytics, most analytics-driven cultures arise in response to the discovery of "natural resources"[7] located in close proximity to a "killer app."

Natural Resources: Naturally occurring impromptu data. By impromptu data, we mean that taking the data out of the ground requires only a little statistical expertise or infrastructure. This contrasts with difficult to extract data, which requires more infrastructure and/or advanced techniques such as simulation, sampling designs, or designed experiments[8] (see Chapter 10).

There is a tendency for killer applications to have these two characteristics:

1. Measureable impact
2. Traceable profit

Measurable Impact: In a functional culture, the quality and accuracy of the analytics are more often and more easily measured. Predictive models predict events that might eventually happen—that is, it is much more common to "experience" the accuracy of the prediction. Also, control groups are more common in a functional culture and can be obtained without great authority. A great deal of data analysis requires a designed experiment[9] to measure its effectiveness—when it can be done.

Traceable Profit: In a functional culture, we must be able to trace large profits back to the analytics. Furthermore, it must be unlikely that these profits could be obtained by non-statistical solutions, such as guessing.

Catalysts and Change

There are a number of catalysts for encouraging an analytics culture, some of which can be created or adjusted:

1. Crisis—heat and pressure to change: A corporation or industry in enough crisis, and not too much, will begin to change. The best way to simulate this catalyst is to build a network of change agents, which is the essence of Six Sigma's network of black belts.
2. Peer pressure: Competitors adopting analytics will stimulate other corporations "to keep up with the Joneses."
3. On-topic training: **Analytics training creates more receptivity to analytics.** General Electric was more receptive to Six Sigma because it is chock full of engineers, scientists, and other analytically oriented thinkers who are comfortable with numbers as facts—left-brain. One reason why Six Sigma underperformed at certain banks and pharmaceuticals is because these corporations have right-brain sales cultures.[10] We will discuss training in Chapter 7, and we do not have *t*-tests in mind.

There are a number of beneficial reactions to striking it rich. Here are some tendencies:

1. Reduced political paralysis: When objective results are shown to make the most money, politics are less likely to force results to match politically inspired conclusions. Measurable impact and traceable profit, the two characteristics above, conspire to render manipulation less politically valuable and some political ambitions are deflected elsewhere.

2. A striking decline in anti-analytics or analytics phobia. When analytics makes us money, it is our friend.

3. Decision makers are more sophisticated. This is because they both become more sophisticated and they are selected because they *are* more sophisticated. They are more skilled and enthusiastic about incorporating analytics into their decisions. Also, they can better discern the quality of analytics. More of the decision makers have more training in statistics. As a result of discerning analytics quality, they can better discern talent from "pretenders with a good story."

4. Analytics talent spreads further into the corporation. More of the statistically trained are hired, promoted, and circulated. Also, the extent of the technical training is better.

5. One final reaction is to raise the analytics content of the culture by adjusting Leadership, Specialization, Delegation, and Incentives (all discussed in Section 2.1).

As previously mentioned, analytics usually grows as a reaction to the environment. Only on rare occasions is there a master plan for building an analytics-driven culture, regardless of the environment. Industries that are well pervaded by the use of analytics may have standard tools and techniques to work with; however, less fertile industries lack the resources to support the development of the techniques they need. They must search for sophisticated techniques in other more analytically mature industries.

Banks struck a rich vein of customer data—the Comstock Load, if you will. In banking, a generation of analytics professionals learned how to build predictive models under favorable conditions. Over time, the industry developed more sophisticated decision makers and tools sophisticated enough to work in other industries too poor to build their own technology.

Industries like accounting have valuable data, but have been unable to leverage it. Even after major scandals[11] created a credibility crisis in the industry, accounting firms could not get past the challenges in predicting fraud. First, the ledger data is crude and requires sophisticated manipulation. Second, there are few examples of actual fraud cases with which to refine predictive models. Third, some companies are understandably sensitive about their ledger data being analyzed. Fourth, this is something new and resistance is omnipresent. Fifth, there are few decision makers familiar with analytics. However, we have learned so much about building predictive models from banking that some of us have been able to build these models under these harsher conditions! And that is how analytics *almost* spread to accounting (see Hakan Gogtas's sidebar in Section 2.3).

Predictive modeling is on the rise in several other industries. It is more pervasive than most other statistical tools. In the corporate world, predictive modeling contrasts sharply with most other data concerns. Predictive modeling is far less likely to be censored or dumbed down, and the results are much more likely to be validated and reviewed. These differences encourage higher quality work than we see elsewhere in a corporate environment just starting to think about certifying analytics professionals.[12]

Two-Trick Pony

It is difficult for corporations to apply a breadth of statistical tools. The manufacturing analytics boom of the 1940s and 1950s was mostly about quality control (QC) charts and Design of Experiments (DoE) with a sprinkling of data visualization tools. Despite a conducive culture and statistical talent, the banking analytics boom of the 1990s was mostly about predictive modeling. There were many opportunities to apply DoE, Design of Samples (DoS), QC, stochastic processes, and other tools.[13] Yet this seldom happened. The banks could not expand their statistical repertoire beyond this single killer application. Sometimes this was due to the inability to measure impact or trace profit. Often it was to due to the inability to connect other statistical tools to new killer applications.

In parallel, Six Sigma has done little to expand its statistical repertoire beyond techniques common to manufacturing.

In Chapters 7 to 9, we will provide tools that will help corporations measure the reliability of analytics and analytics-based decisions—either directly or indirectly. Armed with better measurement, we can extrapolate the value of analytics from past successes to completely different applications. In Chapters 10 to 12, we will discuss three building blocks for better extracting, organizing, and analyzing difficult data. Enabling the mining of less fertile natural resources—messy data.

大　大　大

Section 4.2 The Blend: Mixing Industry Knowledge and Advanced Analytics

> *"Our want of rationality often leads us to confuse desire and reality, and thus to do things without careful planning. Only when our hasty action has ended in failure do we begin to think rationally about it, usually for the purpose of finding excuses for the failure."*
> —Mitsuo Fuchida and Masatake Okumiya[14]

Many corporations are understandably passionate about their current store of industry knowledge. However, this can get in the way of strengthening their analytics capabilities, which ultimately supply new industry knowledge. They dramatically underestimate the technical depth required to facilitate an analytics-based culture.

We need to accept the fact that some information improves with age—wisdom, and other information becomes a liability. The pace at which certain information becomes obsolete will continue to increase. Newer, more dynamic industries tend to be more analytics-driven because they are pressured to embrace the fact that information is transient. Analytics facilitates what econometricians call "creative destruction."[15] This involves challenging current industry knowledge, validating the more accurate legends, and replacing the fairy tales.

We will partition industry knowledge into two parts: general and specific. The general industry knowledge consists of the "common sense" particular to an industry. This common sense provides a language, relevance, and familiar reference points. This under-

> **Concept Box**
>
> *Problem knowledge*—The information specific to a particular business problem. It tends to be more elusive and dynamic. This is not the "common sense" part of Industry Knowledge; it is the problem-specific information. That is, the specific industry expertise that relates to a particular business problem.

standing of the industry shapes our business strategy and from here we first "appreciate" various business problems.[16] The specific industry knowledge consists of the finer details around particular business problems. This problem knowledge is precious for Acts I, III, and IV of business problems lying in Quadrants II and IV. It provides the context for any data analysis, and it remembers past analytics findings and past analytics attempts.

In his book, *Super Crunchers*, Ian Ayres discusses blending industry expertise and analytics. The author provides numerous examples where analytics outperforms industry experts. Similarly, he debunks the absolute hold of the Aristotelian approach—we must first understand the intricate how or the causality of the problem before we can take action. While this is the usual approach, it ignores our ability to "infer" from data.

During the 1990s, a number of established industries courted the idea of adding predictive modeling technology to improve their decision making. They were unable to find a critical mass of people with predictive modeling expertise *and* industry knowledge, which contains some problem knowledge. They wanted each professional to be versed in both skill sets. They chose to hire individuals with adequate industry knowledge and insufficient analytics training. They looked past sophisticated business quants, who did not possess a great deal of industry experience. The brief conversation went something like this:

BA Professional: I can predict your customer behavior!

Industry Intuition: Impossible, you do not understand our business.

Newer, more dynamic industries were more successful. There were no alternative people to hire, who possessed useful industry knowledge.

Industry knowledge is helpful for the Aristotelian approach to problem solving. However, not everyone on the team has to understand everything about the industry. That is, we can infer from the data and rely upon statistical diagnostics to validate our conclusions.

Early in Deming's career, he emphasized the statistics dimension to business problems, claiming that it was the most important part of the puzzle. Later in his career, he came to emphasize the problem knowledge, claiming that it was more important. He was correct both times. We emphasize both and we claim that it is all relative.[17] In Figure 4.1, we place the business problem within these two dimensions: analytics difficulty and business problem difficulty.

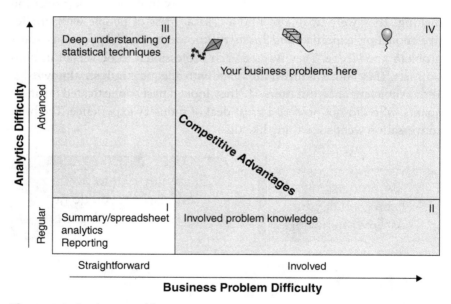

Figure 4.1. Business problems

Cultural Imbalance

Seeking balance is part of the corporate condition. Corporations have too few sales reps, too many sales reps, too little IT, too much IT, and so on. Finding balance in analytics is a challenge. Statistically struggling corporations fail to derive new industry knowledge and defuse old information.[18]

Corporations do a great job of collecting and retaining the industry knowledge[19] needed for Quadrants II and IV. This makes sense because everyone understands and can measure industry knowledge.[20] Unfortunately, our desire for more of something we already possess distracts us from building and empowering analytics ability. For example, occasionally a new analyst misses something simple like the fact that in our industry the work week has six days—so we divide by six.[21] Who knew?[22] Yet this is vital local knowledge—common knowledge, to be respected. Two facts go unnoticed by less analytically driven cultures. First, that the same analytics professional correctly solved the "four-dimensional quadrature"[23] problem. Second, the analyst would know about the six-day work week if this common knowledge resided in the data dictionary where it belongs.

Corporations correctly recognize that there is a powerful synergy between problem knowledge and analytics training. Yet they dramatically underestimate the amount of analytics training required. In place of adequate analytics training, they substitute more industry experience. It has been said that during our third semester of statistics, we understand our second semester of statistics, and so on. The first few semesters of statistics accumulate facts; the latter semesters build the way we think and they provide technique. In the end, there can be little synergism between five or more years of industry experience and only one to three semesters of analytics content. We need problem knowledge combined with a statistical (stochastic) way of thinking and a mastery of analytics techniques.

The primary concern for the professional performing the data analysis should be the data analysis—Act II. Corporations are too fixated on finding professionals who can perform Acts I and III solo.[24] This tends to reduce the statistical training brought to bear in Act II. They have no coverage for the upper two quadrants and plenty of coverage for the bottom right quadrant.[25]

Here is how we can attain balance: Statistically thin corporations need to grow and empower analytics in their culture. The fastest way is to bring in highly trained analytics professionals with cross-industry applied analytics experience[26] and place them on bilingual teams—pairing industry experts with business analysts and business quants. This will address any concerns about Acts I and III.[27]

Some of the more traditional industries are trying to grow their analytics capabilities at the moment. They are likely to struggle and not learn from the foibles of previous industries.[28] They will most likely hold themselves back by under-hiring analytics in favor of more industry knowledge. This makes perfect sense to an extent.[29] The point is that their hiring approach is asymmetrical, covering the quadrants they understand. They will continue to skimp on specialized training like analytics.[30] This retards their assimilation of analytics from other industries.

Here is one likely trajectory: A corporation hires five professionals over three years. All have two to five years in the industry and the equivalent of two to three semesters of statistics. This means no coverage in the top two quadrants—ever.

Alternatively, they could hire three professionals with 3 to 5 years in the industry and the equivalent of 2 to 3 semesters of statistics, and two with cross-industry experience and the equivalent of 10 to 30 semesters of statistical content. If the corporation can provide an adequate data dictionary, then those with no industry knowledge can contribute right away. A whole-hearted attempt will bring them up to speed quickly. This approach covers the more challenging analytics problems in the upper two quadrants.

The Gemini Myths

There are two parallel cultural myths that impede the progression of analytics in Act II. These myths hold back statistically dysfunctional corporations:

1. Data in my industry are different—beyond outsider comprehension.
2. Statistical tools in my industry work differently—beyond outsider comprehension.

The differences between industries lie in the important semantic connections to the numbers—Acts I, III, and IV from Section 3.2. These semantic connections are what people are usually referring to as different. Act II is often seamlessly sandwiched between Acts I and Acts III and IV. Unfortunately, the context can exaggerate the appearance of differences. The real barriers between industries are created by this exaggerated perception of the dependence of analytics on industry[31]... that somehow Act II varies by industry. The missed opportunity is that analytics solutions in one industry are ignored in another.

As a caveat, industries vary by the frequency at which different data structures appear. Manufacturing is known for process data, and finance is known for high-frequency behavioral data. The statistical tools vary with the data structure and the objective.

Marketing analytics and marketing research are recognizable across most industries, using even much of the same terminology. This is because the marketing profession does a better job of communicating across and moving professionals across industries. Marketing is more invariant to industry.

Cross-industry experience can be invaluable for all four acts. There are more helpful similarities across industries than isolating differences. The specifics around the business problem can change more within an industry than across them. Furthermore, we defined Act II to contain only analytics, not requiring the context of the problem knowledge. By our definition, statistical tools in Act II transfer across industries much like addition and subtraction.

By appreciating that we can dissect the analytics business problem into four acts, we can rethink how we hire and how we organize teams. In particular, this elevates the idea of building bilingual teams—pairing industry experts with business analysts and business quants. We are no longer restricted to industry experts with mild analytics training, so we no longer need to skimp on analytics. Similarly, we can leverage analytics solutions from other industries. These advantages enable a number of benefits.

The points are that we routinely have more than enough industry knowledge when what we really want is problem knowledge, and we understate the analytics expertise wanted in the blend.

Notes

1. It is an amazing feat to write a book about a naval battle and tie the outcome to a cultural characteristic. See *Midway: The Battle That Doomed Japan* by Mitsuo Fuchida and Masatake Okumiya (1955).
2. *"Competing on Analytics: The New Science Of Winning," "Analytics At Work: Smarter Decisions, Better Results, Data Driven: Profiting from Your Most Important Business Asset, Super Crunchers: Why Thinking-by-Numbers Is the New Way to Be Smart,* among others, have made it clear that analytics is too understated in the blend.

3. Alright, so this book has footnotes, but some of them are funny.

4. We are just making fun of you a little. Do not be so sensitive.

5. Just make sure no one is looking while you are evolving.

6. This is the right-brainers saying they cannot be bothered to think in a left-brain manner for a single moment.

7. We can hardly confirm the usual urban legends about two guys from some particular college inventing everything. First, they only took credit for inventing it, and second, many discoveries are accidental—except yours and ours, of course. If some of these urban legends were true, then corporations would be more developed in analytics and not focused on a few statistical tools connected to a few killer apps—as we will discuss in the upcoming section, "Two-Trick Pony."

8. These statistical tools are the equivalents of oil rigs and subterranean data-mining.

9. ... *and no one wants that* (this is the sarcasm voice).

10. There were other compelling reasons.

11. Enron and WorldCom, in close proximity.

12. Accountants, physicians, safety engineers, et al. are certified so that you know. Some professions are even bonded.

13. We will discuss the benefits of DoE and DoS in Chapter 11.

14. Which culture were they writing about? See *Midway: The Battle That Doomed Japan* by Mitsuo Fuchida and Masatake Okumiya (1955).

15. The gale of creative destruction as introduced by Werner Sombart in *Krieg und Kapitalismus (War and Capitalism,* 1913) and elaborated and popularized by the Austrian economist Joseph Schumpeter.

16. When we are analyzing the data, there is the potential for further "appreciation" of these business problems.

17. The easy way out.

18. Without the scrutiny of analytics, industry knowledge is more opinion-based and threatened by pervading fairly tales.

19. Usually, walking down the hallway involves passing an encyclopedia of industry knowledge.

20. By how many years you have been in the industry, and how well you can hold a conversation about it.

21. Of course, this only occurs in months with even days.

22. Actually, everyone else knew... and there was probably someone making a big deal out of this to call attention to him- or herself. This "oversight" will not happen for any industry problem knowledge encapsulated into the data dictionary, where it belongs. Anyway, these miscues can be easily caught because this is common knowledge. If we jettison the analyst, who is going

to catch the analytics mistakes or even realize that we are making analytics mistakes?

23. By this we mean just some difficult problem.
24. And then they involve several people anyway.
25. So what was the point?
26. Cross-industry experience is invaluable for mastering a specialization like statistics. Darwin observed that species limited to an island (such as one isolated industry, like publishing) evolve slower and produce smaller offspring than species on the main land.
27. More about this in Section 6.3.
28. After all, that happened in an entirely different industry, and how could that relate to us? Our industry knowledge is different.
29. To the extent to which they can still grow analytics.
30. Corporations tend to hire and promote the same person 50 times.
31. That and every statistical tool must be renamed as if to introduce something novel.

5

Organization: The People Side of the Equation

"... it's the human and organizational aspects of analytics competition that are truly differentiating."
—Davenport and Harris

"It took a full generation to work out the organizational forms best suited to the Industrial Age. One should expect that it will take that long to work out organizational forms fully attuned to the opportunities and challenges of the Information Age."
—Thomas Redman, *Data Driven*

We need to upgrade the corporate infrastructure. We cannot fully leverage business analytics without changing the corporation. **The most important part of this reorganization is to expand the team of analytics professionals to include more leaders and more decision makers.** We need to find the right people and place them in the right roles.

We will focus on four organizational issues:

1. What constitutes the analytics resources (Section 5.1)
2. How to structure the analytics practitioners (Section 5.2)
3. How to lead the analytics practitioners (Section 5.3)
4. Where to place the analytics practitioners (Section 5.4)

Our discussion will describe the characteristics of a successful analytics team, which we define here as a nexus of analytics professionals—investors, consumers, directors, and practitioners. In Section 5.3, we discuss differences between managing and leading as revealed by Warren Bennis.[1] We discuss how to direct analytics capabilities to meet business needs, and the advantages of leadership possessing training in analytics.

Section 5.1 Analytics Resources

We are interested in a number of analytics roles in the corporation as introduced in Table 5.1. These are differentiated by the nature and level of involvement in analytics. In Table 1.1, we set forth four groups in the complete analytics team: Investors, Consumers, Directors, and Practitioners. Now we will break down the latter two groups in a more detailed discussion.

In this section, we will be more specific about the roles of business quants, business analysts, analytics power users, and knowledge workers. We will discuss on-topic business analytics leaders and expert leaders in Section 5.3. We are aligning our discussion of these various roles with the discussion in *Competing on Analytics* by Davenport and Harris.[2]

Table 5.1 Business Analytics Professionals

Talent	Role and Background
Investors	**Business leaders sponsoring business analytics.**
Enterprise-Wide Advocates	Resides at the enterprise-wide level. They might carry a title such as CAO, CDO, CIO, Chief Economist, or CSO. Invests in analytics at the corporate level. Leverages analytics in their decisions.
Mid-Level Advocates	Resides within a business unit of the company. They might be preparing for a role such as CAO, CDO, CIO, Chief Economist, or CSO. Invests in analytics at the business-unit level. Leverages analytics in their decisions.
Consumers	**Those leveraging analytics in the course of performing their duties.**
Ordinary Decision Makers	Makes prominent decisions for steering a business. Might or might not leverage business analytics. Possesses no particular training or commitment for employing analytics.

Talent	Role and Background
Analytics-Based Decision Makers	Makes prominent decisions for steering a business. Leverages business analytics whenever possible. Sufficiently trained to make decisions based upon analytics; collaborates with business analysts and business quants. Trained in statistics up to the business need; knowledgeable of relevant Statistical Diagnostics (Chapter 8).
Knowledge Workers	The critical mass of employees who leverage analytics results in the performance of their duties. Typically possesses one to three semesters of analytics training.
Practitioners	**Those primarily leading and performing the data analysis.**
Business Analysts	Solves analytics problems; mostly in Quadrants I and II. Applies analytics results to business problems.
Analytics Power Users	Solves analytics and some advanced analytics problems (Quadrants I to IV). Applies analytics results to business problems. Usually holds an advanced degree in business or a quant field. We add this role to cover a large group of practitioners, who lie midway between the BAs and the BQs in their emphasis of advanced analytics.
Business Quants	Builds the more advanced analytics models and algorithms in Quadrants III and IV. Advanced degree, usually in a quant field, with post-academic training—should have PSTAT or equivalent certifications. Speaks the languages of business and analytics.
Directors	**Those leading the analytics practitioners.**
Ordinary Managers of Analytics	Has formal authority to manage business analysts and business quants; does not have a great deal of analytics training. Needs to delegate. Speaks the business language.
Expert Leaders	An experienced business quant who leads advanced analytics projects. Speaks the languages of business and analytics. Possesses advanced degree (usually in a quant field) with post academic training; PSTAT certification or equivalent. Focuses on efficiency in Quadrants I and II and solving the problems in Quadrants III and IV. Evaluates Statistical Qualifications, Diagnostics, and Review, and Data Collection, Software, and Management.
On-Topic Business Analytics Leaders (Analytics Champions)	Quantitatively trained leaders of business analysts, business quants, and enterprise-wide analytics initiatives. Reviews corporate analytics needs and capabilities as an input to corporate strategy. Seeks new killer analytics applications. Leads business analytics projects. Bilingual: speaks the languages of business and analytics. Expert Leader + Formal Authority.

Organizational Evolution

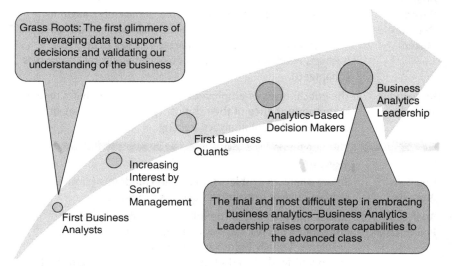

Figure 5.1 Typical analytics progression

To illustrate how analytics evolves inside the corporation, we will discuss one possible progression as illustrated in Figure 5.1. A corporation starts by hiring business analysts within a line of business. The business analysts provide Quadrant I and II capabilities (recall Figures 3.1 and 4.1). These capabilities consist of reporting, tracking, and ad hoc requests. Corporations have had these basic capabilities for a very long time.

At this stage, most of the conversation about analytics occurs among the business analysts, who are performing the data analysis. Eventually, business analytics spreads horizontally to other lines of business, yet there is not much horizontal communication about how to solve problems. The decision makers and business leadership leverage reports and tracking from different lines of business. At some point, these reports need to be standardized so that they can be smartly rolled up to one coherent corporate dashboard or scorecard. This facilitates some horizontal communication about analytics.

In time there is increased interest and greater reliance upon these reports and the tracking of the business. This fosters at least one mid-level advocate facilitating greater use of analytics in their decisions. The mid-level advocate encourages the use of analytics within their business unit—and no further.

An advocate will better focus their reports on key performance indicators, monitoring the corporation's overall strategic performance. Advocates recognize analytics as important to competing in the market place.

Eventually, business quants are hired to perform advanced analytics that one of the company's more innovative competitors has been performing in Quadrants III and IV. Decision makers and an ordinary manager of analytics are being fed more sophisticated analytics. The business quants start proposing all manner of new analytics applications, which are lost on the corporation.

This is where many knowledge-based corporations are located today. There is far more communication about analytics, yet much of this communication is localized and technically limited. In recent years, many corporations invested in IT so that they could build an improved database. Now they are looking for a greater return on this BI investment. This will require further enhancements to the corporate infrastructure.

The next step is for the corporation to acquire or build more sophisticated decision makers. Analytics-based decision makers *want* sophisticated analytics. They are comfortable with more advanced analytics supporting more business decisions. They have thought through the types of decisions they are likely to make and the information that they will need to support these decisions. **Analytics is incorporated into their plan.** They can read Statistical Diagnostics, they can identify business analysts and business quants, and they will lend their influence to ensure that these practitioners have the necessary resources to deliver. At this juncture, analytics is becoming better integrated into the strategy.

Those corporations leading in business analytics possess more fully developed and complete teams of analytics professionals. This achievement is typified by an enterprise-wide advocate, multiple mid-level advocates, analytics-based decision makers, a business analytics leader, and expert leaders. A larger team reflects the greater involvement in business analytics.

An enterprise-wide advocate of analytics and multiple mid-level advocates understand the value proposition. They have expanded business analytics across the corporation. Their conversations better integrate analytics with strategy (see Section 6.1). The leadership expects business analytics presentations to mention more about the analytics tools, to refer to Statistical Diagnostics confirming the results, and to include the practitioners.

Business analytics is used as a strategic resource, and it supports strategic innovation. The focus on how to integrate business analytics into decision making is taken to a next level. Discussions about the technical matters now extend outside the analytics practitioners and into the complete team.

The on-topic business analytics leader and expert leaders possess the training and experience to understand what the analytics team produces and how to fit it into the business. They have a number of partnerships across the entire corporation and they know how to lead the practitioners. They match the rigor to the business problem. They ensure quality and speed through review and they delegate as appropriate.

The business analysts and business quants are highly networked. They seek new analytics business applications and continual improvement of current analytics solutions.

> *"One of the keys to dealing with artists is to be sensitive to their feelings and their needs, to give them their day in court so they can air their grievances or their brilliant ideas."*
>
> —Herb Alpert

Business Quants—Denizens of the Deep

Business quants (people who deal in numbers, quantities) possess specialized training in one or more analytics fields. Davenport and Harris in *Competing on Analytics* write that "there will ... continue to be people in these organizations whose job primarily involves developing and refining analytics"—business quants.[3] "They will either work in a central group or be highly networked, and they'll share approaches and ideas. They will also work to educate the analytical amateurs [what we are terming knowledge workers] of the organizations, who need to understand how analytics models and tools support them in their jobs." These highly capable quants have become hallmarks of change in the way we do business.

The business quant's role is held by the most highly trained professionals. They work in all four quadrants, with their main responsibilities in Quadrants III and IV. This role requires a great deal of academic and post-academic applied training. An advanced degree in a quantitative field will provide most of the desired training and identify those self-selecting for this type of work. Business quants are responsible for building the advanced tools and performing the advanced data analysis. They need the capacity to think critically and to challenge our entrenched assumptions about the business. They need to understand the business without being so deeply immersed that they surrender independent thought.

These professionals need to present their own findings. This will reduce barriers and bring these business quants closer to the decision makers. We want to avoid dumbing down the information to the point that it is irrelevant or harmful for decision making.

Given the proper exposure, business quants can quickly expand their problem knowledge and industry experience. The key is for them to start with enough statistical training, which is typically lacking and very difficult to learn on the job. A strong infrastructure, including a data dictionary and acculturated decision makers, is an important part of that exposure. Those companies that retain and leverage both industry knowledge and statistical expertise will seize the advantage.

Finally, these professionals need to review past analytics decisions and outcomes. They need to examine how the facts were incorporated into the decision and both provide and collect feedback.

Analytics Power Users

This group of professionals blends slightly less analytics into their mix of interests and capabilities. Their focus might not be in performing analytics, yet they are sophisticated enough to apply analytics tools. They might run a great deal of statistical software. Most have an MBA with a quantitative minor, an advanced degree in a quantitative field, an advanced degree in a non-quant field, or a heavy applied statistics degree (B.S.). Some of them are certified and they might want to perform more like business quants. Some will address problems in Quadrants III and IV. By allowing them to present their own findings, we can improve communications and fuel their growth.

Business Analysts

These professionals perform analytics in Quadrants I and II and leverage advanced tools as part of their contribution. They are the most numerous of those performing analytics, and they tend to be more involved in the business side of the problem. While their focus might not be in performing advanced analytics, they are sophisticated enough to apply complicated tools, such as models. Most have an MBA with a quantitative minor, or a heavy applied statistics degree (B.S.). They too need to present their own findings.

Knowledge Workers

A strong group of analytics practitioners is still an incomplete team without the involvement of a critical mass of knowledge workers. Knowledge workers integrate the numbers into the business. They employ some analytics tools, typically within spreadsheets and similar software, and they have a greater understanding of their front line applications in the business.

Knowledge workers serve important functions in the corporation. They need to be networked to the business quants and the business analysts so that their tools are reviewed, updated, and customized. A gap in this communication will suspend continual improvement for an organization and expose the corporation to unnecessary risk. The lines of communication between the knowledge workers, the business analysts, and the business quants create a larger network. Gaps in this communication will diffuse the corporation's effort in competing based upon business analytics.

There Is No Team in I

Section 5.2 Structure of Analytics Practitioners

Now we will discuss the team infrastructure needed for success. Getting the infrastructure right is important in order to lower costs and increase productivity. There is no single organizational structure that fits all corporations and can remain robust over time. We want to design analytics groups that are efficient and insulated from conflicting interests, yet integrated with the business. We think a proper analytics team functions like a MASH (Mobile Army Surgical Hospital) unit.[4] There is specialization, haste, efficiency, a plan, more haste, and no time for theory that does not translate into practice. We want to run the analytics team like an entrepreneurial profit center. This greatly helps with sizing. The analytics team should noticeably produce business results and be measured by the value-add of their completed analyses. An alternative is to arbitrarily ring-fence[5] adequate resources, which is subject to ... subjectivity.

We seek qualified professionals with some outward focus. Practitioners share responsibility for Acts I, III, and IV, and are completely responsible for their work in Act II: Executing the Data Analysis. They should focus on speed, quality, and communication. Finally, they need to oversee and provide visible leadership for the three pillars discussed in Chapters 7 to 9 and the three building blocks covered in Chapters 10 to 12. We will discuss a number of characteristics of teams of analytics practitioners that have proven themselves valuable.

Integration Synergies

As we discussed in Section 4.2, there are synergies in mixing advanced analytics training with involved problem knowledge (see Figures 3.1 and 4.1). An effective team of practitioners must be highly networked to the lines of business.

One particularly efficient structure is to combine a newly arrived expert in data analysis with a company insider—as equals. This is especially effective for statistically emerging corporations, where analytics professionals are less common. A well-matched pair can cut through typical projects faster, and they are capable of sleuthing through those problems where the data says one thing and industry memory says another. We can further leverage this dynamic by pairing company insiders with those already involved in analytics and rotate the expert pair through the corporation. This builds igneous relationships not captured on the organization chart.

Technical Connectivity

One or two people are insufficient to change a culture. By networking a critical mass of business analysts and business quants with the same training, we build the analytics practitioners into a team. This will focus discussions about technical details in one place. This team can promote continual technical improvement, provide one source of the "facts," and find new killer analytics applications. We want to facilitate a highly coordinated effort in Acts I to IV. Furthermore, we want to combine people who like working together and encourage them to create the opportunities. This provides a haven for analytics integrity and specialization. We want the team to contain quants who are ambitious about applying analytics and usually less focused upon self-promotion.

Specialization

The vertical approach to analytics is to treat everyone like a generalist, as illustrated in Figure 5.2. This would be efficient if the tasks were much more alike or people's skills did not vary. For ordinary managers possessing little training in analytics, there is the misperception that all analytics tasks are similar and everyone has the same skill set. Hence, these managers approach projects with assorted parts using professionals with different specializations by making everyone a jack-of-all-trades performing each

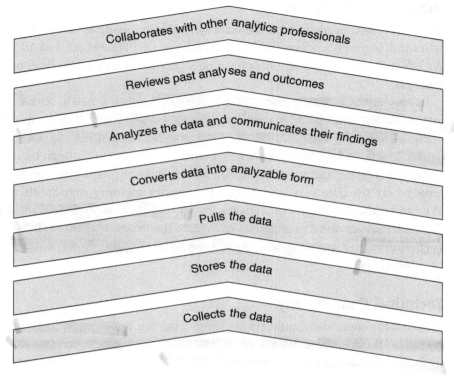

Figure 5.2 The vertical approach

and every task, **like in checkers**. The on-topic business analytics leader recognizes the differences in the tasks and the differences in the professionals' skill sets. These leaders assign professionals to the appropriate tasks. They can coordinate professionals with different skill sets, **like in chess**.[6]

The vertical approach is even more appealing right now because we are in the midst of a multitasking craze. However, research shows that multitasking is not what we think it is. We are not engaging in mental parallel processing. We are just changing the focus of our attention back and forth quickly. This is terribly inefficient for performing numerous assorted high-detail tasks "simultaneously." **We want to multitask only when that makes us more efficient by enhancing our understanding of the business processes, rather than when it merely simplifies the organization chart.**[7] The multitasking craze will likely continue for some time, but die down eventually.

The analytics practitioners, who focus on complex problems, can be far more efficient by allowing them the correct amount of specialization. However, even when the tasks and skills are different, this vertical approach to analytics works just fine when analyses are few and there is not enough repetition to leverage in a horizontal approach. The same person slowly collects the data, stores the data, pulls the data, converts the data into an analyzable form, analyzes the data, communicates their findings, reviews past analyses and outcomes,[8] and collaborates with the other analytics professionals in the corporation—see Figure 5.2.

Once a corporation reaches enough similar analyses with repetitive parts, it is more efficient to increase the specialization. The first split is between the IT oriented tasks around the data warehouse and the BA oriented tasks around decision making. As we continue to increase the specialization, we transition toward a horizontal assembly-line approach. Some regard this as a functional approach or as employing a functional-based organization. Data analysis can involve a tremendous number of details—when we are doing it right. Finding the optimal amount of specialization for a given problem stream requires an understanding of the different functional skills inside and outside of the analytics team. **Person for person, a more horizontal or functional structure can dramatically outproduce a vertical one**.

More specialization has implications for continual improvement as well. By focusing on fewer details, analytics professionals progress much faster and can develop more advanced techniques.

One of the challenges to implementing a more horizontal organization is that those leading the analytics practitioners need to clearly understand the skill sets on the team. They need to be able to match the respective tasks to the business analysts and business quants; and occasionally to IT. They need to understand how the chess pieces function.

Teamwork

Teamwork is one of the greatest inventions of all time.[9] A great deal of recent psychological research is illuminating how teamwork functions within organizations. It appears that corporations are underemphasizing "real" teamwork. Hence, we recommend team incentives, team goals, team-building exercises, and a focused effort on building self-directed teams.

Any student of history can see that we credit our "great" leaders with all of the accomplishments of "their" groups. This myth is made easier to sell because many people fantasize about being that great person. Hardly anyone fantasizes about being a great teammate. Corporations tend to be crazy-mad about individualism. Unfortunately, today's steep individualistic incentives promote self-interests that stymie teamwork.

More thought should be given to motivating a team as a team. Team incentives are important for competitive analytics groups and across professionals belonging to different business units. They pull people together, promote esprit de corps, and foster synergy. Team incentives and team-building exercises inoculate against people problems, which develop between those reviewing each other's work, and thus they maintain the fabric of working relationships. Team incentives facilitate professional norms[10] over market norms, and this is particularly unifying in a like-minded analytics team. Clever incentives will augment leadership. One effective mechanism for building team cohesion across functional boundaries is to allow departments working together to have a voice in the performance reviews of each other's members. This can go a long way toward reducing the number of things that fall through the cracks and it can promote thinking about what makes the organization function as opposed to just the department.

Technical Compatibility

A like-minded analytics group creates a stronger team, which is wanted in a challenging non-analytics culture. The individuals of such a team will become even more specialized and more efficient by trading ideas, techniques, and tasks. We can quickly see this by how fast a compatible crew will start running similar projects through an assembly line. There is a balance between hiring the same econometrician 20 times and hiring one of everything. That is, managers should resist the urge to *build* an overly heterogeneous group that looks like they have everything covered[11]—one econometrician, one statistician, one operations researcher, one industrial engineer, one mathematician, one physicist, one accountant, one nuclear engineer, one agronomist, one brain surgeon, one rocket scientist, et al. This is akin to building an accounting team with people who were all taught different accounting rules. We seek a complementary balance; we need some technical variety without creating a communications deadlock. There is room for everyone, yet we want the chess pieces to speak to each other.

Section 5.3 Building Advanced Analytics Leadership

"Greed, timidity, and lack of vision are rampant among the current crop of pseudo-leaders."

—Warren Bennis

Directing any specialization requires an understanding of its impact and potential. Statistics is the kind of discipline that makes steady contributions with occasional blockbuster innovations. Good leadership is necessary to encourage these major breakthroughs. A positive leader is someone who inspires, motivates, energizes, and unites, while generating loyalty and producing results. Such a leader learns by listening and is integral to the speed with which analytics is performed correctly. There are four strengths that a strong director of advanced analytics will possess:

1. Management and leadership skills
2. Business savvy
3. Communication skills
4. Training and experience up to the technical level of the group

Many corporations perform acceptably in directing regular analytics (Quadrants I and II). However, the same minimums are insufficient for wielding advanced analytics (Quadrants III and IV).

Leadership and Management Skills

Leadership is wanted for directing analytics teams and for working with clients.

Warren Bennis found that organizations that are failing tend to be over-managed and under-led.[12] Both leadership and management have a place in directing analytics. Table 5.2 contains the relative characteristics of leaders and managers as suggested by Mr. Bennis. We provided an ordinal scale for qualifying supervisors of interest.

Management skills get things done. When corporations are struggling, they tend to focus on the short term, which is better optimized by those skills from the management side of the spectrum. Leadership provides more long-term benefits and it softens the autocratic characteristics of management. The old economy of Eastern Europe (1945–1990s) illustrates that autocracy—telling people what to do leads to people who do not know

Table 5.2 Distinctions Between Leadership and Management

Leadership						Management
Innovates ...	5	4	3	2	1	... Administers
Develops ...	5	4	3	2	1	... Maintains
Focuses on people ...	5	4	3	2	1	... Focuses on systems and structures
Inspires trust ...	5	4	3	2	1	... Relies on control
Investigates reality ...	5	4	3	2	1	... Accepts reality
Has a long-range perspective ...	5	4	3	2	1	... Has a short-range view
Asks what and why ...	5	4	3	2	1	... Asks how and when
Has his or her eye on the horizon ...	5	4	3	2	1	... Has his or her eye always on the bottom line
Originates ...	5	4	3	2	1	... Imitates
Challenges status quo ...	5	4	3	2	1	... Accepts status quo
Is his or her own person ...	5	4	3	2	1	... Is the classic good soldier
Does the right thing ...	5	4	3	2	1	... Does things right

what to do.[13] Autocracy is even worse for analytics, which requires some degree of goodwill.

The role of leadership is to increase or at least maintain the productivity of the company's assets—the employees mostly. This is best attained through positive leadership, which requires people skills. The value of positive leadership increases with the complexity of the analytics. Those with on-topic training tend to rely a little less on their management skills because they understand the analytics their team provides.[14] They do not need to exert as much control.

Figure 5.3 illustrates the most effective balance between management and leadership, and the optimal degree of on-topic training. Analytically emerging corporations often select those with less analytics expertise to manage the analytics group. As corporations progress, some of them find leaders with greater analytics expertise. They make finding better leaders a priority. On-topic leadership encourages creativity over mindless process—filling predetermined templates with status quo acceptable answers.

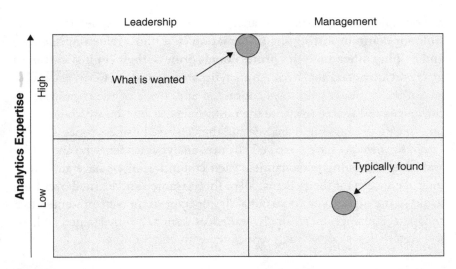

Figure 5.3 Management/leadership—by generalist/on-topic

Mindless process is expensive in terms of opportunity cost, and it is boring. Directors of analytics with on-topic training tend to lead more and delegate more. With the proper incentives, they can both lead and manage.[15]

Business Savvy

Advanced analytics plays a definitive role in the front line where industry knowledge is redefined. In redefining industry knowledge, we are better served by business savvy than past rules of thumb. Business savvy facilitates recognizing how the business is changing. It comprises knowledge and experience combined with independent thought. We want leadership with practical knowledge of how the business functions, people who can think critically and not cling to a fixed set of beliefs about the industry. Business has become too dynamic to expect that rules of thumb will remain static. Instead, we should rely upon general principals of business to remain stable over time, while the particulars change.

Communication Skills

Directors of advanced analytics must communicate across other frontiers. They must understand how others perceive and utilize advanced analytics. At times, they need to articulate statistical methods, the impact of analytics, and strategy. This communication burden does not release others of their responsibility to figure out the analyses. **However, the leader is responsible for communicating the information in a nonthreatening manner and helping other analytics professionals grow in their sophistication to interpret advanced analytics.** An analytics leader must be a good networker within the business who stays connected and aware of the organization's challenges and is able to create the multi-manager buy-in, which is necessary to gain permission to analyze and then change business processes.

In the field, we have observed business analytics leaders who are quirky and have interesting personalities. Their communications have an undertone of concern for their clients. All of this is wanted and learned over time to aid in the digestion of occasional dry or unpleasant facts presented to a generalist audience. Increasingly, audiences want to be entertained and, for some, statistics is not strongly associated with entertainment.

Training and Experience

We have noticed corporations with and without at least some on-topic leadership for their analytics. The most successful business analytics leaders possess training and experience as advanced as the group they are leading. These on-topic leaders are capable of proactively leading analytics, rather than reactively managing it. On-topic training is required to understand the impact and potential of those on the team. An on-topic leader possesses the same way of thinking about the business problem as those performing the analyses. Their training and experience enables them to surpass limits on integrating analytics with the business. Most of the on-topic leaders that we observed are in the more analytically aggressive industries. A knowledge-based economy needs knowledgeable leaders.

On-Topic Leadership by Charlotte Sibley

It's been said that you don't need to be dead to be a good undertaker, but it certainly does help if the group head is sufficiently knowledgeable about the work to be able to perform the key functions of analytics leadership:

- Setting the vision and direction, in line with corporate objectives
- Providing the resources (tools, people)
- Advocating up, down, and across the organization
- Clearing obstacles to success
- Ensuring the individuals/group receives adequate compensation, recognition, and appreciation

---

The objectives of the marketing research and analytics functions are to frame the issue and provide objective insights and recommendations, thereby reducing the risk around decisions. Once the decision has been made, the objective is to optimize the implementation and monitor progress.

If the leader is not an SME (Subject Matter Expert), he or she should hire DRs (Direct Reports) who complement his or her expertise. These DRs can then provide the necessary technical guidance and direction. The burden is on them to lead the group's expertise. In a previous position, Forecasting was one of the departments that reported to me. I did not pretend to completely understand the tools and processes; what I needed to understand was the objective (what is the real issue, not just the question asked?), how we would interact with our business and R&D partners, and how the output would be used. I also needed to be available for consultation if there were issues that arose, such as timelines or unreasonable requests.

The danger is a manager who is not an SME and who is threatened by expertise that he or she does not understand. Innovative new approaches are often stifled. Improvements in the way we run the business are limited to the comfort level, or understanding, of the threatened manager. In one pharmaceutical company, we recommended an alternative targeting scheme to the usual "decile approach"[16] for the launch of a CNS product. Identifying likely early adopters via behavioral and attitudinal market research gave us a list of key targets to call on first. Unfortunately, the sales and business unit heads did not understand this approach and would not agree to try it. However, we did implement our new approach as a "skunk works," but this is not an optimal approach and was not sufficiently robust to make a significant difference in results. So this was a lose-lose situation: the launch was ordinary, because we could not adequately target the likeliest adopters, and the analytics functions suffered because the analytics professionals were discouraged from trying this again with the same group.

Time is one of the greatest issues we face: there's never time to do it right, but there's always time to do it over. Good researchers and analysts need time to get the issue into their marrow and figure out implications and options. We leaders need to ensure that they have the appropriate time—within reason (this is not, after all, academia!).

For all specializations, leaders with subject matter expertise are wanted to customize the leadership to fit the specialization. The head of surgery at a hospital is an example of an on-topic leader. In business, we see a stiff shortage of on-topic leadership directing analytics teams.

The on-topic leader helps the enterprise-wide advocate grow the culture, and regularly collaborates with mid-level advocates to orchestrate analytics in their respective lines of business. They propose the data-analytic vision for the corporation and integrate analytics into the strategy.

Perhaps the most important strength of those directing advanced analytics is their mastery of analytics. On-topic leaders understand the technology so they can delegate better. Analytics needs leadership that can assign the right training to the right problem. We want them to judge the amount of rigor and the time a problem warrants and manage to it, rather than providing too much time for some problems and too little for others. By understanding analytics, on-topic leaders place less burden on the business quants to explain their work. We want them to manage to the strengths of their team and wed the analytics to the business problem.

On-topic leaders have the experience built upon quantitative training. They can leverage this to thoughtfully invest their team's productivity. They value a strong analytics team. On-topic leaders appreciate the importance of maintaining the infrastructure and fostering talent. They guide the analytics team and manage to each team member's strengths. They can identify good data analysis so nothing needs to be dumbed down. The business analysts and business quants can focus on their work rather than managing up.

"Ph.D. with personality."

— Jeanne Harris

Expert Leaders (ELs)—Corporate Trump Cards

In some corporations, there are informal leaders who understand both the business and advanced analytics well enough to wed the two. They know what to do in a crisis and how to create a competitive advantage.[17] If a catastrophe is forthcoming, and there have been many, then the expert leaders are the corporation's best hope for an analytics solution. Similarly, they are the best hope for analytics breakthroughs that create a competitive advantage and there have been many instances of those. As the Information Age evolves, we can expect just as many Wall Street-type emergencies and more analytics competition. We want leaders who can apply their analytics prowess to anticipate, diagnose, and cure important business problems. These leaders compensate for other weaknesses in the corporation. They collect the information concentrate and lessen the dilution or dumbing down of information.

Expert leaders are bilingual, speaking analytics and business. They possess both a high analytics IQ and a high business IQ.

$$\text{Analytics IQ} = \text{Training} \times \text{Experience/Arrogance,}$$
where:

Training = (Courses on applied analytics + MAX [2, courses on theoretical analytics topics] + Post-college learnings)
Experience = (Years of analytics experience + Months applying statistical software to advanced analytics problems)
Arrogance = Just what you think it is

It is difficult to obtain a high analytics IQ without at least two years of applied training in advanced analytics immersed in quants and a few years of intense business experience. There is more to it though; this is a way of thinking about business problems. Academic training from highly touted theory schools on how to perform research for really good scientific papers can only prepare the quant so much.

Expert leaders will usually possess the soft skills and leading business quants is not going to be a problem for them. Yet what is critical is that they possess a commanding understanding of how to apply analytics to the business. We want strong change agents capable of overseeing the important technical aspects of the business. We need to have expert leaders (ELs) oversee and provide visible leadership for the three pillars discussed in Chapters 7 to 9 on Statistical QDR (Qualifications, Diagnostics, and Review) and the three building blocks discussed in Chapters 10 to 12 on Data CSM (Collection, Software, and Management).

For those corporations short on expert leaders, we can develop them by sending their business experts to graduate school in a quantitative discipline or by exposing their business analysts and business quants to the business.

The Blood-Brain Barrier

The highest involvement of the expert leaders and on-topic business analytics leaders in a corporation is indicative of two things: (1) the degree to which the corporation has accepted and integrated analytics, and (2) the corporation's ability to find analytics people capable of leading.

The clarity with which a corporation understands complex analytics dissipates as we move further from those practicing analytics. This holds for other disciplines as well: accounting, law, brain surgery, rocket science,

IT, and so on. We should be reluctant to place an off-topic manager directly in charge of those performing these specializations. For many applications, the highest on-topic leader is the point below which analytics is truly applied. If it is low, then applications are tactical. If it is high, then applications are strategic. We do not expect the C-level management in a large corporation to be expert in every topic that is a corporate concern. We expect decisions to be delegated to those close to the information. In that advanced analytics facilitates better business decisions, some decisions need to be close to the analytics. In dysfunctional corporations, layers of "business experts" act as insulation and tend to dilute the information. An enterprise-wide analytics group can help with some of these problems by better facilitating seamless communication.

For specializations, the most common management limitation is the difficulty in delegating what we do not understand.[18] This management limitation becomes a technical limitation when the analytics group is restricted by the leadership from pursuing problems beyond a few semesters of statistical content. This discourages the most valuable product of an analytics team—innovation. The worst-case scenario occurs when a manager consistently discounts long-term growth in favor of short-term perception.

However, these limitations can be avoided by placing experts in leadership roles. This maximizes the effectiveness of the quantitative group. Results no longer need to be dumbed down to such an extent, or unduly delayed for explanations.[19] We can make good progress.

For the quants, when their fearless team leader understands analytics, they do not need to spend valuable time reexplaining complexities. This counterproductive burden is reduced, and there is more time to spend with analytics-based decision makers and fitting the analysis to the business problem.

> *"The nonstatistician can not always recognize a statistical problem when he[/she] sees one."*
>
> —W. Edwards Deming

Advantages of On-Topic Business Analytics Leaders

As the Information Age continues to evolve, it will become paramount that corporations find or develop on-topic leaders. We need business professionals who have both the authority and the ability to solve the strategic business analytics problems. They will possess the training and experience in applying statistics to the business combined with the usual proficiencies in communication, organization, leadership, industry knowledge, and business savvy. We want them to turn "reactive analytics" into proactive analytics. When needed, we want them to lead the corporation out of the Decisive Circle,[20] even if it means cannibalizing our own business. We want to run analytics like an entrepreneurial profit center.

Management Types by David Young

Today, a large number of analytics groups are managed by someone with little training in analytics. Their role is to provide a comfortable report for their manager and direct the analytics team's efforts toward business goals. This structure has always reminded me of the days when managers did not know how to type and they dictated everything to secretaries. Today, no one would hire a manager who couldn't type, because it is so clearly inefficient. The same inefficiency applies to analytics, but is actually much greater because the non-analytics manager doesn't understand the analytics trade-offs he or she is making, while the prior generation of managers did understand what needed to be typed.

Separating the knowledge pools of "what to do" and "how to do it" is always a method of last resort. At some point, the manager of analytics needs to be versed in the business's needs and be equipped with the analytics skills to understand and manage the process of meeting those needs.

In the scientific world, workers initially focus on technically demanding tasks and over time move on to managerial and strategic roles, but in the business world, the process is often cut short, by the creation of an analytics group with a non-analytics business manager. The rapid growth in demand for advanced analytics propelled this tiered system forward as non-analytics business managers were easy to find and statistically trained ones were not, but it brought with it many long-term consequences.

Non-analytics managers limit the complexity of the tools that can be applied and therefore negate a large portion of the benefit of having an analytics group. Quantitative workers, who see that their manager doesn't appreciate the difference between a good analysis and a mediocre one, lack one incentive to do a good job. And the class system that is created by separating the management function from the work being done, encourages feelings of inadequacy on both sides, limiting information sharing, and increasing turnover among quantitative workers as they search elsewhere for opportunities to grow.

> It's easy to see why many businesses established this structure, as it was often the only choice, based on a short supply of experienced statistically trained professionals, but it's equally clear why businesses should continue to transition away from a tiered structure as the analytics boom matures. Corporations unable to make this transition will find themselves trying to compete using only poorly trained business managers, who do not recognize solvable problems when they see them. Today, most managers of analytics are underperformers in this role and will be more productive elsewhere. Corporations need leaders who are bilingual—they understand the business and they possess years of training in analytics.

A manager, who is struggling with the technical side of leading an analytics team, is just in the wrong role. However, they have accumulated experience corporations want in other roles. Perhaps, they should be promoted to a mid-level advocate or a coach for decision makers—or they can become an analytics-based decision maker.

The analytics team needs a leader. On-topic business analytics leaders are the most profitable directors of analytics. They can raise the productivity of the entire analytics team. Figure 5.4 illustrates one possible organizational structure. At present, any shortage in statistical talent is exacerbated by the shortage in analytics leadership. Statistically strong corporations find a business analytics leader, who can recruit and leverage talent.

Effective analytics leaders might require some sculpting to fit into such a difficult role. They must master all phases of the game and not just the "sound bites." They might need to strengthen their soft skills. On-topic leaders must be significantly better communicators to vault over certain barriers. They can build some of these skills through Toastmasters. At the advanced level of Toastmasters, there are training manuals designed especially for those with technical backgrounds.

We need to do more than just sculpt the business analytics leader. We need to build a nexus for the business analytics leader and the other analytics professionals. This involves reorganization and changing the corporate culture. A business analytics leader, working in concert with other leaders, can provide a number of advantages.

First, they can recognize, attract, empower,[21] and retain[22] the best talent—the most profitable leadership can sometimes be identified by their low turnover. To accomplish anything of significance, we must have

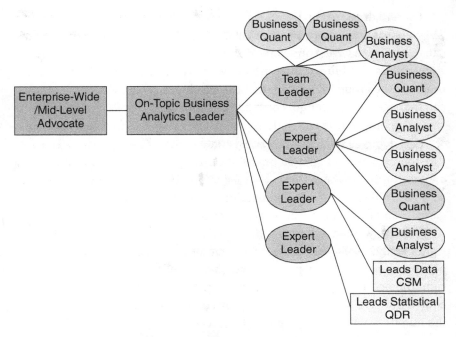

Figure 5.4 Team structure leveraging business analytics leader

the right people! We want a business analytics leader who is people-oriented and positioned well to lead business analysts and business quants. This requires an appreciation of the inner workings of the analytics team.

The business analysts, business quants, and expert leaders need an on-topic leader, who can:

1. Provide them with opportunities to lead and to present their results.
2. Keep others, who are trying to get to the top of the corporation, from trampling on them.
3. Assign an expert leader to oversee the three pillars for Best Statistical Practice: Statistical Qualifications, Statistical Diagnostics, and Statistical Review (Chapters 7 to 9).
4. Assign an Expert Leader to oversee the three building blocks for supporting analytics: Data Collection, Data Software, and Data Management (Chapter 10 to 12).
5. Clarify what, in the quant's academic training applies, what does not, and what they need to learn going forward.

Second, business analytics leaders know how to help a team execute. They comprehend the subtleties of the analytics specialization, and they can delegate what they understand. They know how an analytics team functions and its capabilities. They are not an extra burden to the staff. They can organize the group into a team that can produce like an assembly line. They can manage to the strengths of the team's members. They can wisely invest resources on projects worth doing from a business technical point of view.

Third, business analytics leaders can facilitate an analytics-driven culture that will expand current capabilities. They can figure out how to create an environment where ideas will proliferate. When called upon, they can serve as midwives for idea incubation. This enables the hunt for the "big game"[23] and furthers the entrepreneurial aspect of the role.

Fourth, we can rely upon business analytics leaders to get the facts right. Analytics is a mindset; it is a way of thinking that is already their occupational mantra or possibly their raison d'être. Getting the numbers right the first time, saves time and money. A panicked manager with inadequate training will gladly sacrifice any competitive advantage afforded by the numbers, which they might not appreciate.

A technical group can only progress so far without an on-topic business analytics leader.

Section 5.4 Location, Location, Location of Analytics Practitioners

The best locations for analytics practitioners are not necessarily near the decision making and not necessarily far from conflicts of interest. While there might not be one right location for analytics resources, we have observed a number of rules of thumb. The analytics team should:

1. Be integral to the decision making.
2. Have a reporting structure separate from their clients[24]—one conflict of interest to be avoided when possible.
3. Be insulated from all other conflicts of interest.
4. Be highly connected to other analytics professionals.
5. Be well connected to the data.

Ideally, the data should be freely accessible to those using it. Hence, we will assume that there is no advantage to placing analytics near the data or near IT.

If we are going to apply a fact-based approach to locating analytics resources, then there are a number of considerations. What should be the reporting structure? Who finances the analytics team? Who claims credit for the fruits of analytics? Who reviews the data analysis and the analytics-based decisions? How can we increase the sophistication of our decision makers? How can we help them improve their decisions?

A major concern in choosing the location is the flow of information. W. Edwards Deming advocated that information reflecting the performance of certain middle management should go directly to senior management. There needs to be some communication lines that can avoid most conflicts of interest.

We would like to discuss three locations for analytics and a hybrid of the three. First, we can draw analytics services from outside the corporation. Second, analytics can report into local leadership—within the line-of-business or business function. Third, analytics can be centralized or enterprise-wide.[25] Finally, we can construct a hybrid by combining these three locations.

Outsourcing Analytics

It can make sense to outsource specialized tasks when the needs warrant it. An increasing number of consulting companies can perform reasonable analytics. It is somewhat efficient for them to invest in these specialized skill sets and market them to numerous corporations. Leveraging consultants to perform analytics is double-edged. First let's enumerate the rewards:

1. Certain consultants can provide superior analytics.
2. For a struggling corporation, consultants provide a rapid way around analytics dysfunction.
3. A smaller corporation's analytics needs might not be large enough to justify this investment—no critical mass.
4. Consultants can help meet spikes in a corporation's labor demand or add flexibility to its labor force.
5. When properly engaged, consultants provide a source of objectivity.
6. Consultants bring innovation from competitors and other industries.

There are a few risks involved in leveraging consultants:

1. Involving consultants exposes proprietary information—including innovations in analytics.[26]
2. It might be more difficult to screen the quality of the work.[27]

3. The shortcomings of the outside consultants are less familiar than our own.

4. Consulting companies might be pressured to make their results fit the political conclusion, yet so can internal resources (see Brian Wynn's sidebar in Chapter 2).

Here are our guidelines for getting the most from consultants:

1. We should manage the analytics experts with our own analytics experts.[28] We want to communicate as much as possible with those performing the analytics. This will protect us from mistakes and counterfeit analysis.[29] Even the most trustworthy consultants have to compete. If we enable an environment where one consulting company can sell substandard work, then we are responsible for facilitating lower quality, counterfeit analysis, and unethical behavior.

2. Hire the expert not the brand name.[30] Certified, quantitatively trained veterans are expensive, and some consultants routinely lack properly trained personnel or they employ bait and switch to stretch more expensive resources. Non-discerning clients will struggle to identify experts. Ensure the consulting company involves trained veterans to oversee the work, too, and be mindful that the business model of some consulting companies is to train fresh graduates at our expense.

3. Look for cross-industry consulting companies that do not silo their talent and, in fact, encourage their business quants to work in multiple industries. These consultants have a greater mix of analytics ideas combined with technology from more statistically demanding industries. This breadth is particularly valuable for clients who have little exposure to other industries.

4. Look for consulting companies with reasonable leadership. Try to find leadership that is as interested in solving your problem as they are in sending you an invoice.

Dispersed or Local Groups

A local reporting structure is ubiquitous in large corporations. For example, marketing analytics reports into the marketing head, manufacturing analytics reports into the manufacturing head, clinical analytics reports into the clinical head, and so on. The analytics resources are located in isolated "analytics pockets" within lines of business or business functions. These pockets are born and grow organically from the local needs. *If the resources are competent and well led*, then the principal advantage is speed.

A local reporting structure is usually more responsive and comfortable at the expense of being frail in developing analytics. **This structure functions a bit better for tracking/reporting than for advanced analytics.** A single small pocket of business analysts is less likely to warrant a business analytics leader to boost their productivity. This local reporting structure is subject to conflicts with local interests, such as local opinions or traditions. The most common conflict involves measuring local performance. For example, a group in a medium-sized pharmaceutical was performing poorly within its line of business. As a solution, a senior manager removed the business analysts measuring their performance. This dramatically improved the performance of his friends in that group. We refer to such altered analysis, or lack of analysis, as filtered information. The local structure fosters "information screening" on the way up. This leads to no bad news, no instances of "I do not know," and no one gets hurt—except the shareholders and the employees losing their jobs when the corporation fails.

The success of a local structure can hinge on the incentives and the sophistication of the analytics-based decision makers. In a politically charged environment, the line-of-business structure can degenerate into a statistical underground,[31] which some may refer to as "the dog playing ball with itself" or "the rogue statistician."

Central or Enterprise-Wide Groups[32]

For many corporations, a natural next step is to build a centralized analytics function led by a business analytics leader, who reports high into the corporate tree. A centralized structure provides an organization that owns analytics investments over the long term, and centralization enables enterprise-wide benefits. The advantages include the following:

1. Reduces the filtering of information traveling upward through corporate ductwork[33]
2. Facilitates a central clearinghouse for solving more advanced statistical problems
3. Provides more insulation from local political interests
4. Addresses concerns about information getting siloed within business units
5. Provides a place for reviewing important analyses

6. Strengthens analytics-based decision making
7. Simplifies ensuring that analytics resources are invested wisely
8. Facilitates helping overworked or struggling decision makers
9. Separates the boss from the client
10. Enables better connectivity between those performing data analysis

The sought-after value of reducing the filtering of the information has a long-standing precedent. Decades ago, W. Edwards Deming, a leader of the quality revolution, recognized the value of direct information. He supported the organizational structure shown in Figure 5.5, which justified an enterprise-wide advocate.[34] This structure originated from Dr. Morris H. Hansen in the U.S. Bureau of the Census, circa 1940.

Adding a centralized analytics function will take many corporations to the next plateau of analytics. As mentioned in Chapter 1, there is a great deal of embellishment about the degree to which corporations are successful in leveraging analytics—marketing. One measure of analytics strength is if they have an enterprise-wide analytics team when they should have one. Another is the degree to which this team has enough influence to help the corporation. Finally, a centralized or enterprise-wide analytics function might require a C-level leader, and this leader's approach will be indicative of the corporation's focus.

There is a growing number of C-level titles[35] that might vie for the responsibility of leading an enterprise-wide analytics group. The ascending chief analytics officer is responsible for the analysis of data within the organization. The chief data officer manages the corporation's data processing and data maintenance needs. There are a number

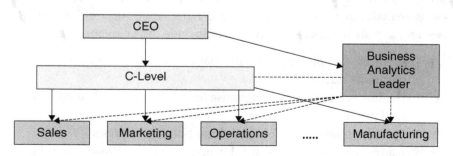

Figure 5.5 Dr. Morris H. Hansen's organization

of other possible leaders with different emphases: the chief information officer, the chief decision officer, the chief economist, the chief statistical officer, etc.

The chief information officer is traditionally responsible for the infrastructure to process information. Many corporations have reached a plateau where they are seeking a greater return on their data investment. For some corporations, it might make sense to expand the CIO role a little to add analytics. This might improve the value proposition of the IT silo. For many other corporations, this will be at best a baby step in the right direction. For this to succeed, we must address a number of poorly understood challenges associated with this structure. There are grave incompatibilities between IT and BA. **Business analytics starts with the business problem and then looks for the data.** We must avoid a structure that shifts our business analytics' focus from seeking data based upon business needs to offering only solutions made possible by the data available. Also, IT has different priorities, skill sets, software, and cultural values.[36] **A smaller business analytics team will dissolve when mixed in with a large IT culture.**

If centralization offers so many advantages, why is it still absent from so many corporations? Here are some of the popular reasons:

A. Analytics is perceived as a functional skill that is bound to a business context. That is, data analysis is perceived as "context dependent"—as if a regression analysis within marketing is a "marketing regression" and a regression analysis within manufacturing is a "manufacturing regression."

B. The central reporting structure might need physical proximity to the decision makers in order to provide synergy and speed up the process. This is a challenge for large corporations spread all over the world.

C. There is a desire to delegate the responsibility to the local level. At the extreme this enables plausible deniability. The need for plausible deniability is an impediment to supplying the information directly to senior management.

D. No one has made a strong enough case for the power of analytics. The analytics professionals need to provide compelling examples of salient profitable business solutions—killer apps.

Hybrid: Outside + Local + Enterprise-Wide

The goal of hybrid structures is to leverage the best characteristics of all three locations. A hybrid organizational structure enables the resources of the central group to be stronger technically and the local groups to focus upon speed in delivery and the local relationships. This structure is much better at facilitating communication and avoiding conflicts of interest. Combining the three locations is flexible enough for most businesses. The enterprise-wide group can be leveraged to stitch together the disparate analytics pockets. While this structure is powerful, combining the enterprise-wide group to the local analytics pockets is not always politically practicable.

Notes

1. See *On Becoming A Leader* by Warren Bennis.
2. However, our definitions and our viewpoint might not perfectly coincide.
3. We use the term "business quant," whereas *Competing On Analytics* uses "analytics professional," and we use "analytics professional" as a broader, more inclusive term.
4. We yearn for the maelstrom of meatball surgery.
5. To set aside resources for a separate purpose.
6. Quants are not interchangeable parts; thinking the same way and using the same techniques.
7. A brain surgeon leaves the anesthesia to another professional. A master chef does not start preparing a tasty meal by planting corn that they will feed to chickens that they will slaughter, and so on. The chef starts with somewhat prepared ingredients.
8. Another time to think about the performance of past decisions and analyses is prior to making a decision.
9. Teamwork predates Homo sapiens so there is no dispute over "priority"—that is, who invented it first.
10. As long as we are performing at our best, we can allow professional norms to run amok inside the analytics groups.
11. In the meatball surgery of corporate data analysis, we have larger concerns than collecting majors.
12. Although some over-management might be in response to failure, Bennis suggests that it is one cause of failures.
13. Or care about doing it.
14. The real corporate danger is the off-topic manager told to reorganize analytics.

15. We think the bar is not set that high and it is much easier to lead what you understand.

16. This is a simple approach for assigning sales visits to physicians relative to their prescribing volume. Physicians who prescribe more (so called high-decile physicians) are targeted for more visits.

17. For many corporations, the promise of CRM (Customer Relationship Management) has never been realized. It fizzled because they lacked competent on-topic leadership to identify the required resources and execute.

18. This reminds us of the second type of being lost. The first type is when we realize that we are lost.

19. Some of the more interesting explanations are in *The Cartoon Guide to Statistics* by Larry Gonick and Wolcott Smith (1993).

20. Oh, that Decisive Circle mentioned in Chapter 3. This occurs when a corporation repeatedly faces the same business problem and makes the same decision as last time—the circle. Although it makes each decision "decisively," it fails to incorporate new contradictory information that would lead to a much better decision. This is common with decisions that need to be made annually.

21. We routinely see talent that is misunderstood or not motivated. The on-topic leader can get the business quants to buy in. Those who are "all in" will go "all out."

22. We have seen technical staff even follow an able on-topic leader to a new company. A feat that seldom happens with technical staff—except in hyperbole.

23. Big game = analytics breakthroughs with significant economic benefit; or killer applications.

24. For example, there is a conflict when statistical resources measure the performance of the group into which they report.

25. The local and central locations for analytics and combining them are also discussed in *The Deciding Factor* by Larry Rosenberger and John Nash (2009).

26. One consulting paradigm is to borrow an innovative idea from one of their customers and harvest it as next year's crop to be sold to their portfolio of clients.

27. Some consulting companies like it that way.

28. In the absence of our own experts, we can hire another consulting company to oversee the work—preferably one that specializes in analytics and is not a major competitor of the former consulting company.

29. Smaller corporations in particular will be tempted to forego this technical oversight. Despite this risk, some of these corporations will survive.

30. Put the expert's name on the contract when possible.

31. Have you been contacted yet? If not, welcome to the statistical underground. We are organized in threes, and instead of secret decoder rings and secret

handshakes, you must be able to explain the importance of the Central Limit Theory or some such concept.

32. These are sometimes referred to as a Center of Expertise or a Center of Excellence.

33. This tosses out "plausible deniability," which is wanted for those who wish to avoid culpability through the bliss of ignorance.

34. More specifically, Deming thought it made sense for the CEO to interact directly with a statistician, see p. 467 of *Out of the Crisis*.

35. The C-level is a crowded place.

36. As discussed in *Business Analytics for Managers* by Gert Laursen and Jesper Thorlund (2010), pp. 195–196.

6

Developing Competitive Advantage

"Plans are worthless. Planning is essential."
—Dwight D. Eisenhower

We want to develop an analytics plan as part of the overall business strategy. This plan will organize our analytics needs, identify our analytics opportunities, and provide a strategy for competing on analytics. Corporations regularly invest resources into reorganizing. Part of rethinking the next organizational structure should include a retrospective on past analytics-based decisions, how the reorganization could improve decision making, and how reorganization redefines the business analytics plan.

A business analytics plan needs to be thorough enough to accommodate the pace of decision making and flexible enough to address unanticipated needs. By leveraging their experience, analytics-based decision makers, on-topic business analytics leaders, and expert leaders can anticipate certain types of needs and prepare the corresponding parts of our infrastructure. The pace of decision making does not allow us the luxury of delaying planning until we ascertain all of the information that is wanted. We need to be proactive. Most of the time, we can infer some of the required preparation and thus reduce the hazardous lag in reaction time. Planning facilitates avoidance of rushed or unnecessary analyses.

Approach for Identifying Gaps in Analytics

The basic approach is to derive current needs; evaluate current capabilities; and juxtapose the two. Deriving current needs is easier to envision once we have seen it done. Our approach is to follow the business flow. We can follow money, customers, products, or services. Once we inventory our needs, we can evaluate capabilities by counting the BAs (Business Analysts) and BQs (Business Quants), assessing their leadership and resources, and evaluating the approach of the decision makers.

Strategy

The overarching objective is to integrate business analytics into the business strategy. Laursen and Thorlund explain it thusly: "If a company does not use information as a strategic asset, it will not, in the strategic implementation plans, have descriptions of how the competitive advantages should be gained via the use of information. If a company does use information as a strategic asset, then next to the objectives of the strategy it will also provide directions of how the objectives should be reached via the use of information."[1] Our strategy incorporates the use of analytics to improve our performance in the marketplace.

Protecting Intellectual Property

Keeping proprietary information secret is part of our competitive advantage. We want to keep our business analytics plan, strategy, tactics, and technology to ourselves. Back in the 1990s, Fair Isaac demonstrated its modeling techniques worked for predicting loan risk. This helped it increase sales in the short run. In the long run, they were rewarded by their clients, who then built their own in-house analytics groups and lessened their dependency on Fair Isaac.[2] The technology was not that advanced, yet some of these banks needed this nudge to take the next steps.

This chapter will blend the ideas from the first five chapters and lead into the tactical ideas in the next six chapters. We begin by discussing how to assess our corporation's information needs. Next we will discuss evaluating the corporation's analysis capabilities. We end with suggestions for accelerating innovation and bringing about changes in analytics and by analytics.

Section 6.1 Triage: Assessing Business Needs

We want to assess the information needs of the corporation. One approach is for a business analytics leader, working in concert with the senior leadership, analytics-based decision makers, expert leaders, and other analytics professionals to inventory the data analyses needed to support business decisions. Many corporations already have a company scorecard and a set of critical tracking reports. These are good places to start because they are close to the corporate strategy. We can usually find ways to improve these tools and thereby develop trust. We want to search further afield for projects with high ROI (return on investment) or "killer applications." These applications represent the most economically impactful decisions that need the support of data analysis.

Process Mapping of Analytics Needs

One route to mapping analytics opportunities is to chart the customer flow. Figure 6.1 outlines a basic customer flow, with which most industries can relate. We have embedded a number of analytics opportunities, which can directly support decisions and provide business insights.

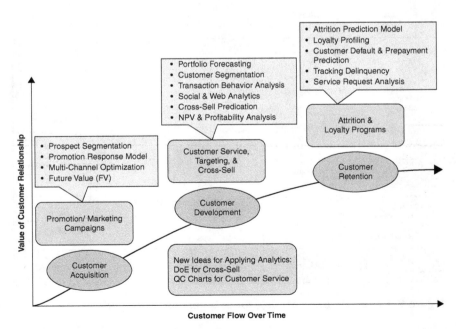

Figure 6.1 Analytics along customer flow[3]

As a second example, Figure 6.2 provides a customer flow specific to an automobile loan portfolio. This illustrates the location in the customer flow where we should use various data analyses to support business decisions.

Another more enterprise-wide approach is to build a value diagram as depicted in Figure 6.3, outlining the flow of value within the corporation.

In Table 6.1, we inventoried some of the business problems. We mapped them from the basic customer flow in Figure 6.1 to the anticipated analytics needs. We characterized these analyses by the parameters of value-add, desired accuracy, and desired reliability. We added the last two rows as placeholders for general business needs such as exploratory data analysis or addressing questions "in the moment." We want to have contingencies for unexpected needs.

Judging accuracy and reliability leads to thinking through how to better design the solutions. We need to focus more on supporting the most important decisions. Within the confines of the desired accuracy, we need to consider how to make novel problems more routine and how to better leverage the infrastructure we have on hand.

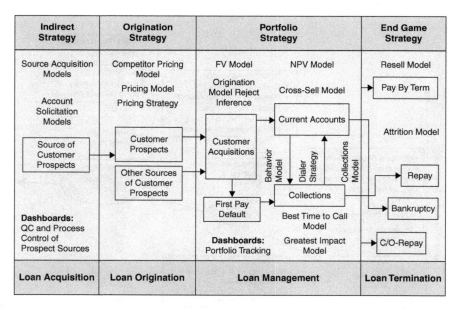

Figure 6.2 Mapping customer flow for an automobile loan portfolio

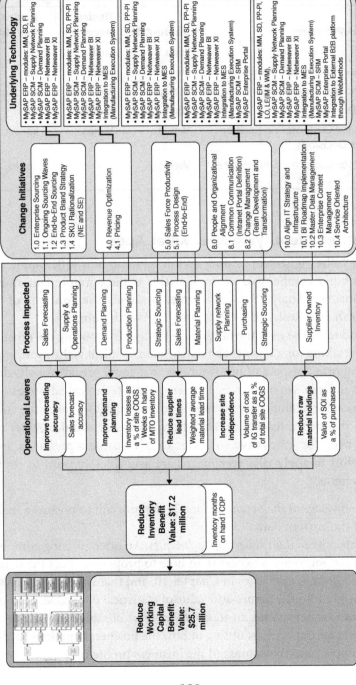

The following describes the content of the value diagram (Figure 6.3):

Why is this important to shareholders?

Reduce Working Capital Benefit Value: $25.7 million

What to Transform & how to measure it?

Reduce Inventory Benefit Value: $17.2 million
- Inventory months on hand I CDP

Operational Levers / Process Impacted

Improve forecasting accuracy
- Sales forecast accuracy
- Sales Forecasting
- Supply & Operations Planning

Improve demand planning
- Inventory losses as a % of site COGS
- I Weeks on hand of MTO inventory
- Demand Planning
- Production Planning

Reduce supplier lead times
- Weighted average material lead time
- Strategic Sourcing
- Sales Forecasting
- Material Planning

Increase site independence
- Volume of cost of IG transfer as a % of total site COGS
- Supply network Planning
- Purchasing
- Strategic Sourcing

Reduce raw material holdings
- Value of SOI as a % of purchases
- Supplier Owned Inventory

How do you effect the transformation? — Change Initiatives

1.0 Enterprise Sourcing
1.1 Ongoing Sourcing Waves
1.2 End-to-End Sourcing
1.3 Product Brand Strategy
1.4 SKU Rationalization (NE and SE)

4.0 Revenue Optimization
4.1 Pricing

5.0 Sales Force Productivity
5.1 Process Design (End-to-End)

8.0 People and Organizational Alignment
8.1 Common Communication (Intranet Portal Definition)
8.2 Change Management (Team Development and Transformation)

10.0 Align IT Strategy and Infrastructure
10.1 BI Roadmap Implementation
10.2 Master Data Management
10.3 Enterprise Content Management
10.4 Service Oriented Architecture

Underlying Technology

- MySAP ERP – process modules: MM, SD, FI
- MySAP SCM – Supply Network Planning
- MySAP SCM – Demand Planning
- MySAP ERP – Netweaver BI
- MySAP ERP – Netweaver XI

- MySAP ERP – modules: MM, SD, PP-PI
- MySAP SCM – Supply Network Planning
- MySAP SCM – Demand Planning
- MySAP ERP – Netweaver BI
- MySAP ERP – Netweaver XI
- Integration to MES (Manufacturing Execution System)

- MySAP ERP – modules: MM, SD, PP-PI
- MySAP SCM – Supply Network Planning
- MySAP SCM – Demand Planning
- MySAP ERP – Netweaver BI
- MySAP ERP – Netweaver XI
- Integration to MES (Manufacturing Execution System)

- MySAP ERP – modules MM, SD, PP-PI
- MySAP SCM – Supply Network Planning
- MySAP SCM – Demand Planning
- MySAP ERP – Netweaver BI
- MySAP ERP – Netweaver XI
- Integration to MES (Manufacturing Execution System)
- MySAP SCM – SRM
- MySAP Enterprise Portal

- MySAP ERP – modules: MM, SD, PP-PI, LO, LE(IM & WM),
- MySAP SCM – Supply Network Planning
- MySAP SCM – Demand Planning
- MySAP ERP – Netweaver BI
- MySAP ERP – Netweaver XI
- Integration to MES (Manufacturing Execution System)
- MySAP SCM – SRM
- MySAP Enterprise Portal
- Integration to External B2B platform through WebMethods

Figure 6.3 Value diagram

Value Diagram is Infosys proprietary intellectual property and should not be reproduced, adapted, or reused in any form without written permission from Infosys Limited

119

Table 6.1 Analysis Inventory

Analysis Problem	Value-Add	Desired Accuracy	Desired Reliability
Prospect Segmentation	High	High	High
Promotion Response Model	High	Medium	High
Multi-Channel Optimization	Medium	Medium	Medium
Future Value (FV)	High	Medium	High
Support for Customer Acquisition Business Decisions	Varies	Varies	Varies
Support for Customer Development Business Decisions	Varies	Varies	Varies

Innovation: Identifying New Killer Apps

We want to be vigilant in finding and developing new killer applications that will build competitive advantage. This is the entrepreneurial aspect of the Business Analytics Leader's role. We apply the concepts of Real-Win-Worth. Is it Real; can we Win; and is it Worth doing?

Introducing the new, the faster, the stronger is probably the most difficult undertaking for a business analytics team. While it is the most impactful, an important aspect of innovation is that some breakthroughs do not happen suddenly. We need to make incremental technical advances—each of which can be a temporary economic failure—until we reach the coveted final one that generates wealth. The Information Age should further motivate the need for innovative solutions to our business problems. In our all-out effort to apply whatever means are available, we want to combine these strengths:

1. *Knowledge of the potential data.* It is important to possess a mastery of the current data.
2. *Expertise in data collection techniques.* An often missing component in corporations is expertise in how to properly collect the data. We will discuss the basics in Chapter 10, and that should provide some insight into the nature and value of statistical data collection.
3. *Business savvy and an understanding of our business.* We need to leverage our understanding of how the business functions, and fully comprehend the context of the business problem.

4. *Competitive intelligence.* Part of planning involves competitive intelligence regarding rival analytics capabilities.[4] This, incidentally, is notoriously prone to bias from embellishment and a lack of understanding.

5. *Cross-industry experience.* Cross-industry experience is particularly invaluable for hunting killer apps. This facilitates considering applications, which are more common in completely different industries. The problem in getting these applications accepted still remains because industries focus on how they are different from each other. Similarly, knowledge of other industries supports a fresh view of our business, a phenomenon that encourages reevaluation of long-held assumptions.

6. *A broad repertoire in statistical techniques.* Such a range of techniques is invaluable, though often lacking. Most corporations tend to overuse their most popular data analysis techniques—as mentioned in Section 4.1, "Two-Trick Pony." Part of embracing the serendipity of statistics is to experiment with all of the statistical tools at hand, thus making it important that we have most of them at hand. We should consider the types of statistical problems natural to certain types of decisions.

7. *Advanced training in statistics.* Advanced statistical training is critical for recognizing business problems that can be solved using statistics.

Scrutinizing the Inventory

We want to run analytics like a profit center. For each analysis, we should consider its value-add to the business and strive to estimate the ROI. Our inventory is likely to be dynamic, so this can be an ongoing challenge.

We experience a continuum of business needs spanning from high-value, surgically precise one-off analyses at one corner to quick-and-clean mass-produced analyses providing ballpark estimates at another corner of the plane.[5] For Table 6.2, we want to consider the desired rigor, amount of problem knowledge, and amount of analytics expertise for the inventory from Table 6.1. Also, we may want to group similar analytics problems and think about who should review the various analyses. We have added two new analyses to this table: DoE for Cross-Sell Prediction and Quality Control Charts for Customer Service, both from Figure 6.1. Today, these types of analyses are largely underutilized in business.

Table 6.2 Scrutinizing the Inventory

Analysis Problem	Degree of Rigor	Problem Knowledge	Analytics Expertise	Groups
Prospect Segmentation	Medium	Medium	Medium, Quadrant IV	Methodology Group
Promotion Response Model	High	Medium	High, Quadrant IV	Modeling Group
Multi-Channel Optimization	High	Medium	High, Quadrant IV	Modeling Group
Future Value (FV)	Medium	Low	Medium, Quadrant III	Modeling Group
Support for Customer Acquisition Business Decisions	Varies	Varies	Varies	"In The Moment"
Support for Customer Development Business Decisions	Varies	Varies	Varies	"In The Moment"
DoE for Cross-Sell Prediction	High	Medium	High, Quadrant IV	DoE Group
Quality Control Charts for Customer Service	Medium	Low	Medium, Quadrant III	QC Group

In scrutinizing our inventory of business needs, we can:

1. Judge the required problem knowledge, value-add, and analytics sophistication needed—today and during the life of the analysis.
2. Group together similar analyses to build them more efficiently.
3. Eliminate unnecessary analyses.

Ideally, for every analysis we want to be able to demonstrate how we will use the results. The corresponding trade-off is between avoiding unnecessary analyses and missing those opportunities, which lack "pre" demonstrable benefits. The value-add of an analysis can be relative to its accuracy and reliability. We may need to choose between many less-accurate analyses or a few more-accurate ones.

By grouping together similar analyses, we can make similar business problems more routine, and possibly build the infrastructure needed for mass production. This can help lower the overall cost of analytics and, as a by-product, improve accuracy and reliability.

Someone, presumably **a business analytics leader, needs to make the difficult decisions involved in not analyzing everything**. There are unnecessary analyses, the quantities of which vary dramatically by corporation. The typical reasons for these are (1) we cannot solve the business analytics problem well enough to justify the resources, (2) we do not have the data or other resources available to undertake the analysis, and (3) the analysis cannot add value because it will not influence the decision, which may have already occurred—"toy analyses." We will define a toy analysis as one that must fit a conclusion. The purpose of toy analyses is to lend credibility to a committed opinion-based decision. Hence, performing data analysis will not add value to a past decision. Identifying toy analyses[6] might force senior management to cull them or at least reduce their drain on resources.

Assigning Rigor and Deducing Resources

The next level of the plan is to assign rigor and deduce required resources. We should be able to place the business problems in the correct quadrants in Figure 6.4.

The position in which we post the analysis will vary with the desired accuracy and reliability. We acknowledge that it is difficult to accurately

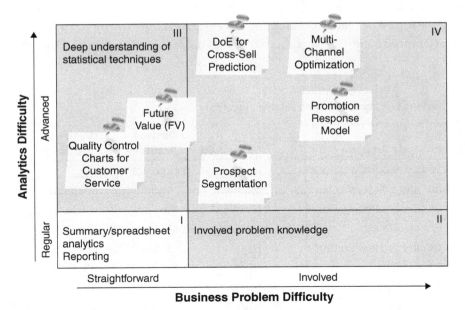

Figure 6.4 Business problems (high-hanging fruit)

place analyses; that is not the point of this graph. The graph is intended purely to help us to think strategically.

Now we will repeat the last two steps again using select business problems from the automobile loan portfolio in Figure 6.2.

The challenge is in assessing the amounts of accuracy and reliability needed to economically solve the business problems. We often see the waste of too much rigor allocated to some projects and both the risk and waste[7] of too little rigor allocated to other projects. Matching the right amount of time and thoroughness to the business problem will have the greatest impact. This is especially difficult to gauge for less familiar business applications. Getting the rigor right requires training and experience. Even then, this can be more time-consuming and expensive than just providing ample rigor.

In Figure 6.5, we post the business analytics problems on the capabilities chart. We expect that the originations model will need to be built to exacting standards. This model is the critical gatekeeper for managing risk by predicting it.

Directors of analytics approach rigor based, more or less, on their degree of quantitative training. Those managers with less quantitative training find it more difficult to judge the right amount of rigor needed to provide the most value. Their best option is to delegate these decisions. They tend to be too conservative in assigning rigor—less is more. On-topic leaders are even more conservative, adhering to the "more is less" maxim and thereby

Table 6.3 Automobile Loan Analysis Inventory

Analysis Problem	Value-Add	Desired Accuracy	Desired Reliability
Source Acquisition Models	High	High	High
Account Solicitation Models	Medium	Medium	Medium
Competitor Pricing Model	High	Medium	High
Pricing Strategy	Medium	Medium	Medium
QC and Process Control	High	Medium	High
FV Model	High	Medium	High
Originations Model	High	Medium	High
Portfolio Tracking	High	Medium	High

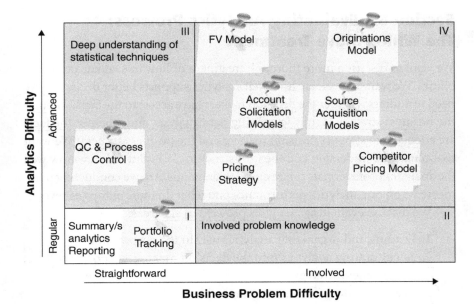

Figure 6.5 Automobile loan business problems (high-hanging fruit)—Loan business problems (high-hanging ftruit)

minimizing the risk that the analyses will be inadequate. On-topic leaders are not stingy with rigor. They are stingy with assuming superfluous risk. They are experts at business analytics and, for their analytics teams, rigor is less expensive anyway. It is thus conservative for them to lather on too much as opposed to too little rigor. One way to think about this is that every decision has a probability of failure. As we reduce rigor, the probability of a poor decision rises. For 100 decisions with a failure probability of 0.1, we expect 10 lousy decisions.

Finally, if assessing the needed rigor is so difficult, then we recommend building an infrastructure, which will lower the cost of rigor—and lower costs in general through economies of scale. We wish to identify those situations where we can build models in assembly-line fashion rather than hand-crafting each one from data collection onward.[8]

Now that we have reviewed our data analysis needs on the way to developing an analytics plan, the next step is to count the practitioners against the identified needs.

Section 6.2 Evaluating Analytics Prowess: The White-Glove Treatment

We want to discuss a more thorough treatment of how to evaluate our capabilities. We want to evaluate how well analytics supports better decisions. We need to address whether the decision makers have access to the facts, whether the business strategy is fully leveraging data analysis, and whether the facts are adequate to support decision making and the business strategy. We want to evaluate the leadership and the infrastructure. We want to know how well the analytics professionals can respond to demands. Are we conducting postmortems on our analytics performance and what do these autopsies reveal?

We discuss evaluating analytics prowess in six areas:

1. Leading and organizing analytics within the corporation
2. Acculturating analytics into the decision making, corporate culture, and business strategy
3. Evaluating decision-making capabilities
4. Evaluating technical coverage
5. Executing Best Statistical Practice—applying Statistical Qualifications, Statistical Diagnostics, and Statistical Review
6. Constructing effective building blocks to support analytics—Data Collection, Data Software, and Data Management

Leading and Organizing

We need to evaluate the strength of the leadership and the appropriateness of the current organization as discussed in Chapters 2 and 5. The most important ingredient for implementing change is a strong, confident advocating leadership. The typical concerns are around having enough analytics professionals, an efficient structure and adequate leadership, and an effective location—most likely with some centralization.

For a large corporation, we are likely to want an enterprise-wide advocate, a business analytics leader, a handful of expert leaders, an enterprise-wide analytics group, and a plethora of analytics-based decision makers. As mentioned in Chapter 5, it is important to have expert leaders oversee and provide visible leadership for the three pillars discussed in Chapters 7 to 9: Statistical Qualifications, Statistical Diagnostics, and Statistical Review, and the three building blocks discussed in Chapters 10 to 12: Data Collection, Data Software, and Data Management.

In assessing the organization, we need to verify that information is free flowing and without too many unwanted additives or impurities.

Progress in Acculturating Analytics

In Section 6.1, we discussed integrating analytics into the business strategy. We want to evaluate the degree to which our corporation makes solid analytics-based decisions (Chapter 3), the effectiveness of our decision making, and the extent of our analytics-driven culture (Chapter 4). We can identify where mistakes are occurring and how well we are functioning within each of the four acts described in the analytics-based decision making process. We need to think through how we make decisions and how we incorporate data analysis into decision making. These are the hard questions.

We need to evaluate the acceptance of analytics in the corporation. This includes measuring how well the corporation converts analytics into industry knowledge. We may need to train the staff in a manner similar to Six Sigma training.

Evaluating Decision-Making Capabilities

We need to identify the largest decision makers, then consider their analytics sophistication and training needs. We want to understand their analytics usage, their comfort level, their humility in accepting new contradictory information, and their analytics knowledge. We want to help decision makers understand Statistical Diagnostics (Chapter 8) and better wield analytics. We can identify the types of analyses that correspond to poor decision making. We might expect our corporation's best decision-making performance to occur for business problems in the lower left corner of Figure 6.6.

Evaluating Technical Coverage

As corporations expand their team of analytics professionals, they grow their capabilities as illustrated in Figures 6.6 to 6.9. Let the stepped areas in the bottom left corner represent a corporation's technical reach. (These graphs are for illustrative purposes; in truth, there is a great deal of synergism that is difficult to capture in these simple step-by-step portrayals.) We can partition the quadrants as finely as we need to look for gaps. We need to think about how to keep the practitioners at optimal productivity. We want to ensure that we are applying the full depth and breadth of our statistical capabilities.[9]

Today, we cannot imagine a corporation surviving very long without the basic analytics capabilities afforded by adding business analysts, as illustrated in Figure 6.6. Most corporations took this initial step long ago and the productivity of the business analysts has risen dramatically.

Today, we cannot imagine certain corporations in certain industries surviving very long without the capabilities provided by business quants, illustrated in Figure 6.7.

Tomorrow, it will be difficult for corporations to survive without more sophisticated decision makers. Analytics-based decision makers will unleash the practitioners, facilitating greater productivity and higher innovation as illustrated in Figure 6.8.

The final step in covering analytics needs is to add an on-topic business analytics leader. Figure 6.9 shows the resulting coverage.

Adding an enterprise-wide advocate does more to spread analytics across the corporation. Centralizing at least part of the analytics practitioners can further facilitate these benefits.

Executing Best Statistical Practice

We want to evaluate our ability to execute Best Statistical Practice when solving business analytics problems. In Part II of this book (Chapters 7 to 9), we will discuss the three pillars for Best Statistical Practice—Statistical

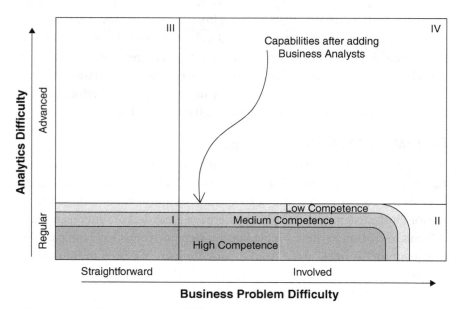

Figure 6.6 Analytics capabilities after adding business analysts

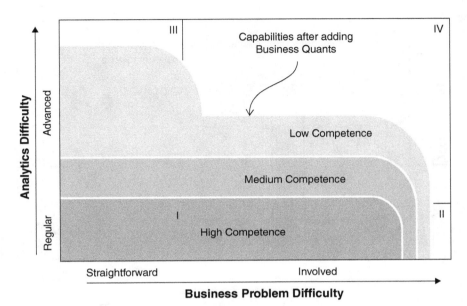

Figure 6.7 Analytics capabilities after adding business quants

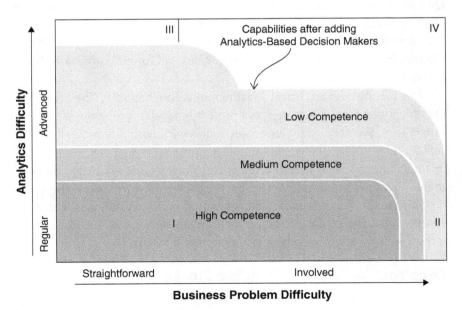

Figure 6.8 Analytics capabilities after adding analytics-based decision makers

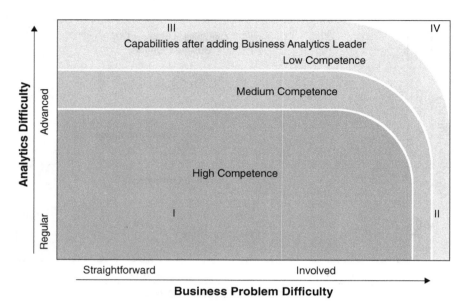

Figure 6.9 Analytics capabilities after adding a business analytics leader

Qualifications, Statistical Diagnostics, and Statistical Review. We want to confirm that a business analytics leader or an expert leader is overseeing the needed Statistical Qualifications, Diagnostics, and Review so that our capabilities will meet the needs of our current and future business problem inventories.

We will discuss Statistical Qualifications in Chapter 7. The Statistical Qualifications among our analytics professionals determine our corporate capabilities. We need analytics professionals with both technical skills and soft skills.

In Chapter 8, we will outline Statistical Diagnostics and discuss a few of them. There are many techniques for measuring performance—the accuracy and reliability of a particular data analysis. We will discuss Statistical Review in Chapter 9. This is an opportunity to perform a "self-diagnostic" of how well we are solving business analytics problems.

Constructing Effective Building Blocks

We want to evaluate three critical building blocks that support analytics. In Part III of this book (Chapters 10 to 12), we will discuss Data Collection, Data Software, and Data Management. We want a business analytics

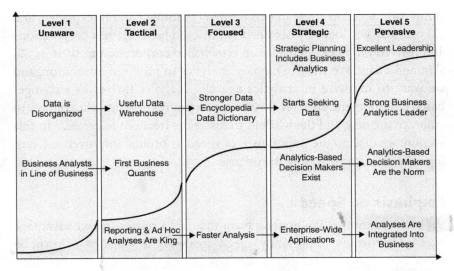

Figure 6.10 Business analytics maturity model

leader or an expert leader to evaluate the extent to which these three building blocks are going to meet our current and future statistical needs. We
want to know how much value is lost in (1) going without data that we can
collect, (2) compensating for insufficient software, and (3) struggling with
data or computer support that is not customer-centric. It is not unusual for
inefficiencies to consume 20% to 60% of productivity.

Business Analytics Maturity Model

We end this section by presenting a Business Analytics Maturity Model,
Figure 6.10.

Section 6.3 Innovation and Change from a Producer on the Edge

"Innovation comes from the producer—not from the customer."[10]
　　　　　　　　　　　　　　　　　　　—W. Edwards Deming

*"Nothing changes at the center. Change only occurs at the edges and
works its way in."*
　　　　　　　　　　　　　　　　　　　—Russell Banks[11]

Innovation tends to come in two flavors: (1) sudden and unexpected, and (2) planned, yet doggedly obtained. Innovation has built new corporations and revived old ones. It enables an established corporation to shed its old skin and adapt. We want to employ analytics to promote innovation, and we want to innovate in analytics as well. Analytics thrives in a change-based environment. Such an environment requires humility, the courage to embrace the new, and the wisdom to foster the freedom to create.[12] In this section, we discuss the importance of speed, continual improvement, and ingredients for accelerating the offense.

Emphasis on Speed

Speed is the thing.[13] We prefer a team that has a relative speed advantage over other virtues. Importantly, speed creates time that can, in turn, be spent developing bigger advantages—such as greater speed. Many decisions must be made quickly, and so reaction time can be critical. We want a team that can react quickly and can anticipate the needed facts prior to decision making. This does not mean that we need to sprint back and forth from our desk all day. Simply put, we need to think about how we make a viable analytics-based decision faster.[14]

The primary solution to obtain greater speed is an improved infrastructure. We want a trained organized team with the software and hardware infrastructure to mass-produce, react quickly, and anticipate as much as possible. That is why we wrote three chapters on Statistical QDR and three more on the Data CSM.

Continual Improvement[15]

Integral to our strategy is to create competitive advantage by continually improving our ability to make analytics-based decisions. Building this competitive advantage involves a long-term investment in capabilities for making decisions faster, better, and less expensive. We want to integrate continual improvement into every project. We have already discussed a few of the important topics for supporting continual improvement: Leadership, Specialization, Delegation, and Incentives (Chapter 2); analytics-based decision making (Chapter 3); the corporate culture (Chapter 4); and organization and leadership (Chapter 5). As mentioned in Chapter 3, there can be a fifth act in the analytics-based decision making process, which is to prepare for future business problems by learning from the present one at hand.[16] This fifth act is covered by Statistical Review (Chapter 9), and there are no new causes of death.

The thrust of continual improvement is to learn from doing. Based on past decisions and analyses, we want to continually improve our infrastructure to accommodate greater analytics breadth, better solutions, and more speed. The downstream benefits include less expensive rigor, more flexibility, faster turnaround (speed), and greater breadth in addressing business needs.[17] Naturally, we want to emphasize making those improvements that will produce the greatest ROI. This usually involves leveraging economies of scope and scale. Continual improvement is an ongoing commitment, for which we may need to ring-fence resources. We cannot allow the problems of the day or short-term incentives to interfere.

In particular, Statistical Review, as discussed in Chapter 9, is *the* major force in continual improvement. Statistical Review not only enhances and ensures the quality of the current decision but also looks forward to improving future decision-making performance. In some instances, we perform autopsies to find out what went right and what went wrong. This is about more than just checking the data and the data analysis. The focus should be on the quality of the solution for the business problem and the analytics-based decision. As we discussed in Chapter 1, the data analysis is a technical problem within the business problem. We need to review the entire context including the broader business needs: Timeliness, Client Expectation, Accuracy, Reliability, and Cost—Best Statistical Practice. We must review how well we solved this problem within its constraints and provide that as feedback to improve the infrastructure.

Another point we wish to make is that some problems require incremental gains. Before we can build an economically powerful super model or business strategy, we may need to go through several generations of mediocre ones. Worst case, we might need to fail in a very public manner—to fall forward.

Accelerating the Offense—For Those Who Are Struggling

Some corporations are on course to take generations to acclimate to the Information Age, a delay that puts them on a path to oblivion. These corporations need to take thoughtful aggressive steps beyond just throwing resources at the problem. There are likely to be many corporations that fail to execute. We need to genuinely understand how the "machine" works if we are going to speed it up. Most statistically struggling corporations are psychologically predisposed to gently add analytics reactively and this timidity can be fatal. Again, we need to be aggressive. With the new and/ or unknown, there can be a psychological draw toward a moderate though inadequate approach.

A good first step is to look at the big picture. As discussed, we need to review how analytics fits into the business strategy, assess our business needs, and evaluate our capabilities. From here on, we can rethink our overall approach. If we are struggling with incorporating analytics, then we will most likely want to reorganize—an application of the "gale of creative destruction" as introduced by Werner Sombart. As part of our restructuring, we should consider (1) bringing in new talent, (2) erecting an improved infrastructure, (3) training our staff about analytics, and (4) reviewing how we execute the four acts in analytics-based decision making.

Bringing in new talent can completely change the dynamic. One aggressive option is to hire an intact team of analytics professionals—an enterprise-wide advocate, mid-level advocates, analytics-based decision makers, an on-topic business analytics leader, expert leaders, and a cadre of business analysts and business quants. We want to hire in a group that thinks alike and can work well together. They are more valuable if they already know each other—especially the decision makers and the practitioners—as this preserves their culture. We want this new group to report high in the corporate tree, and we would eventually want to circulate the members all over the corporation.

A completely different tack is to bring back talent that left when we were not ready to change. They already know the lay of the land and what we need to do to improve our analytics.

Now for what we need to stop doing: we tend to repeatedly hire and promote "ourselves"—that is, professionals with similar backgrounds. So those with little statistical training hire and promote those with, at best, slightly better statistical training.[18] Similarly, if we are in an industry that is weak in analytics, then we need to stop lowering our analytics standards to (1) be comparable with industry norms, and (2) accommodate our appetite for more of what we already possess—industry knowledge. More industry knowledge adds far less value in an industry that has a greater need for analytics. In this situation, we should recruit from other more statistically aggressive industries and look for quant qualifications and certifications.

With regard to infrastructure, it is a Herculean task to take the data analysis that supports decision making all the way from a cottage industry to mass production. While addressing needs as they come in the door, we need to build large-scale investments that emphasize speed. The initial resources to build additional infrastructure could come from postponing or canceling certain other analyses.

Improvements in infrastructure will generate greater productivity that we can shrewdly reinvest in generating more productivity. We need to ring-fence this newly created resource reserve and regard "unfinanced" unanticipated in-the-moment spending as deficit spending. We should continue to reinvest with a focus on creating efficiencies first and then making the results more reliable.

Another option for acceleration is to employ wholesale training of the staff—Six Sigma style. We want the larger team to be more comfortable and effective in applying analytics to decision making. The training needs for analytics practitioners will be very different, focusing on leadership and communication. We will discuss training needs further in Chapter 7.

Another way to jump-start our analytics is by starting a review capability. We can begin by only reviewing the company scorecard and a random sample of tracking reports and analyses to see how well our corporation is performing. We may need to house an analytics governance team in the corporate governance arm of the company—an independent and centralized function like legal, compliance, or finance. This facilitates high-level objective reporting.

Acceleration should not be an excuse for losing sight of the details or unknowingly compromising on customer service. Fast does not imply sloppy. Limited resources might mean doing one highly profitable analysis very well or many less profitable analyses in an acceptable fashion. Acceleration depends on the corporate strategy and the economics.

In the next six chapters we will introduce Statistical QDR (Chapters 7 to 9) for improving decision making and data analyses, and Data CSM (Chapters 10 to 12) for supporting analytics.

Notes

1. *See Business Analytics for Managers: Taking Business Intelligence Beyond Reporting* by Gert Laursen and Jesper Thorlund ((2010).
2. The alternative of not explaining the technology might have been worse.

3. At some corporations, CRM failed during this phase because they struggled with adequately mapping the analysis requirements and supplying all of the analyses needed.
4. This information should be taken with a bucket of salt.
5. Most of the activity lies with either the one-off analyses or the mass-produced ones.
6. A hazardous proposition.
7. Analyses performed with too little rigor will either underperform or be of no value. We are missing many opportunities where rigor could make a difference. Some of these are instances where the corporation needs an analytics solution to extricate itself from the Decisive Circle mentioned in Chapter 3.
8. For many corporations, model building is still a cottage industry.
9. We will give anyone who can do this a passing grade.
10. There is much more innovation from healthy producers with numerous competitors.
11. *Mark Twain: "A Film Directed by Ken Burns,"* directed by Ken Burns (2000).
12. Think Walt Disney.
13. Shakespeare had it wrong.
14. Again, we measure the time of a footrace beginning from the starting gunshot to when the runner crosses the finish line (attains a viable answer, decision, or result) rather than when the runner stops.
15. Continual improvement includes both continuously improving a current approach (continuous improvement) and looking for new means for solving current problems. We are open to completely changing how we solve the problem. In a word . . . humility.
16. Deming regarded continual improvement (and continuous improvement) as part of the process.
17. Through attaining strategic competence.
18. When playing poker, if "you don't know who the patsy is, you're the patsy."

Part II

The Three Pillars of Best Statistical Practice

When corporations struggle with business analytics, it can be due to chronic deficiencies with decision making or data analysis. We can meet these challenges with a strong infrastructure: Statistical Qualifications (Chapter 7), Statistical Diagnostics (Chapter 8), and Statistical Review (Chapters 9). One of the benefits of a strong infrastructure is in establishing the appropriate level of rigor. We struggle with estimating how accurate and how reliable we need our results to be. Also, we occasionally need to justify how much rigor we propose for solving a business analytics problem. One strategy for addressing the problem of assigning enough rigor is to make rigor so inexpensive that other business solutions, such as guesswork, have a discernibly smaller RAROC (risk-adjusted return on capital).

These difficulties in getting the analytics right are exacerbated by the motivation to (1) pretend everything is proceeding famously, and (2) declare "mission accomplished" even though the mission is not yet finished. Most of us have seen the growth in these two phenomena, which appears to be related to the drive to impress investors and, in some countries, a growing emphasis on hierarchy. In the case of analytics, we hear or read about these great analytics "achievements" in the media—some of which make sense, while others resonate as unlikely or implausible. It can be much later that, for some of these stories, we learn from competent sources close to the matter that certain achievements were "make-believe."

Stock analysts should ascertain analytics capabilities by looking at the fundamentals[1] rather than listening to "difficult to corroborate" stories.

Blind Man's Russian Roulette Bluff

Here is how we play Blind Man's Russian Roulette Bluff. Place the following accoutrements on the table in a large boardroom: one blindfold, one headache pill, your company's data analyses, and one revolver. Swallow the headache pill whole in one gulp. Put the blindfold on. Spin yourself around until you are disoriented. Now, we will pretend that the reliable data analyses are blanks and the unreliable data analyses are live rounds. Grope around on the table and insert one questionable data analysis into the revolver. Spin the chamber and point the revolver somewhere. Try not to point it at your own head. (Hopefully, you are not that disoriented.) Pull the trigger, that is, make an analytics-based decision. Depending on what happens, select the next round.

Being guided by unreliable analyses is tantamount to playing with deadly "toys." There are countless examples of corporations that closed their doors or were severely impacted by a single poor decision, let alone a series of them. We want to watch the high-impact decisions closely, to push decisions to those professionals who are in the best position to make them, and to orchestrate our ability to make analytics-based decisions—as discussed in Acts I to IV of Chapter 3.

Part II will introduce the three pillars for Best Statistical Practice: Statistical Qualifications, Diagnostics, and Review. These pillars facilitate supporting higher quality decisions by measuring and therefore improving our performance in Acts I to IV. Statistical Qualifications are wanted (1) as a surrogate for measuring the reliability of decisions and data analyses, and (2) to identify the training necessary to properly execute the decisions and analyses. Statistical Diagnostics are essential for measuring the reliability of the data analysis in Act II: Executing the Data Analysis. Part of our definition of analytics-based decision makers is that they comprehend Statistical Qualifications and Statistical Diagnostics. Statistical Review[2] is a self-diagnostic that identifies concerns and creates synergistic growth. We can wield review in broad strokes or as a microscope performing autopsies.

|♻| |♻| |♻|

7

Statistical Qualifications

$$E = MC^2 + \varepsilon$$

"What would you say the odds [are of] our getting out of here?"
— Captain Kirk

"Difficult to be precise, Captain. I should say approximately 7,824.7 to 1."
— Mr. Spock[3]

We look for qualifications comprising four skills: leadership, communication, analytics training, and analytics-based decision making. We have observed that the cost of overtraining is usually less than the cost of under-training.[4]

Statistical Qualifications are extremely helpful for making decisions based upon advanced analytics. They are necessary, yet not sufficient for performing advanced analytics. Applied statistical training supplies the tools and the way to think about business analytics problems[5] with imperfect and often incomplete information.[6] We look for advanced training to lend credibility to the results. Experience working with other analytics professionals and from analytically aggressive industries is also helpful.

Many corporations struggle to identify qualified analytics professionals. The growing pressure to compete based upon analytics has encouraged more companies to look for tangible measures of ability. This is leading to new certifications (such as the CAP, GradStat, GStat, PSTAT, or P.Stat) to help identify those with adequate statistical training and fit them into the most productive roles. Mistakes in decision making and data analysis are not always easy to trace to inadequate Statistical Qualifications.

Section 7.1 Leadership and Communications for Analytics Professionals

We look for more than just abilities to make analytics-based decisions and perform the analysis well. We want analytics professionals to have leadership and communication skills. A great deal has already been written elsewhere about leadership[7] and communication. We will discuss the important peculiarities for analytics professionals.

Leadership

Leadership is wanted to help socialize findings and direct people toward analytics-based decision making. Leadership exudes confidence in the approach even though there will be distracting anecdotes. We have observed corporate concerns about over-analysis to be a leadership problem. We need leadership that does not flinch at advanced analytics. We want business analytics leaders who understand analytics enough to judge the amount of rigor wanted for each data analysis.

Communication

Communication is not optional. Communication skills are imperative for expressing complex results in a simple manner and for relationship building—both of which are facilitated by having analytics professionals present their own results and encouraging them to master the business. Ideally, we want analytics professionals to present their own work so that there are no additional communication barriers. This is the last step in the analysis and the first step in the next analysis. An adequately trained audience will understand business analysts and business quants and a shrewd audience will want them there. It is appropriate to bundle the identity and qualifications of the source with the results. The same bundling holds for safety inspections of airplanes, elevators, restaurants, and nuclear power plants. The credentials are part of the statistical results and should appear with them. This encourages communication and increases the value of the findings.

Some of the analytics professionals must be bilingual. That is, they must be adroit in two types of communications: collaborating with other business professionals and discussing technical results. Currently, it is typical for there to be a communication burden on the business analysts and business quants to bridge the gap between those who understand analytics and those who do not. This is often out of necessity. The most egregious communication error an analytics professional can make is to try explaining complex technical results when it is unnecessary and unwanted. Talking business is the preferred language for most audiences—try that first. Business quants need to understand the vocabulary and how the business works. Everyone needs to evolve outward.

Leadership and Communication Training

Many analytics professionals do not have sufficient opportunities to build their leadership and communication skills. The first place to start is to have analytics professionals lead groups and present their own results. There are other opportunities outside the corporation, including presenting at conferences and reading business books[8] and journals.

Additionally, Toastmasters is an easily accessible choice for developing great leaders and great communicators. Toastmasters provides a curriculum for leading, motivating, mentoring, evaluating, speaking, listening, and presenting.

Section 7.2 Training for Making Analytics-Based Decisions

"When statistics are not based on strictly accurate calculations, they mislead instead of guide. The mind easily lets itself be taken in by the false appearance of exactitude which statistics retain in their mistakes, and confidently adopts errors clothed in the form of truth."
—Alexis de Tocqueville

The usual requirements for decision making include knowing what information we need, where to get the information, when to delegate the decision, and how to make decisions within the context of time and other related decisions. Analytics-based decisions can be more complex requiring us to interpret the analytics, judge the accuracy and reliability of the information, incorporate utility functions, and deal with uncertainty. Past managers of analytics practitioners can make excellent analytics-based decision makers.

One tactic is to conduct on-site training from the business analysts and business quants to the analytics-based decision makers and from analytics-based decision makers right back to the business analysts and business quants. On-site training can decrease the distance between the various analytics professionals, thereby facilitating better communication and vocabulary sharing. Training should include corporate examples that illustrate the workings of the left and right brains. For some of the examples, we want to go through Acts I to IV and dissect the team's approach to the problem. Analytics-based decision makers need to fully understand the concepts so as to consume analytics appropriately as well as to delegate wisely.

In training analytics-based decision makers, there are a number of helpful topics:

1. *Decision impairments* (discussed in Section 3.3):   Analytics-based decision makers can improve their performance by going through examples of these pitfalls, syndromes, and plagues.

2. *Interpretation of analytics results: first, what not to review*: Very few analytics-based decision makers will benefit from reviewing how to calculate statistical tests. We have seen on-the-job training[9] attempt to raise statistical prowess through teaching the masses the *t*-test ceremony.[10] This "flash training" loses about half of the audience and does too little to help anyone understand the concepts—a fact that is supported by the continuing plethora of incorrectly interpreted results. Anyway, software does the usual calculations now, so we can leave the formulae buried in pedantic statistics books.[11]

   Second, What to Review: We need to discuss how to interpret statistical results, and Statistical Diagnostics in particular. We should go through slides of past business problems, dissecting our approach and presenting all manner of alternatives. Solid analytics-based decision makers thrive on reviewing past analytics-based decisions. We want to better integrate analytics into the business.

   An analytics-based decision maker should be able to understand a business quant's presentation and will not need someone else to present or interpret that person's work. We want to lessen any dependence upon communicating through "interpreters," who have never practiced. We want to close the distance between the various analytics professionals.

One reason why industries tend to be two-trick ponies is because analytics-based decision makers are too few and regular decision makers have little breadth in the usage of statistical tools. Sophisticated decision makers should be familiar with basic methodological tools for collecting data, designing experiments, monitoring processes, predicting, forecasting, and so on.

3. *Judging reliability*: We need to consider the source. Analytics-based decision makers should be trained to look for conflicts of interest and the appropriate qualifications to go with the analytics results. This is part of the process for judging the reliability of the results. The other part is to understand the Statistical Diagnostics, which will be outlined in Chapter 8. Analytics-based decision makers should leverage these diagnostics to appreciate the accuracy and reliability of an analysis.

4. *Utility functions:* In the advanced class, analytics-based decision makers need to know how to incorporate results into utility functions like those we often associate with econometrics. That is, they need to be able to think through more complex situations. For example, they might want to make a decision that will minimize the maximum loss that we can incur. This would imply a Minimax utility function.

"You sell it, we'll build it."

—Consulting company

Statistical "Mythodologies"

Many statistical "mythodologies" are introduced through an absence of proper training and some are exacted through charlatans. After a time, ordinary decision makers internalize the statistical mythodologies and believe the counterfeit analysis over the genuine article. For example, one consulting company sold the idea of creating synthetic one-to-one "control groups" from observational data as an *equivalent* substitute for building a control group in a designed experiment. They would search observational data for consumers, who did not receive some promotion (control group) and map them to consumers, who did receive the promotion (treatment group). For some of their clients, it sounds better if the mapping is one-to-one, so they arbitrarily used that approach. While not without merit, these synthetic "observational control groups" are not really the same as those in a designed experiment (see Section 10.4).

☙ ☙ ☙

Section 7.3: Statistical Training for Performing Advanced Analytics[14]

"Superiority lies with him[/her] who is reared in the severest school."[12]
— Thucydides[13]

"It seems to me that the people with an educational match to the practical experience turn out to be the best combination."
—Don Ritchey

The reliability and style of each data analysis is dictated by the training that facilitated it. Qualifications are implicitly bundled with the results. That is, we can think of an analysis as coming from a set of credentials, as if the credentials generated that result based on that data. In this section, we discuss the technical training needs for performing data analysis and their direct leadership—the needs are the same.

For business quants, we think that academic and post-academic training should cover these five topics:

1. *Analytics-based decision making:* How to make decisions based upon data analysis.
2. *Professional interaction:* How to collaborate with experts from other topics. This includes both relationship building and communicating findings with an emphasis on the former.
3. *Advanced analytics:* The how-to in applying techniques to data-analysis problems.
4. *Statistical software:* How to leverage statistical software, both packages and programming languages, to analyze all kinds of data for all kinds of applications.
5. *Theory:* The underlying statistical basis for analyzing often inexact and often incomplete data.

When practice is built upon a foundation of on-topic training, there is a multiplicative effect between the two: Training × Experience.[15] Without appropriate training, the off-topic practitioner is forced to rediscover and blindly navigate the pitfalls chartered during past decades.[16] As a result, some off-topic professionals invent new "methods" and create all manner of arbitrary rules for evaluating data numerically, something similar to writing rules for a parlor game. Sometimes off-topic colleagues request that we reproduce one of these new methods and end by saying, "What? You do not know the banana-moon technique? I thought you had a quant degree! Go ask so-and-so—they can teach you how to perform statistical techniques."[17]

Training in advanced analytics contains the distilled experience of previous generations. Suppose that mathematics, statistics, and algorithmic techniques were taught chronologically. One semester could cover the significant applied analytics breakthroughs made from 1951 to 1960. Suppose that these breakthroughs represented the work of a mere 1,000 researchers working a mere 2,000 hours a year. Ergo, the content of that single semester would be the "concentrate" from 20,000,000 hours of toil ... and some people want to try to rediscover this on their own? Well, we can rely upon statistical software to contain some of this distilled knowledge.

The Benefits of Training

It is the training that makes the quant. For universities teaching statistics, their struggle is with keeping it applied and not dogmatic. For corporations applying statistics, their struggle is with identifying and leading talent. Unfortunately, we do not always hire people with the right training.[18]

Even for regular analytics, we see occasional mistakes within the corporation, while for advanced analytics we see more serious problems. Advanced analytics requires advanced training, and corporations today need much more analytics expertise, yet in the right places. The benefits of advanced training include the following:

1. Greater speed
2. Expanded business and analytics capabilities
3. Improved accuracy
4. Fewer mistakes
5. An enhanced ability to detect mistakes

Speed is the most important benefit. Training facilitates greater speed through faster execution, better focus on aspects of the analysis that matter, the ability to mass-produce, and the ability to finish the problem. This last point is often overlooked. As stated before, in a timed race to solve a problem, the race ends only when we produce a viable answer. Simply blurting out "42!," though astonishingly fast, does not cross the finish line.

Qualified professionals realize that they are performing analyses within the confines of assumptions. Their training enables them to know when it is safe to skip steps and the corresponding consequences. Qualified professionals can figure out what can be mass-produced and how to automate it. They have a greater understanding of their technical limitations.

During Statistical Review, we see marked differences between advanced data analyses performed by those with two semesters of training as opposed to qualified professionals.[19] Mistakes occur when there is a gap between statistical difficulty and statistical ability. Without review, most mistakes go unnoticed because the training required to avoid the mistake is the training required to recognize it. Frequent unrecognized mistakes are an unrecognized symptom of a qualification problem.[20] Not every problem requires a full-bird[21] econometrician, industrial engineer, operations researcher, statistician, et al. to solve it. We can stretch our resources by having the qualified professionals judge the amount of rigor required and assign problems appropriately, thus minimizing the gap between qualifications and difficulty.

> "Instructors of statistics courses do not teach applied statistics, instructors of engineering courses do not teach statistics, engineering professors are not statistically literate, and [industry] is not happy."
> —Craig Barrett, CEO of Intel (1989)[22]

Academic Training[23]

Yes, universities teach too much theory.[24] Each teaching generation prepares us for a future that resembles their past. Hence, our education system, from preschool onward, does a great job of producing university professors. It is a pity that we, in this book, are the first[25] to recognize a need for changing academic training for quants. Oh, wait, maybe there was something before. See Bishop (1964); Armstrong (1973); Bartholomew (1973); Boardman, Hahn, Hill, Hocking, Hunter, Lawton, Ott, Snee, and Strawderman (1980); Eldridge, Wallman, Wulfsberg, Bailar, Bishop, Kibler, Orleans, Rice, Schaible, Selig, and Sirken (1982); Wulfsberg and Eldridge (1982); Zahn (1982); Minton (1983); McCulloch, Boroto, Meeter, Polland, and Zahn (1985); Currie, Gough, Hole, Drotki, Lussier, and

Maranda (1986); Allen (1987); Fong (1989); Snee (1993); Garfield (1994); Morris (1994); Bailar (1995); Bickel (1995); Clark and Schuchardt (1995); Hoerl and Snee (1995); Hole, Lee, and Jones (1995); Kettenring (1995); Killion (1995); Lethoczy (1995); Ross (1995); AmStat News (2001); Bryce, Gould, Notz, and Peck (2001); Tarpey, Acuna, Cobb, De Veaux (2002); and Bryce (2005).[26] Dr. Ronald Snee said, "There is a growing consensus that the 'content side' of statistical education should move away from the mathematical and probabilistic approach and place greater emphasis on data collection, understanding and modeling variation, graphical display of data, design of experiments, surveys, problem solving, and process improvement." Unfortunately, all of these presidents of ASA (American Statistical Association), distinguished professors, educators, et al. did not know anyone in a position to influence change.[27]

The point of divergence is that academic incentives emphasize theoretical research and publishing. Many of these publications pursue the aforementioned mathematical and probabilistic approach. They do not discuss actual or simulated data! One rationalization for stressing so much theory is the desire to prepare professionals, who can solve, or at least recognize, an obscure original problem. Teaching theory is expensive. In particular, it takes a great deal of time. Meanwhile, there is an unmet need for training quants to analyze data, particularly within the business context.[28] This need almost requires a separate faculty of professors with more applied field experience. If we want to change the status quo, we need to raise the prestige of applied statistics (relative to theory) in academia and modify the "publishing" incentive structure.[29]

We know that there are numerous well-meaning applied professors who want to train and acculturate quants and, more specifically, the type of business quants that we need. Their level of interest is reflected by the numerous references and meetings on how to better teach applied statistics. There are many wanted skills that are difficult to teach. Also, each department is tasked with preparing quants to address multiple sets of requirements—research, academia, and those of different industries. Perhaps, a BS in a quant degree such as statistics (six courses in applied statistics, three courses in computing and statistical software, and two courses in theory, which require five courses in mathematics for support), taught to a large group of students, is the closest to the ideal technical training for a business quant. To address this deficiency in applied statistical training, we are looking to Internet courses, iTunes offerings, etc. to make applied training

Table 7.1 Progress from Academic Training

Training Areas	BS[30] in Quant (uncommon)	MS[31] in Quant	Ph.D. in Quant	MBA	Post-Academic Training
Analytics-Based Decision Making	30–50%	40–60%	+10–50%	+0–30%	Remainder of Training
Client Interaction	0–10%	20–30%	+20–60%	+30–60%	Remainder of Training
Analytics (Basic Algorithms, Statistics, and Mathematics)	Plenty	Plenty	Plenty	+30–100%	NA
Advanced Analytics	30–60%	30–60%	+5–20%	+0%	Remainder of Training
Statistical Software	60–80%	40–80%	+0–100%	+0–20%	Remainder of Training
Theory	200–300%	0–500%	+100–500%	+0%	Never Happen

Notes: We regard a BS or MS in a quant degree as containing mathematics, 10+ semesters of applied statistical content, and software training. **Statistical content can be found in many degree programs.** This table treats Ph.D. and MBA degrees as addendums to a quantitative master's degree.

more accessible and we are looking to the new MS in Analytics to combine applied statistical training with business training.

Today, we think academia is only one stage in training business quants, which touches upon the five topics mentioned above: Analytics-Based Decision Making, Professional Interaction, Advanced Analytics, Statistical Software, and Theory. Based upon our engagements with other quants, we will venture a guess in Table 7.1 as to the extent that academic preparation covers these areas. This table is intended to provide some basic insight into the situation, and it is not meant to be relied upon for accuracy.

We regard the applied courses and the immediate underlying theory as preparation for data analysis and the excess theoretical classes as to enablers for publishing and scholarly work. Some theory is essential for understanding the underlying assumptions of applied tools.[32]

To adequately cover this objective, we need the equivalent of two, possibly three, semesters integrated into the applied coursework. Applied statistics is a rough-edged dirty business. Academia has domesticated it to an extreme by removing too many practical, and often anecdotal, lessons.[33]

Post-Academic Training—Best Statistical Practice

Like many other fields, applied business quants are self-made. The final stage in their development occurs in the real world. Typically, they need to learn much much more about building relationships and communicating findings; more about making decisions based upon analytics; more about other advanced techniques—they have mastered some of them by now; and continue updating their statistical software skills—this is a moving target. It is assumed that, since they self-selected themselves into this profession, if they liked what they learned so far and if they have the opportunity, they are going to continue their training.

Quants will build off their academic training by pouring through how-to books and applying them to business problems, by attending conferences and workshops, by building relationships and communicating findings, by adapting academic training to work in the business world, and by solving the whole business problem rather than just the data analysis problem inside it (Best Statistical Practice). The fastest growth comes from working with expert leaders (ELs) within a large quant group. Although it is a slow road paved with unlearning the publishing training, they can make it with the proper leadership.

Training Through Review

The final word in on-the-job training is review. Even those with dead-on training can benefit. We advise review, not from those with political agendas, those enforcing their pecking order, or those with diametrically opposed training. Instead, we recommend review from those interested in promoting growth. Toastmasters provides a functional paradigm for how to review others. We want expert leaders who know what they are doing to review and coach those coming out of graduate school—exiting theory boot camp.

The idea is that ELs can develop new quants by acculturating them from academia to business. Business quants have many opportunities to learn from peers and too few to learn from leaders.

Section 7.4 Certification for Analytics Professionals

"The purpose of accreditation is not only to distinguish good practitioners,[34] but to encourage growth and improved statistical practice."
—Ronald L. Wasserstein, Ph.D.

Certification does more than help identify qualified professionals and qualify the quality of the data analysis. It promotes growth within the necessary skill sets. There is a need for analytics professionals to be certified in leadership, communication, performing analytics, and analytics-based decision making. Toastmasters and other organizations provide certification for leadership and communication. Perhaps the more urgent need is to help identify those skilled at performing analytics and making analytics-based decisions. There is a training gap. As we will mention again in Chapter 11, software once served as a surrogate for certification in practicing analytics. This barrier held back the floodgates of statistical malfeasance and misinformation. Now statistical software is so much easier to use that the gates, dams, and corps of engineers have been swept away.

As for analytics-based decision making, we have only just begun to incorporate analytics into decision making. A few industries have been employing advanced analytics long enough to educate decision makers, yet the sophistication usually does not extend beyond a few analytics tools.

Meanwhile, "market forces" are pressuring the quality of analytics and analytics-based decision making. As mentioned in Chapter 3, ordinary decision makers judge the reliability of data analysis with the following criteria:

1. Source is trusted/historically "demonstrated."
2. Custom—that is, because they always use that type of analysis, it must be reliable.
3. Results fit business experience.
4. Results come with depth of explanation.
5. Popular source/well-presented source projects confidence.
6. Source has industry experience.

To help decision makers better discern the reliability of the data analysis, we can help them better discern the capabilities of the source. Certification provides a more objective means for identifying competent practitioners. Certification holds the potential for enabling analytics-based decision makers to better discern the reliability of the data analysis. The analysis is bundled with the certifications, just like other vocations such as brain surgeon, risk manager, bridge inspector, airplane pilot, and so on. This raises the quality of the work by enabling the consumer to discern competence and by encouraging professional norms.

Professional accreditation needs to be bundled with the analytics results. **The data analysis is reliable to the business quant's integrity and his or her level of certification.** Credentials of this nature should lead and follow statistical results in presentations, as these serve wonderfully to validate the data analysis.

One of the greatest business concerns is having inadequately trained professionals in the wrong roles. In addition to the direct waste, we develop people with experience and "know-how" to incorrectly perform data analysis and to make ill-advised decisions. This leads to fairy tales about how to perform analysis[35] and about how to run the business.

Another important role for accredited professionals is to work with the teams of knowledge workers. Like anyone else, knowledge workers do not know what they do not know. They need guidance to better apply analytics in their jobs and to grow their analytics skills. We should train knowledge workers to know when to seek counsel and when to delegate.

The PSTAT® (ASA) (Professional Statistician)—ASA's New Accreditation by Ronald L. Wasserstein, Ph.D.

Analytics needs to be part of the decisions. Those trained in statistics need to be at the table when data are being used to make decisions. The American Statistical Association (ASA) is working on this in a variety of ways. One way is to join previous statistical organizations in providing an accreditation program:

- Hong Kong Statistical Society: Certified Statistician (CStat), and Graduate Statistician (GradStat)
- Royal Statistical Society: Chartered Statistician (CStat) and Graduate Statistician (GradStat)
- Statistical Society of Australia: Accredited Statistician (AStat) and Graduate Statistician (GStat)
- Statistical Society of Canada: Professional Statistician (P.Stat) and Associate Statistician (A.Stat).

INFORMS (Institute for Operations Research and the Management Sciences) will offer a CAP (Certified Analytics Professional) in 2013.

> Individually, statisticians should be growing as professionals within their organizations in such a way as to be building the level of trust needed to become a sought-out voice. If we're happy sitting at our desks doing analysis and writing reports, that won't happen. But I don't think many statisticians work that way. The modern statistician is a collaborator, not a "data flunky."
>
> The question of bad practice will always be with us, as it is in many professions. Accreditation is one way to encourage good practice. We ask two very important things of accredited members: (1) participate in the statistics community through ASA membership, and (2) complete 60 hours of continuing professional development each year. Regarding the first, we want accredited members to be part of the larger statistical community, and to experience the growth that comes from interacting with colleagues. Second, we want accredited members to continue learning leadership, communication, analytics, and decision-making skills. And speaking of growth, it seems somewhat unlikely that charlatans will want to devote serious time to professional development. However, I prefer to think about this positively. That is, the purpose of accreditation is not only to distinguish good practitioners but to encourage growth and improved statistical practice.

"The ones who are least trained are the easiest to manipulate."
—James Wright, Ph.D. (Statistics)

"Honesty is the best policy—when there is money in it."
—Mark Twain

Professionalism

Part of the motivation for certification is to protect professionalism from "market forces." Unfortunately, professionalism has declined over the last 30 years. Journalism and accounting provide notorious examples of how market forces have crushed overall professional norms[36] by redefining norms to accommodate short-term incentives. Practically all professions have moved further away from stewardship and ever closer to salesmanship.[37]

Market incentives alone are insufficient for guaranteeing quality where it is difficult to measure. The economy depends on professional norms in order to function. These norms are strongest with those individuals who make an investment of years in training and practice. Certification offers some minor protection for those who want to practice professionally and for those who want to consume analytics. Also, it comes with ethical obligations.

We believe that professionalism is inextricably tied to ethical obligations and that integrity and responsibility are parts of the long-term profit equation.

Notes

1. Count the analytics professionals and look for the degree to which analytics is integrated into the leadership and corporate strategy.
2. Sometimes the term model validation is synonymous with model review.
3. *Star Trek*, "Errand Of Mercy," written by Gene L. Coon.
4. Some of you are training right now.
5. Think stochastically, not deterministically.
6. The universe is essentially stochastic and only deterministic within some localities. where some of the variables are held constant. Looking for causation can be a distraction at times.
7. See *On Becoming a Leader* by Warren Bennis (2009).
8. This book has some intriguing references.
9. A consultant comes in for a day of calculating t-tests and such.
10. Oh, the t-test ceremony! Understanding how to calculate something is helpful. Dwelling upon the t ceremony likens it to calligraphy and flower arrangement. This dwelling came about due to our pedantic mathematical and probabilistic approach to teaching statistics and our need to grade students.
11. These books are like "chalk and cardboard" sandwiches.
12. We wish this were true, yet it appears that the faculty just wanted to make us work hard. Great quants can come from anywhere, even the theory schools.
13. See *The Landmark Thucydides: A Comprehensive Guide to the Peloponnesian War*." Edited by Robert B. Strassler, Translated by Richard Crawley. New York: Free Press, 1998.
14. If someone has been performing data analysis incorrectly for the past ten years, then how many years of experience do they possess?
15. A Training-Experience Multiple.
16. This is not only unnecessary, it is a Herculean task for some great idle intellect.
17. One response is to gently mention that most techniques have multiple names and to ask the client to show us the technique in a statistical dictionary or statistical encyclopedia (see *Encyclopedia of Research Design*) in order to avoid the hyperbole of the Internet or word of mouth.
18. It takes adequate training to spot adequate training.
19. Also, we see differences in strengths and styles based upon the type of training.

20. We recognize this.
21. About as trained as possible.
22. This was partially addressed by ABET—The Accreditation Board for Engineering and Technology, which forced universities offering engineering degrees to include a statistics course in order to retain their program accreditation. This was hugely successful! We are ready for next steps now.
23. The first formal statistics course was taught by George Snedecor (Iowa State University) in 1915! Almost 100 years ago, he led us down a path in applying statistical techniques, largely to the agricultural experiments of the day.
24. The textbooks render a mathematical and probabilistic approach to the subject. This sharply differs from student expectations.
25. In keeping with the tradition of authors taking credit for originating ideas that in truth predate the authors.
26. We apologize for leaving out many authors. We had space considerations.
27. Or in a position to terminate accreditation at those colleges that offer statistics degrees without teaching applied statistics.
28. While it is noble to want to train more researchers, the dominant institutions are corporations and most corporations are slow to value these specializations.
29. In the fullness of time, the great super-intelligence or technological singularity will certainly change the status quo. This is the hypothesized future point in time where artificial intelligence begets an intelligence explosion whereby AI produces most new information. We are sure that the luddites cannot wait. See I. J. Good, et al.
30. A BS in operations research, statistics, or similar are the logical prerequisites for the MS quant degree. Unfortunately, these degrees are not offered at many universities. Quants need a mathematical, a statistical, *and* a computational foundation.
31. Academia needs to redefine the MS in applied statistics as a terminal degree and stop thinking of it as a consolation prize for not going on to the Ph.D. Those who stop at the MS do so for two reasons: (1) they cannot stand to go another day, and (2) they are smart enough to know better. By the time the student makes the decision to end at the MS, they are taking derivatives of log likelihood equations in their sleep.
32. What really matters is the quant's ability to successfully apply the statistical tool.
33. In a similar vein, foil fencing is the domesticated version of fighting techniques taken from Western martial arts. The techniques and accoutrements (a wire-mesh helmet, white pajamas, tennis shoes, and brandishing a "wire" sword) are just as impractical for storming a castle as the Law of Large Numbers is useful for analyzing data.

34. From bad?
35. Statistical mythodologies.
36. We admire those exceptions who have held-out—those "Molly McGuires" of journalism and accounting, who value their integrity above the money.
37. Except for sales.

8

Statistical Diagnostics

"What gets measured, gets done."

—W. Edwards Deming

"I have a soft spot for secret passageways, bookshelves that open into silence, staircases that go down into a void, and hidden safes. I even have one myself, but I won't tell you where. At the other end of the spectrum are statistics which I hate with all my heart."

—Luis Buñuel

"Probability."[1]

—H. O. "HOH" Hartley

S tatistical Diagnostics measure the quality of the data analysis. They provide five broad benefits:

1. Detecting mistakes or weaknesses—foibles
2. Measuring the accuracy of an analysis
3. Measuring the reliability of an analysis
4. Providing insight into interpreting the results
5. Providing insight into potential improved solutions

Statistical Diagnostics are important for any analysis upon which we want to make large-dollar business decisions. Diagnostics assess aspects of the data analysis, unearthing the shortcomings. The insight they provide conveys the relative strengths of the components of the data analysis. This can lead to completely new solutions or to iterative improvements. We test that which is testable and merits testing. We evaluate the statistical analysis within the context of the business problem, that is, within our Best Statistical Practice constraints presented in Chapter 1: Timeliness, Client Expectation, Accuracy, Reliability, and Cost. Naturally, the effectiveness of Statistical Diagnostics varies with the problem.

Unfortunately, there are many instances in business, especially amid the "fog of war," when an analysis is unreliable. After a failure, it is common to hear anecdotal explanations such as "the population changed"[2] or "the data were off." For every failure-occurrence, there is no shortage of these potential "explanations,"[3] all of which mask frailties with the analysis that could be ascertained using Statistical Diagnostics.

The Model Overfitting Problem

Model overfitting is one of the common problems that we assess through diagnostics. We build models by identifying a pattern in the data and finding a structure to express and replicate this pattern. A pattern could be a linear trend or a monthly cycle in the data. We want to find a pattern that will repeat itself in future applications. Unfortunately, there is a strong tendency to fit a model to more than just repeatable part of a pattern. This is called overfitting. That is, our model is overfit to the data upon which it was developed. Part of the pattern it has captured is not repeatable. Statistical Diagnostics provide feedback on the degree to which a model is overfit. These techniques quantify a model's strength and guide us in refining the model so that it will better fit the data.

Section 8.1 Overview of Diagnostic Techniques

"The more closely a model approaches the complexity of real life, the more difficult it is to distinguish genuine rare emergent events from programming deficiencies."

—Doug Samuelson's Theorem

A detailed discussion of Statistical Diagnostics is well beyond this book.[4] Table 8.1 contains a representative set of the families of diagnostic tools. Many of these diagnostic tools are known within the modeling paradigm, and some are generally applicable.

We can combine tools from multiple families—for example, a lift chart from the diagnostics family, Tools for Performance Measurement, is often

Table 8.1 Diagnostic Families: Tool Sets and Themes

Diagnostic Family	Description
External Numbers	Sometimes we have the luxury of using external numbers from outside the analysis to validate parts of or all of the results.
Juxtaposing Results	Solving a problem two or more times, usually in a different manner. We then compare or juxtapose the results. This is similar to creating "external" numbers.
Data Splitting (Cross-Validation)	Data splitting methodologies use part of the data for the analysis and a different part of the data to evaluate or "validate" the veracity of the results.
Resampling Techniques with Replacement	These techniques reanalyze different partitions of the same dataset—with replacement. This creates a distribution of results.
Simulation/Stress Testing	Approaches for finding the properties of the results under various possible scenarios.
Tools for Performance Measurement	A huge family of tools for all manner of applications. This is part of the core of statistics.
Tests for Statistical Assumptions	Tools for testing assumptions arising from the particular statistical technique employed.
Tests for Business Assumptions	Tools for testing assumptions arising from the business situation.
Intervals and Regions	Intervals and regions surrounding point estimates such as the mean or predictions; or around a population.
DoS (Design of Samples)	Sample designs with a self-diagnostic quality due to using randomization. These designs validate that the sample is representative of the population.
DoE (Design of Experiments)	Designed experiments with a self-diagnostic quality due to using randomization. These designs validate that the analysis and the data collected are representative of a causal relationship.

combined with Data Splitting. We will discuss particular statistical diagnostics in Sections 8.2 and 8.3.

External Numbers

When available, external numbers provide an independent means of checking values and results. External numbers are from outside the data analysis, are provided independently, and are often obtained prior to the data analysis. External numbers include intermediate and occasionally final numbers, which are usually in the form of rough benchmarks. There is usually a reason why these external numbers cannot serve as the final answer—such as incompleteness. External numbers are often used for validating forecasts and predictions. Intermediate external numbers are particularly valuable for understanding mechanistic models.

These numbers might originate from similar business problems, presaged industry knowledge, and ancillary information. In this situation, we are using the external numbers to vet the analysis rather than the other way around. The strength of these diagnostics varies a great deal. For models that are tracked historically, we can strengthen the results by comparing a more numerous series of point estimates with their external counterparts. Also, we can look at the confidence or predictive intervals for the differences.

We need to avoid confusing virtuous "independent" external numbers with post hoc rationalized values. A far less rigorous approach is to finish the analysis and then rationalize whether the results make sense. We do this informally all the time. This reactive approach does have its risks.

Example

Figure 8.1 juxtaposes two quarterly sales forecasts (Colossus and Guardian) with the actual sales results. The graph shows that, for most quarters, the Colossus forecasts are too high and Guardian's forecasts are too low. Monthly data, a more numerous series, would provide a better comparison. Also, we should look at the interval of the differences between pairs of values. In addition to comparing the two forecasts to external numbers (actual sales), we can gain insight by comparing them to each other. This idea is discussed next in "Juxtaposing Results."

Juxtaposing Results

When useful external numbers are not available, we can juxtapose different analyses of the same data. This is somewhat like creating our own external numbers. For each repeated analysis, we can solve the problem in exactly the same manner or we can vary the method, the business quant performing the analysis, and/or the entire approach.

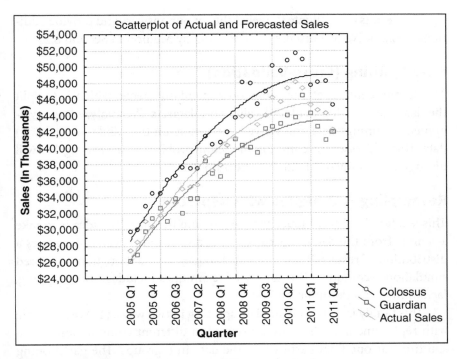

Figure 8.1 Scatterplot of colossus, guardian, and actuals

There are four categories of juxtaposition:

By Method—Analyzing the same data multiple times with different methods.

By Quant—Analyzing the same data multiple times with different business quants.

By Approach—Involves comparing completely different approaches starting with the data collection—for example, modeling data from customers, who were surveyed regarding their perceived purchasing behavior juxtaposed by modeling a sample of actual purchase data. Juxtaposing results includes comparing an analysis to the results from a meta-analysis of existing external analyses.

By Repetition—Solving the analysis multiple times with the same method, quant, and approach.[5] This includes iteratively re-solving the problem to refine our technique and building multiple models with different input variables from the same dataset.

The results can validate the reliability of our answers and provide additional insight. We will discuss Juxtaposition by Method in Section 8.2.

Data Splitting (Cross-Validation)

This family consists of variations on a standard theme, which is to split the data into development and validation datasets. We analyze the development (training) data and we vet[6] the results on the validation (testing) data. This addresses the common modeling problem of overfitting. We will discuss this Family of Methods in Section 8.3.

Resampling Techniques with Replacement

This is a family of techniques that regurgitate the data. The idea is to take a sample from the dataset, perform an analysis, and repeat. This creates a distribution of results. Resampling techniques can be thought of as inbred simulation techniques. This family of techniques includes Bootstrapping, Jackknifing, and Permutation Tests.

This family is distinct from data splitting in two ways: (1) We resample with replacement so the data are reused in different combinations. Data splitting has one final partition of the data into groups. The partitioning can be complex, yet data in the same group are always analyzed together. There is no replacement or reselection. (2) Resampling always creates a distribution of results for comparison purposes and the essence of data splitting is to compare results from static development and validation groups.

Bootstrapping is a popular resampling technique where the data are resampled with replacement. It is extremely popular for validating results for small datasets, and it has some statistical advantages over data splitting. We advise bootstrapping the few, and data splitting the many.

Standard Errors for Model-Based Group Differences: Bootstrapping to the Rescue[7] by James W. Hardin, Ph.D.

To evaluate the efficacy of an intervention on risky sexual behavior of adolescent females, I was provided data on approximately 600 enrolled participants recruited at a free clinic. The sexually active young women were randomized to one of two treatment groups: a control group received the usual source of care for clients of the clinic, and an intervention group received the usual source of care plus an education-based intervention consisting of three live (interactive) classes. The classes aimed to increase knowledge, reduce risky behaviors, and alter attitudes among the participants.

Each participant provided information through an Audio Computer Assisted Self-Interview (ACASI). Biological specimens were collected from each participant so that bacterial STIs (Sexually Transmitted Infections: gonorrhea, trichomoniasis, and chlamydia) could be identified and treated. ACASI and biological information were collected at baseline (at enrollment), 6-months post-enrollment, and 12-months post-enrollment. Thus, analyses utilize baseline values as a covariate while treating the two follow-up data points as repeated measures.

One of the aims of the study was to determine whether the intervention significantly reduced STIs. Independent of fitting data to a model based on Generalized Estimating Equations (GEE), random effects, or a pooled independence model, we always identified a significant effect of group membership which supported that the intervention treatment was protective; that is, that the intervention group had lower incidence rates of STIs. We chose to interpret specific results of whether the participant had an STI based on a logistic GEE model. Exponentiated coefficients have a clear interpretation as an odds ratio, but health researchers typically prefer to interpret risk ratios. Although one can approximate risk ratios from odds ratios, the client requested that we estimate the relative reduction of the intervention group incidence rates $(p_2 - p_1)/p_1$, where p_1 is the adjusted incidence rate of the control group and p_2 is the adjusted incidence rate of the intervention group. This can be estimated using the adjusted means from the fitted model. The adjusted means (linear predictors) are converted to probabilities via the logit link function.

The advantage of the client's preferred summary statistic is its clear interpretation. Missing from this, however, is an associated standard error or p-value. The point estimate unambiguously represents the reduction in STIs associated with the intervention, but without a standard error, one can't be sure that the difference is statistically significant.

Faced with an absence of formulas for this function of adjusted means, we recognized that the data could be *re*-used to yield the desired results. We repeatedly resampled the data at the person level (all observations on a person included or excluded depending on whether the person was sampled). For each of 200 bootstrap samples, we estimated a logistic GEE model and then calculated the incidence rate difference. This approach yielded an empirical distribution of the incidence rate difference from which we could easily construct confidence intervals from the percentiles of the collection of rates. While constructing such a confidence interval does not necessarily result in a symmetric interval about the point estimate, the data-driven result was straightforward to calculate and provided the necessary support to justify our conclusions for reviewers at the *Journal of the American Medical Association.*

A kernel density estimate of the 199 bootstrap values illustrates the bimodal (non-normal) distribution of empirical values (Figure 8.2). The point estimate of the relative reduction was 19.08%. The empirical 95% confidence interval was (1.31%, 41.54%), illustrating that the relative reduction was significantly different from zero (participating in the intervention was protective), which matched inference on the coefficient of the logistic generalized estimating equations fitted model. This technical example, our business examples are proprietary, illustrates that bootstrapping can create confidence intervals for difficult problems.

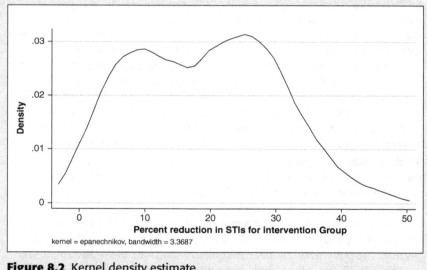

Figure 8.2 Kernel density estimate

Simulation/Stress Testing

Simulation involves generating insight into a business problem by simulating an environment or some aspect of it. The purpose is to understand the typical behavior or the performance under adverse or interesting conditions. There are many types of simulations. Some involve sampling random inputs from known distributions, simulating what will happen based upon these inputs, and generating synthetic performance data. Designed experiments can be thought of as a sophisticated type of simulation.

Stress testing involves measuring model performance under simulated conditions of interest, which are usually adverse. This type of simulation tests our understanding of how a model will perform under these conditions. This includes stressing the variables in the model to understand the conditions under which they will fail and the overall effect of each failure. One common application of stress testing is to back-test a VaR (Value at Risk) model, as illustrated in Figure 8.3.

Tools for Performance Measurement

This huge family of tools addresses a broad set of applications. There are a number of univariate and multivariate diagnostics for exploring the data and measuring performance. This includes EDA (exploratory data analysis), data quality checks, and a rather large group of model building diagnostics. EDA consists of simple techniques to provide insight into the essence of the data. These overlap with data quality checks, which protect us from garbage in, garbage out. Model building diagnostics include likelihood statistics, concordance statistics, collinearity diagnostics, graphical representations such as residual plots and lift charts,

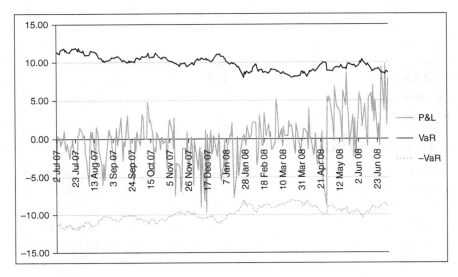

Figure 8.3 Value at risk (VaR) back-testing for profit and loss (P&L)

goodness-of-fit tests, outlier diagnostics, R^2 for regression models, model calibration tools, and validation-fit statistics, among others. Such diagnostics provide insight or some degree of validation for some aspect of an analysis. These tools are particularly important for data mining or observational analysis.

Tests for Statistical Assumptions

This family of tests checks the degree to which the underlying methodological assumptions are supported by the data. In the course of applying a method to a data analysis problem, we need to make assumptions. Even non-parametric or so-called "distribution-free" tools have implicit assumptions. Although this family of tools overlaps with the tools for performance measurement mentioned above, we want to recognize this as a separate theme. For example, one common assumption is that the underlying variance is homogeneous. For this common concern, we can apply Bartlett's Test or Levene's Test for the homogeneity of variance. Other commonly applied tools include studentized residual plots, Anscombe residual plots, influence statistics, pair-wise correlation estimates, and box-plots.

Tests for Business Assumptions

This is more of a theme than a fixed set of tools. The tools will overlap with those already mentioned, yet we want to recognize this paradigm separately to provide enough focus. For example, in Section 2.2, Brian Wynne provided us with an example where the business was willing to assume that future promotional activities would be more effective than those in the past. We could devise a test for this assumption early in a promotional campaign.

Intervals and Regions

Rather than relying solely upon a location estimate, such as the mean, we can construct an interval around the point estimate. For example, an election poll for a candidate might be reported as, say, 48% with a $\pm 3\%$ margin of error. This indicates that this candidate has anywhere between 45% to 51% of the vote. This interval conveys more information than just a point estimate of 48%. Such intervals help us to better envision the uncertainty around a point estimate.

This concept can be expanded in three ways. First, we can place an interval around a line estimate, such as a regression model, as well as around a point estimate, such as a mean. Second, we can build intervals in more than two dimensions—regions. Third, there are three types of intervals: confidence, prediction, and tolerance. Confidence intervals surround point or line estimates. Prediction intervals surround predicted values. Tolerance intervals surround a portion of the population values.

Interval estimates are incorporated into more sophisticated tools such as quality control charts (see Figure 8.4), process control charts, and box plots (see Figure 2.3).

DoS (Design of Samples)

DoS (Design of Samples) is a family of self-validating data collection designs, which validate that the sample is representative. The secret is to know how to make the most of randomization. We will discuss DoS in Chapter 10.

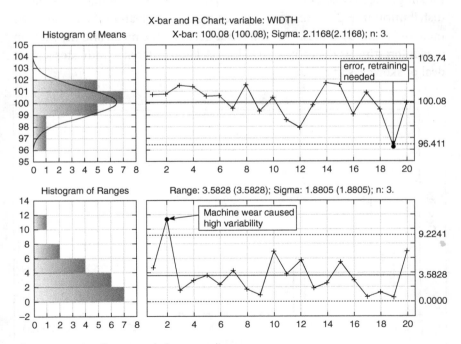

Figure 8.4 Quality control chart

DoE (Design of Experiments)

DoE (Design of Experiments) is a family of self-validating designs that combine data collection and analysis of causal relationships. Again, as in the case of DoS, the secret is to know how to make the most of randomization. We will discuss DoE in Chapter 10.

In the next two sections, we discuss Juxtaposition by Method and the family of Data Splitting techniques, both of which are underutilized and deserve further attention.

Section 8.2 Juxtaposition by Method

The typical application is to perform an analysis on the same data using two methods. The two methods have different underlying assumptions and different results will reflect those assumptions. This provides two perspectives and can raise intriguing questions. We apply this approach frequently for simple needs like estimating the location of a population. For the salary distribution in Figure 8.5, we might compare the mean ($78,726) and the median ($72,579) values. The difference between the mean and the median is as interesting as the estimated values. A large difference indicates a great deal of skewness in the data.

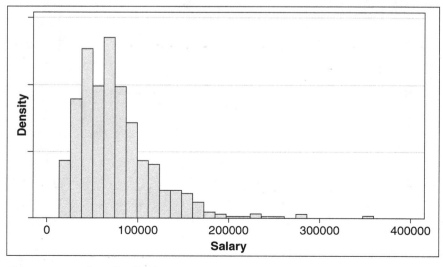

Figure 8.5. Salary distribution

This is a simple case for illustration purposes. Juxtaposition by Method is far more valuable for complex methods, where we might not have the luxury of an illustrative graph like Figure 8.5. Also, we can make different types of comparisons. We can contrast well-understood or well-behaved models with black box models[8] or with more powerful yet less stable models. We can learn a great deal by comparing models with different assumptions and other properties. The genius is in the juxtaposition.

A completely different tack is to consider the sensitivity of the business decision to the different methods.

Paired Statistical Models

One application of Juxtaposition by Method is to apply two different models to the same problem on an ongoing basis. Multiple models are warranted for many prediction problems.[9] In Figure 8.1, the two predictive models illustrate how one model can validate the results of another. The second model validates the first model's overall performance and its specific performance for particular cases.[10]

We suggest the paradigm of a sophisticated primary model on the front line and a simplistic confirming model as a backup. The primary model should be more accurate at the expense of additional unwanted complexity.[11] It does not need to be simple enough for everyone to understand. The confirming model might be more transparent[12] and make simpler assumptions.

While there can be compelling reasons to make the transparent model the secondary one, in practice this decision is driven by the culture's acceptance of technology.[13] This is a case where the arts of trust building and delegation can have large financial payoffs—for the shareholder.

Section 8.3 Data Splitting

Data Splitting is a family of techniques with a common theme: partitioning the data into development and validation datasets. There is no sampling with replacement. That is, data in the same group are always analyzed together. The data from one group might be combined with that of another, but there is one final partition for which the data within a group are never separated—no resampling. The analysis, which is often a model, and its components, is built on development data and "proven" on "pristine" validation data.

If the validation indicates poor model performance, we leverage this information to rebuild. Lift charts like the one in Figure 8.6 are routinely used to illustrate the performance of a new model on the development and validation datasets. The lift chart in Figure 8.6 reveals that the new model performs equally well using the validation data and that the new model outperforms the current model. In practice, we would complement this with more rigorous Statistical Diagnostics to confirm these results.

Once we obtain a validated model, we usually combine the development and validation datasets and re-estimate the results. As cited by Harrell,[14] data splitting "only validates the development model, but not the final whole-data model." Hence, it is often a good idea to compare the validated results based upon the development data and the results based upon the entire dataset to ensure that the difference is minor. For a well-validated model, there will be a small difference and we might consider this a small improvement in our results. If the difference is large enough to have economic ramifications, then we have our answer—trouble. Just how well was the model validated? The trepidation around this comparison is less concerning for large datasets.

The Data Splitting family comprises a number of highly stylized adaptations. We use out-of-time validation to better predict the future.

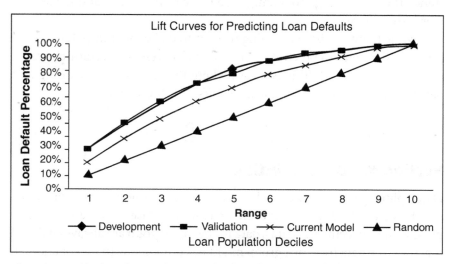

Figure 8.6 Lift chart for predicting loan defaults

For factor analysis, we perform an exploratory factor analysis to provide a conceptual structure. This is followed by a confirmatory factor analysis performed on a separately collected dataset to confirm or reject the prior conceptual structure. This is de facto data splitting. We employ k-fold cross-validation to rotate the development and validation roles across k groups. We apply "sequential" validation to build a hierarchy of layered validation groups.

Even with the presence of other powerful techniques such as bootstrapping, there remain business situations where we want to engage in data splitting:

1. We need to outsource the work to a separate unproven group.[15]
2. We think there is an advantage to explaining data splitting, as opposed to bootstrapping, to those with which we are collaborating.
3. We want to validate an analysis that is difficult or computationally intensive in such a way that it is unfriendly to bootstrapping and other techniques.
4. We want to take certain liberties in performing the analysis—for instance, we want to leverage the response to select variables for a model.

Coping with Hazards

In practice, we will do just about anything with the development data, but playing games with the validation data is verboten.[16] The purpose of the validation data is to measure performance; it must not be used to select or estimate anything it will eventually validate. Never, ever, ever break this rule.[17]

There are desperate situations when we cannot create an effective validation dataset, such as when the out-of-time dataset is too small for validation, or when a binomial response has one category with a small frequency. For these difficult situations, we should reconsider other methods. If other methods are not possible, then maybe an underpowered validation (too few observations) might be the best that we can achieve. The next-to-last option is to abandon the dream and settle for an unvalidated model—combining the development and validation data. If, for some reason, an unvalidated model is deemed unworthy,[18] then our final option is to drop it and move gracefully on to the next approach or project.

Another pitfall to avoid is not splitting the data soon enough. For straightforward applications, we will split the data at the onset of our work. There are complex situations when we need to split the data with some restriction on the randomization.

Finally, the greatest hazard with data splitting is that it is often circumvented. Data that is supposed to be reserved for validation is included in the development dataset and then the results are "validated" on the contaminated data. This is an expensive problem.

K-Fold Cross-Validation

This is an approach that produces a distribution or set of results—cross-validation within resampling with replacement. First, we split the dataset into k equal parts. We develop the analysis on $k-1$ of the parts and validate on the remaining part. We repeat this k times,[19] using each of the k parts to validate the result. K-fold validation is cross-validation taken to the k. This approach is excellent for clustered (repeated measures) data.

For the special case where $k = 2$, we have something like a crossover design in DoE. For $k = n$, we have leave-one-out cross-validation, which equals the jackknife.

Sequential Validation (with Three or More Splits)

For large enough datasets, we can layer our validation. This layering allows us to assess the layers of the model as we build them. At the bottom layers, we validate the functional form or derive working components such as splines, time series functions, coefficients, variable transformations, and so on. As we validate model components, we combine lower layers of the validation[20] with development data into larger development datasets.[21] The extra data splits provide proving grounds for intermediate results. Eventually, we perform a final validation of the model's performance on the final layer of the validation data. Figure 8.7 illustrates our approach in taking this idea to the k-th.

For example:

1. Build the response and predictors in Development 1—test them on Validation 1.
2. Build some models with a few functional forms and compare new predictor variables to the response using Development 2—test them on Validation 2.

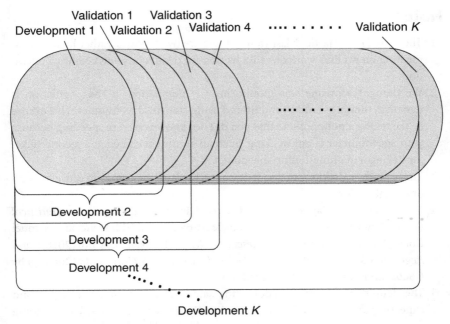

Figure 8.7 Sequential validation plot

3. Build more models in Development 3—pick the best using Validation 3.
4. Rebuild the winning two models using Development 4—perform final validation on Validation 4.
5. In case both of these models fail, we can rebuild two more models using Development 5 and perform a final final validation on Validation 5.
6. Finally, we re-estimate the two models based upon the combined Development 5 and Validation 5 datasets—the complete dataset.
7. As a check on work, we compare the results from the two final models built upon Development 5 to their results when built upon the complete dataset.

In the era of Big Data, we often have the luxury of discarding development datasets after each use. More data has become disposable.

Notes

1. These are HOH Hartley's last words. There are two theories. Either he was commenting on his life's work or, sadly, he was referring to his botched heart operation.

2. We thought someone was monitoring the population. If the population is dynamic, then it should be monitored using statistical techniques. This excuse is like telling a police officer that you did not know you were speeding because your speedometer is not working. Such an argument can elicit a second ticket for having a malfunctioning speedometer.

3. Those on the sidelines can find patterns to "explain" the common cause for a set of a single failure.

4. Many statistical diagnostics are discussed in the *Encyclopedia of Statistical Sciences* by Campbell B. Read, N. Balakrishnan, Brani Vidakovic, and Samuel Kotz (2005); *Encyclopedia of Research Design* by Neil Salkind (2010); and *Regression Models for Categorical Dependent Variables Using Stata* (2nd ed.) by J. Scott Long, and Jeremy Freese (2005).

5. The definition of insanity—doing the same thing over and over again and expecting different results, does not directly apply to statistics. We are doing the same thing; it's just that there are additional components that are not the same.

6. This vetting is akin to performing a simulation on the validation data.

7. It is difficult to publish our business examples because of their proprietary nature. This example is fairly technical, and we would not present this much detail to certain audiences.

8. Sometimes called opaque models.

9. Modeling shops need to be efficient enough that they can build multiple models to cover critical needs.

10. It is important to make the distinction between a composite model that employs multiple models as one tool and a set of models, where one model serves to validate or juxtapose the results of the other.

11. Otherwise, there would be no melodrama.

12. Not only is this simpler for less sophisticated decision makers, it is easier to understand during a crisis.

13. Ah, the white-knuckled control of those stressed because they do not understand how the model works and the dour-faced disapproval when the model works and yet defies status quo expectation. If you possess some of these understandable stresses, then maybe this book will help you let go.

14. *Regression Modeling Strategies with Applications to Linear Models, Logistic Regression, and Survival Analysis* by Frank Harrell.

15. Put your validation data into a safe, drop the safe down a deep hole, and cover the hole with cement mixed with radioactive waste. When the other party delivers the model and you are ready to test it on the validation data, all that remains is the small matter of retrieving the safe.

16. This safeguard is often violated, resulting in one of the assorted anecdotal explanations—the population changed, the model was misunderstood, the data did it, and so on.

17. What if you need to break this rule? First, consider other Statistical Diagnostics such as bootstrapping.

18. Some models are worth more dead than alive.

19. This is like Ring Around the Rosie.

20. No longer pristine.

21. This can be thought of as sequential validation.

9

Statistical Review–Act V

"Inspect what you expect."[1]

—W. Edwards Deming

"You gotta make decisions, you gotta keep making decisions even if they are wrong decisions. ... If you don't make decisions, you're stuffed."

—Joe Simpson[2]

"I think the essence of the scientific method is the willingness to admit you are wrong, the willingness to abandon ideas that don't work."

—Carl Sagan

Statistical Review is a powerful tool for assisting a corporation in progressing to the next level. This book focuses upon using analytics for decision making. We will discuss applying Statistical Review in the context of checking the process involved in making an analytics-based business decision or a set of related decisions. This will include the data, the software (including spreadsheets), the assumptions, the Statistical Qualifications, the Statistical Diagnostics, the results (including dashboards), the analytics-based decision(s), and so on. We need to review the complete business problem including the broader needs: Timeliness, Client Expectation, Accuracy, Reliability, and Cost—Best Statistical Practice.

Under Statistical Review, poor decisions and frail data analyses routinely snap like a plastic fork.[3] Many corporations, such as The Associates/Citigroup mentioned in Section 2.3, have leveraged review to raise the level of analytics and to meet regulatory requirements.

While our focus is on the decision-making process, findings can lead to strategic concerns about the organization, the data, and so forth. All important[4] analytics-based decisions merit review. Most corporations are squeamish about reviewing decisions, yet here is where the money resides. As we mentioned in Section 6.3, Statistical Review is a major force in continual improvement.

Statistical Review can be performed by internal or external resources—an important decision. Corporations that are less passionate about applying analytics will need external assistance with review. The benefits of Statistical Review are both immediate and long-term. In addition to continually raising our analytics aptitude, Statistical Review provides numerous downstream benefits such as:

1. Improves decision making.
2. Ensures the rigor of the results, thereby enhancing reliability.
3. Reveals insight into the problem—even a partial review can reveal insight, which can be leveraged to find better solutions.
4. Provides on-the-job training, hones analytics professionals.
5. Fosters collaboration between reviewers and those reviewed.
6. Protects the findings from political aspirations.
7. Sterilizes one source of political growth.
8. Eradicates expensive and dangerous fairy tales about how to run the company.
9. Discourages negligence, charlatans, and counterfeit analysis.
10. Encourages speedier execution.

Finally, Statistical Review is "think time." This is an opportunity for more than measuring the reliability of the analytics-based decision. We need to think about how we can do everything better—Continual Improvement. This is especially important for our most difficult business problems. We can learn from our mistakes if we can invest in reviewing our work. This investment facilitates improvements in all four Analytics-Based Decision Making Acts.

Élan

It is not enough to be trained to think critically. It is paramount to want to get the analysis right. The right problem-solving mindset is necessary for competent data analysis, yet less tangible to identify. It can be derived through acculturation in a large group of quants during graduate school or while working in industry. It can be lost by placing the professional in a complacent environment. The review process will detect and encourage the appropriate, unassuming test-and-learn mindset.

Qualifications and Roles of Reviewers

It is easy to criticize and difficult to review. At the people level, review is about praising and encouraging.[5] The quality of the review depends on the qualifications (see Chapter 7) and the motivations of the reviewers. Reviewer qualifications need to be comparable to or stronger than those of the reviewed. Review is an advanced leadership role (Chapter 5). It takes tact and care to promote self-esteem.

Professional integrity and the proper incentives are necessary for this role. Review can develop teams and the professionals within them—each person who is reviewed should assume the reviewer role. This is not to be a popularity or intelligence contest. It is not about creating unnecessary hierarchy. Review should be an upbeat, collegial opportunity to encourage professional norms, an opportunity for nurturing technical competence in others. We should find out what went right and suggest what we can do better. Review is a development opportunity and should not be executed like annual performance reviews, which are destroying our corporations. We need to evaluate the analysis, not the person.

Many reviews should be held privately between a manageable number of qualified peers—two are enough. Advanced analytics is proprietary, so small groups are warranted. Some aspects of the data analysis might be out-of-scope from the review. **Quants should not be forced to divulge their secret techniques or coerced into training others.** There are uncommon circumstances when double-blind review is appropriate.[6] We look for a Business Analytics Leader or an Expert Leader to verify the objectivity and veracity of the review process.

Statistical Malpractice

There is a tremendous need for Statistical Review in medicine. In a recent scandal, a number of researchers claimed that a group of gene signatures could predict which patients are likely to benefit from adjuvant chemotherapy for early-stage lung cancer. The findings were published in and later retracted by seven medical journals *(Journal of Clinical Oncology, Nature, The Lancet Oncology,*[7] *The New England Journal of Medicine, Blood, PLOS ONE, and Proceedings of the National Academy of Sciences (PNAS))*. At this writing, an eighth journal, *The Journal of the American Medical Association (JAMA)*, has yet to retract either of its two papers. In addition, three large clinical trials were launched to prospectively apply these findings in the treatment of patients. In the event that the research findings were incorrect, these trials might assign patients the wrong treatments and expose them to greater risk than that of conventional treatments.

It appears that for this research the Statistical Qualifications, Diagnostics, and Review were inadequate to the task. Two very unwelcome independent biostatisticians (Keith Baggerly and Kevin Coombes) could not reproduce the data analysis. Eventually it was confirmed that no one could reproduce the data analysis or even the data. There were data errors, missing data, and serious modeling errors.[8] The clinical trials were suspended and patients have brought suit against the university conducting the trials.

This is an extremely unusual case in that someone tried to reproduce the data analysis; they made their concerns public; and after lengthy public scrutiny, the situation was eventually addressed. The interested reader might study the manner in which this was handled by journal editors and university administrators. The conclusions of this type of research hinge on the data analysis. Such publications merit knowing which of the authors was responsible for the data analysis, who independently reviewed the data analysis, and both sets of credentials for doing so.

Another example is the once perceived linkage between fiber and colon cancer. Starting about 30 years ago, a high fiber intake was regularly recommended as one way to lower the risk for colon cancer. Corporations designed and marketed products that were high in fiber. Consumers diverted their purchases and dining pleasures toward these products. This recommendation was largely based on observations that populations with a high fiber intake tended to have lower rates of colon cancer than those found in populations with a low fiber intake.[9] What just happened? It turns out that the methodology is good enough to supply "best information," but not robust enough to withstand the scrutiny of Statistical Review. Descriptive studies are insufficient for providing definitive information about the complex causes of colon cancer. They cannot address all of the factors that might account for differences in rates of disease. Years later, a number of randomized perspective cohort studies have largely failed to show a link between fiber intake and colon cancer.[10]

In general, supplying best information is a service to healthcare and preferred over no information. In hindsight, the healthcare and economic ramifications due to the supposed benefit of a high fiber intake would have justified a more rigorous study decades earlier. Instead, our search for the causes of colon cancer was delayed by the distraction of observational results involving dietary fiber intake.

Data analysis that is poorly performed or poorly reviewed is statistical malpractice, and in a world of evidence-based medicine, this could be described as medical malpractice, too. Despite their best intentions and all of their problem knowledge, an M.D. with less than ten semesters of statistical content is not qualified to perform or lead complex analyses. A data analysis is not a medical opinion or the vehicle for one. It is about having the appropriate expertise to conduct the analysis, and we should carefully review complex analyses when those qualifications are absent. Furthermore, the status of "independent reviewer" must be elevated.

While alluring and certainly glamorous, these are treacherous waters. Even though there is room for contributions from everywhere, evidence-based medicine requires qualified epidemiologists, biostatisticians, statisticians, and similar professionals—those who are trained to handle the evidence. There needs to be greater collaboration between M.D.s and independent quants with adequate training.[11] With more relevant training, we are more likely to reach a conclusion that will prove to be useful and life saving in years to come.

Section 9.1 Purpose and Scope of the Review

We set the purpose and scope of the review to fit the business needs. One common business need is to review the first three acts to support an analytics-based decision in Act IV. Another reason for review is to meet a regulatory obligation—such as Basel II/III in banking, the U.S. Tele-communication Act of 1996 in telecommunications; and, the U.S. Health Insurance Portability and Accountability Act (HIPAA) of 1996 in health-care; and others. One valuable by-product of review is to continually improve our decision-making process.

Purpose

The usual purposes of a review are to verify the integrity of the decision or analysis and to find alternatives. The essence of review is validating the approach taken for making a smart decision. We will search for ways to improve our decisions, to diagnose an acknowledged problem, or to train staff. Usually, our work comprises a postmortem, yet we should not overlook the opportunity to use review as a tool prior to initiating a project—a premortem. While all data analyses are reproducible up to a point, we do not expect unique answers for some methods, and there are components that we cannot always reproduce, such as experiments, simulations, and sample selections.

To better comprehend the particular application, we need to understand the economic implications of the decision/analysis. This helps us to gauge the wanted thoroughness of the review. For models, it is always helpful to know the nature (such as if it is a primary or a confirming model) and purpose (whether the model must predict outcomes, estimate coefficients, rank order units, or classify items). We need to identify interdependencies between decisions or between analyses. The desired output from an analysis can be an input to an equation or another model.

Scope

The scope is shaped by what makes sense within the confines of our resources (including time), the complexity of the work, and our projected benefits. At the onset of the review, we should sketch an overview of the business problem. We want to include the economic importance and the complexity, which drive the intensity of the review. A clearly defined scope improves the review, because it helps us to focus on specific areas and to think through what needs to be included. In practice, there are business problems where some aspects have already been mastered or are otherwise straightforward. There might not be any benefit in re-reviewing everything each time.

Here is a typical checklist tailored for conducting a particular review:

1. Purpose of Decision/Analysis
2. Thoroughness of Review
3. Statistical Qualifications
4. Underlying Assumptions
5. Analysis Structure
6. Statistical Diagnostics

 7. Alternative Solutions
 8. Timeliness, Client Expectation, Accuracy, Reliability, and Cost—
    BSP (Best Statistical Practice) List
 9. Decision Results
10. Recommendations for Future Enhancements
11. Rejoinder

Here is a different kind of checklist:

1. Business assumptions
2. Statistical assumptions
3. Development data
4. Model calibration
5. Decision
6. Implementation

Another approach might be to map an analytics-based decision-making process into acts:

Act I: Framing the business problem.
Act II: Executing the data analysis.
Act III: Interpreting the results.
Act IV: Making analytics-based decisions.

We can follow this mapping with checking for the usual causes of death as presented in Chapter 3.

Causes of Death

- (A), (D), (F), and (H). The necessary qualifications were absent or underutilized—check all four acts.
- (B). The team did not comprehend all the details and ramifications of the business problem. This can be understandable for some complex problems. The team might have realized from the onset that they did not completely understand the problem or the business problem might have taken a surprising twist.
- (C). The team did not adequately plan the data analysis or develop an adequate profit equation.
- (E). The business analysts and business quants were insufficiently resourced with statistical software, adequate time, and/or access to appropriate or reliable data.
- (G). The team misinterpreted the data analysis.

- (I). The decision makers inadequately or incorrectly incorporated the findings into the decision. This includes not leveraging the findings at all or misinterpreting said findings.

We should consider situations where we have a broader scope. Many reviews are performed within the context of larger project reviews or case studies. All too often, these reviews do not cover the analytics issues: decision making and data analysis.

For strategic reasons, we should include timeliness and the quality of the collaboration within the scope of the project. We often hear, "Why did it take so long?" The review should fine-tune the mix of rigor and speed. To emphasize speed, we need to evaluate how long each component took and how to speed this up while maintaining reasonable rigor. This is where we will note that the data arrived after the analysis was due. As to collaboration, we have to know how well the various analytics professionals and others worked together as a team.

Context

We need to review the decision and the analysis within the business context. Both are sually part of a bigger picture, which we can map. Figure 9.1 repeats our automobile loan customer flow from Figure 6.2. This illustrates

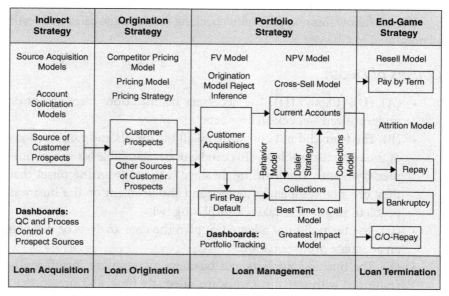

Figure 9.1 Mapping customer flow for auto finance

the flow of customers from external sources through origination, through their payment history, and into the customer end game. We might review decision making and analytics along the course of this process.

Mapping the anticipated analytics needs lays a good foundation for review. In Chapter 6, we demonstrated how to inventory a set of analyses.

$$\text{ᚋ} \quad \text{ᚋ} \quad \text{ᚋ}$$

Section 9.2 Reviewing Analytics-Based Decision Making—Acts I to IV

We begin by framing the business problem and translating a part of it into a statistical one. The larger problem must address all of the tenets of Best Statistical Practice: Timeliness, Client Expectation, Accuracy, Reliability, and Cost. At its most difficult, marrying business and analytics can take the skills of a team containing a business analytics leader. If a thorough review is wanted, then this will require bilingual skills—speaking business and statistics. If we are going to solve this or similar problems in the future, we should use the review to improve our problem knowledge. We should consider investigating how this aspect of the business truly functions. For example, when we launch a new product, we want to understand how various marketing channels will work together to position the product and to cover potential customers. We would like to design an experiment that tests different combinations of promotional spend or, better yet, design a low-maintenance ongoing experiment that incorporates each new product launch.

We want to verify that the data, data analysis, business strategy, and profit equation match the business problem.

Reviewing Qualifications of Analytics Professionals— Checking the Q in QDR

We review qualifications for two reasons.[12] First, the qualifications of the analytics professionals are a part of the credibility of the decision/analysis. Decisions and analyses performed by trained professionals are more reliable[13] and will better weather unanticipated demands. Second, knowing the qualifications of the analytics professionals helps to understand their style and provides the appropriate direction toward the right areas to review. We want to know if the analytics professionals possess mastery of the problem knowledge, the data, the Statistical Diagnostics, and so on. After enough reviews, patterns will start to emerge.

Restrictions Imposed on the Analysis

The solutions for many business problems are subject to restrictions. The typical restrictions arise from regulatory, accounting, legal, management, resources, proprietary information, and so on. For example, anti-discrimination laws restrict the use of data that could be used unethically. Also, privacy regulations protect individuals from having their personal medical information publicized (e.g., HIPPA in the United States). An example of an accounting restriction occurs when corporations cannot recognize a "loss" until certain accounting rules are satisfied. Finally, there are resource restrictions such as time, software, data, and the training possessed by those performing or interpreting the analyses. We must accommodate all manner of restrictions in performing and leveraging the data analysis.

Appropriate and Reliable Data

Another paramount concern regards whether the data or data collection can address the business problem. Some data are complex and yet so important that they merit review. The input data should be evaluated for:

1. Appropriateness for the application;
2. Integrity of the numbers and the reliability of the quality checking methodology;
3. Availability of the data on a timely basis; and
4. Support from the data dictionary and data encyclopedia (see Section 12.2).

Many business mishaps can be traced back to the data. Regarding data integrity, we should verify that the appropriate care went into scrutinizing and repairing the data. We must avoid "discretizing" the data—this unnecessary activity of rounding to discrete values may harmonize with our neatness, yet it definitely plays havoc with our downstream analyses. As for data availability, there are many examples of when the data has arrived so late that the analysis was already overdue. A last concern is with regard to misinterpreting the data. We can reduce this risk by employing a strong data dictionary. We will discuss data management in Chapter 12.

Analytics Software

We should assess the reliability, accuracy, and efficiency of the software platform for this business problem. This is especially important for complex/simulation models where we recommend taking the time to obtain a holistic view by mapping out the software modules.

Analytics software is designed and vetted for quantitative applications. It is less likely to generate or contribute toward the deficiencies mentioned above. For business problems that evolve in sophistication, we need to consider future needs. We will discuss software for data applications in Chapter 11.

Reasonableness of Data Analysis Methodology

We want to assess the appropriateness of the methodology for addressing this business problem. Our objective is to assess whether this approach will obtain the desired rigor. We look to Acts I and IV for guidance on how much rigor is desired. For complex analyses, we recommend an overall and component-by-component evaluation of the methodology. This is especially important for mechanistic and simulation models. We must evaluate the methodology within the context of the business problem.

For models and most analyses, we consider the reasonableness of five aspects of the methodology:

1. Functional Form/Weighting Structure;
2. Underlying Assumptions;
3. Approach Relative to Alternative Solutions;
4. Parameter Estimation; and
5. Interval Estimation.

1. *Functional form/weighting structure:* For many problems, changing the model changes the answer. We look for functional forms in a tabular representation as well as routine parametric forms, special-built curves, and weighting structures. We recommend paying special attention to the use of curves.[14] We check anchors and inflection points upon which a curve is based.

Weighting provides another method for structuring the data. In this case, observations are not treated equally for estimation purposes. For example, suppose we want to evaluate the reasonableness of weighting for loan-default curves. Newer loan originations are generally considered

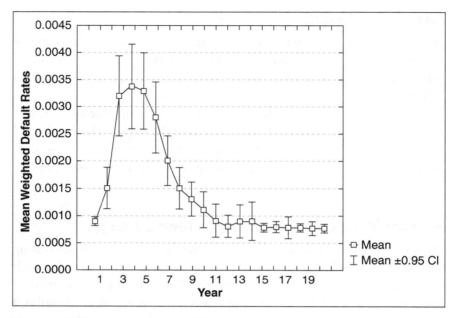

Figure 9.2 Means for mortgage default rates

more indicative of near-term future performance in modeling single-family-home defaults. Older loan originations are necessary to fill out performance information for the years farthest away from origination, thus capturing more macroeconomic breadth. Hence, a weighting structure is a convenient way to place more emphasis on newer loans for modeling more recent loan behavior.

Figure 9.2 illustrates a default curve based upon equally weighted available default-rate information. Each year's default rate is based upon the data available. So default rates in Year 1 might be based upon a weighted average of 30 years of data, with no emphasis on the most recent years, whereas default rates in Year 21 might be based upon a weighted average of 10 years of data.

For all of these approaches, we want to understand the basic structure, identify any variables involved, and enumerate the assumed underlying distributions.

2. *Underlying assumptions:* There are numerous implicit and explicit assumptions underlying each decision and each analysis. Violating assumptions impairs the quality of the decision. Functional forms (the choice of

the model equation) are nests of parametric assumptions[15] and weighting structures bring their own big detailed assumption. Even non-parametric tools have underlying assumptions. We want to leverage our experience in evaluating their plausibility and the impact if the assumptions are false. Sensitivity analysis relies upon a family of tools for investigating how model performance is related to violations of the assumptions and variation in the quality of the inputs.

3. *Approach relative to alternative solutions:* This is our opportunity to think outside the box. We have a tendency to stick with the same analytics solution for similar problems, and sometimes this choice was arbitrary in the first place. We should consider other versions of the analysis and, possibly, completely different solutions. We want to consider the alternative solutions relative to the context provided by the business problem. Reviewing the current approach might provide insight into the potential of certain alternatives.

4. *Parameter estimation:* Populations are described by parameters such as the mean and variance. These two parameters respectively describe a population's location and spread. There are a number of techniques for estimating parameters.

5. *Interval estimation:* This includes confidence intervals, prediction intervals, and tolerance intervals, as discussed in Chapter 8. Interval estimation is underutilized. We should consider whether an interval estimate would be an improvement over a point estimate. We want to verify the application of the proper interval. Note that interval estimates have their own assumptions and not every approach can assume an underlying normal distribution.

Reasonableness of Data Analysis Implementation

Implementation is where the Analytics Practitioners' training rings true.

This topic considers any changes to the data analysis methodology as a consequence of implementing it, usually in software. Our work reviewing the implementation often leads right back to the appropriateness of the methodology. For a thorough review, there are advantages to running through the reasonableness of the methodology followed by the reasonableness of the implementation of the methodology. Reviewing these separately improves our focus on the issues and provides a second pass through them.

There are a number of areas to review, some of which are Statistical Diagnostics. They include:

1. Model fitting diagnostics
2. Parameter estimation
3. Calibrations
4. Weighting calculations and other calculations as implemented
5. Curve estimation
6. Interval estimation
7. Quality assurance procedures
8. Suitability of downstream applications, such as another model or a profit equation

There are several situations when an analysis can stray. We want to review the typical causes of death and look for opportunities to improve this solution and future analyses. We explore the sensitivity of the results to assumptions and techniques as implemented. We check the most likely suspects—missed opportunities for Statistical Diagnostics and statistical techniques; and the occasional calculation errors and lapses in logic.

"80% of cited statistics are merely statistical babble."

Statistical Diagnostics—Checking the D in QDR

Performance is relative. We should review the Statistical Diagnostic techniques applied, and ascertain whether the analysis could use more diagnostics. We measure accuracy and reliability in the context of the application and perhaps within the context of historical performance. We seek assurance that the model or analysis is reliable and that the results are adequate for their purpose. That purpose might be an input to a direct business decision, to a profit equation, to another model, or to some other next step. We discussed Statistical Diagnostics for evaluating performance in Chapter 8.

Interpreting the Results (Transformation Back), Act III

The objective of Act III is to interpret the results back into the business context. This stage in the analytics-based decision making process is critical and varies in difficulty. This is a common failure point. Sometimes we need Quadrant IV[16] competence in order to properly interpret the results.

Needless misinterpretations are often due to a lack of analytics involvement, or domain knowledge. We recommend a generous involvement of

Analytics Practitioners in translating the findings back to the business problem. Also, we want to review the Statistical Diagnostics and judge the reliability of the results. This protects the corporation and provides the business quants with invaluable insight. We want to test everything that is testable. Finally, this is a good time to reflect on how long it took for the various aspects of the analytics-based decision-making process.

Reviewing Analytics-Based Decision Making, Act IV

Success hinges on the analytics-based decision maker's ability to identify needed information and to differentiate between reliable and unreliable analyses. Our review of Act IV serves the dual purposes of evaluating the current decision and preparing for future decisions. Many corporations do an astounding job in the first three acts, yet they chronically make mistakes in Act IV. For these corporations, we need to emphasize continuity in skills and personnel.

It is insufficient to "judge" decisions on results only. Often, results are at most partially determined by the decision. To make an informative assessment, we should incorporate the context of the decision. To develop the skills of decision makers, we have to check:

1. Collaboration with the business quants
2. Ability to identify business analysts and business quants
3. Understanding of problem knowledge
4. Mastery of interpreting analytics results and Statistical Diagnostics
5. The presence of decision impairments described in Section 3.3.

We want decision makers to have functional relationships with business quants. We need to understand how the analyses are leveraged in making the decision, and how we can foster this synergy between the two skill sets. This synergy will improve future decision making.

Closing Considerations—Documentation, Maintenance, Recommendations, and Rejoinder

We want to review four closing considerations:

1. *Documentation:* We need to check the accuracy, completeness, and clarity of the documentation.
2. *Maintenance plan:* We want to assess the reliability of any maintenance plan needed to maintain software, data, models, and so on.

This is partly a software issue and partly a custodial or governance issue. We should review software that performs some of the maintenance, for instance, automatic quality control charts. Also, we must judge the degree to which results are sensitive to future inputs

3. *Recommendations for future enhancements:* Recommendations for future enhancements can be invaluable for advancing the corporation's capabilities. Many recommendations arise from the review process. This can provide immediate and long-term economic benefits.

4. *Rejoinder:* A rejoinder is a proper response from those reviewed, addressing the content of the review. A rejoinder clarifies complex details and keeps the review fair and relevant, thus preventing any unreasonable burden on the claimant. Reviews should be mutually respectful and interactive.

ⓜ   ⓜ   ⓜ

Notes

1. This common saying has evolved from his original statement, "You can expect what you inspect."
2. Mountaineer from the film *Touching the Void.*
3. The old brittle kind of plastic.
4. If a decision is not important, then we should question supporting it with analytics. Analysis for political purposes does not merit review.
5. A demonstration of this approach can be found in Toastmasters.
6. Mistakes in poorly reviewed journals provide public lessons for the benefits of Statistical Review. Increasingly, publications require reproducibility and access to the data.
7. This paper was typical in that it had 19 authors, 12 of which were M.D.s.
8. Not the kind we have come to accept!
9. *Epidemiology of Cancer of the Colon and Rectum* by D. Burkitt. *Cancer* 28: 3–13 (1971).
10. *Dietary Fiber Intake and Risk of Colorectal Cancer: A Pooled Analysis of Prospective Cohort Studies* by Yikyung Park, et.al., *The Journal of the American Medical Association (JAMA)* 2005; 294 (22): 2849–2857.
11. We regularly see medical publications where the so-called quant has inadequate training.

12. We are not looking for wrong answers.
13. In addition to the presumed benefits of speedier turnaround.
14. Otherwise you might be thrown one.
15. Assumptions are called "parametric" when they are implied by assuming a functional form.
16. See Figures 3.1, 3.2, 4.1, 6.4, and 6.5.

Part III

Building Blocks for Supporting Analytics

Infrastructure is fundamental. Analysis, re-analysis, and missed decisions are expensive. Infrastructure is the cornerstone for continually improving the support for analytics. We want to build a strong infrastructure that supports quick and economical data analysis and at the same time better meets our continuum of needs.

Part III discusses three building blocks: Data Collection (Chapter 10), Data Software (Chapter 11), and Data Management (Chapter 12) for an infrastructure that can support Best Statistical Practice. These building blocks facilitate higher-quality decisions by supporting the analytics behind them. Most corporations can easily improve all three building blocks. We begin by outlining the different tools for collecting data—from simulation to the Herculean Design of Experiments (DoE) to Design of Samples (DoS) to mere observation (Chapter 10). Next, we discuss the power of software (Chapter 11). Finally, we close by discussing how to manage those invaluable data assets—from the perspective of those analyzing data (Chapter 12).

In the meatball surgery of performing data analysis, we must strike a balance between accuracy and reliability, and the efficiency in completing the analysis. Infrastructure helps us to obtain both. We seek to create an infrastructure that is user-friendly and customizable to the analytics professional.[1] This environment enables faster turnaround. We must master the cutting of corners and designing automation tools with which to bake in as much technical judgment as possible. As we build the infrastructure, we can expand or enhance its capabilities.[2] While our mass-produced data analyses can be elegant on an individual basis, the objectives of a strong infrastructure are (1) to reduce the cost per analysis, (2) to automate some of the technical expertise and most of the tedium, and (3) to perform analyses en mass. Speed is essential because quick turnaround saves more time to construct the infrastructure ... which facilitates quicker turnaround times.

兀   兀   兀

10

Data Collection

"When you can measure what you are speaking about, and express it in numbers, you know something about it; but when you cannot measure it, when you cannot express it in numbers, your knowledge is of a meager and unsatisfactory kind. It may be the beginning of knowledge, but you have scarcely, in your thoughts, advanced to the stage of science."

—William Thompson Kelvin

Data is money. Our objective is to invest in data to support smarter business decisions. This chapter will help corporations avoid the usual foibles of data collection, which are, for the most part, forms of inaction:

1. Failing to involve the proper Statistical Qualifications
2. Overusing anecdotal sampling
3. Not leveraging interval estimation
4. Maintaining a rigid "census-taking mentality"
5. Failing to obtain a representative sample
6. Not learning about measurement error
7. Withholding data acquisition for unreasonable proof that it will add value
8. Denying the nonresponse problem
9. Not taking advantage of more advanced designs that will lower costs and add capabilities
10. Failing to statistically validate results from observational data

The economic benefits and the avoidance of pitfalls justify delegating data collection to quant specialists, who are typically expert leaders possessing more specialized training in DoS or DoE. They can deduce the most efficient designs, run smarter simulations, and find the minimum sample sizes, which are just as likely to be smaller than expected.

We collect data to estimate population values such as the mean, total, variance, and so on. We estimate locations like the mean using either point estimates or preferably interval estimates.

> **Concept Box**
>
> *Population*—An entire collection of elements about which we want to make inferences.
>
> *Element*—The smallest unit of interest, e.g., customers, transactions, patients, et al. in a population. These are the units that we want to measure and make inferences regarding.
>
> *Data*—We define data as rows of observations that describe elements in a population and columns of variables (measurements of characteristics of each observation).

For the purposes of a successful project, we must define the population of interest. This will avoid holes that can weaken our solutions.

Passively collected data are often called observational data. We will compare this against five approaches for actively collecting data: Census Taking, Anecdotal Sampling, DoS—Design of Samples (Statistical Sampling), DoE—Design of Experiments (Experimentation), and Simulation. We will describe the resulting six types of data and later juxtapose some of them.

1. *Observational:* Running a business passively generates data that may or may not be complete and often have rough edges. Many statistical techniques are built for analyzing observational data; most are referred to as data mining tools. In exploring the degree to which the data are representative, we need to understand how the data are generated. This will provide a feel for the accuracy and reliability of the data. Statistical Diagnostics are particularly important for observational data.

2. *Census taking:* A census consists of measurements on every element in a population. In practice, censual data are often collected passively by conducting business, yet there are many instances where we need to collect censual data deliberately. When censual data is measured accurately, we can use mathematical tools without making statistical

assumptions. Otherwise, the censual data is said to be measured with error. Statistical tools are built to analyze data measured with error. We can still use mathematical tools, but we will be making explicit or implicit statistical assumptions. For example, we might implicitly assume that the measurement error will not change the answer, or we might explicitly assume that we can get a reasonable answer by making some kind of adjustment.

3. *Anecdotal sampling or nonrepresentative sampling:* These data are usually valuable because they generate insight into "the possible," and they are usually conveniently collected. Despite claims to the contrary, the results are not intended to be "directional" or representative of the parent population. There is no design and no randomization (see Randomization).

4. *DoS (Design of Samples)[3] or statistical sampling:* The objective of drawing a statistical sample is to collect a representative set of observations that will support estimation. We employ a design so that every element in the population has a chance of selection.[4] The design randomly selects elements from the population. The elements might be selected in a simple or complex fashion. A sample can trade completeness for accuracy in measurement. The secret to sampling is to know how to make the most of randomization. Sampling makes sense when we obtain more information relative to the cost.

5. *DoE (Design of Experiments)[5] or experimentation:* A controlled estimation of the relationship between a response (dependent) variable and other explanatory (independent) variables—called factors. The response measures performance and for every DoE, at least one of the explanatory variables can be controlled. We control an explanatory variable by "assigning" different treatments to elements in the population. This is dictated by a design. DoE is the most aggressive approach toward estimation, and it is the only way to solve the chicken-and-egg causal problems.[6] Again, the secret is to know how to make the most of randomization.

6. *Simulation:* Simulation leverages a model to generate outcomes data. The model simulates a business situation we are trying to understand. This is a well understood and under-applied approach. It can be extremely challenging to build a relevant model. Also, we can regard DoE as a simulation tool. This is all the more impor-

tant because some decision makers cannot abide by conducting an experiment. Whereas, conducting a simulation might be acceptable. When employing simulation, again, randomization plays an important role.

Now we juxtapose pairs of these data types to clarify the most common misunderstandings.

Anecdotal Sampling Versus DoS: The difference is that an anecdotal sample provides insight into the possible; a statistical sample is representative and provides insight into the probable. Each element in a DoS has a probability (not necessarily an equal probability) of selection, and we can leverage this information to infer the shape of the overall population.

In some situations, distinguishing between an anecdotal sample and a representative one may require training. This is the same training required to understand the consequences. The most routine mistake is to depend on an anecdotal sample to be representative.

DoS Versus Census: A census is not always preferable. There are a number of reasons for opting for a sample over a census:

1. *Greater simplicity:* For many situations it is difficult or impossible to conduct a census. Even government population censuses, upon which businesses make trillion-dollar decisions, are not usually complete censuses. Censuses usually have a nonresponse problem that makes them incomplete. This is solved by augmenting the partial census with a sample to represent nonresponders.
2. *Lower cost:* A sample usually costs less; sometimes substantially less. Businesses waste incredible sums taking unnecessary censuses. A medium-sized corporation missed its opportunity to be the leader in measuring marketing impact based upon internet click-stream data. They canceled their lucrative contracts because they did not know how to take complex representative samples.[7]
3. *Greater accuracy:* The smaller size of a sample can facilitate more accurate measurement of the elements in the population, and it provides a better opportunity to address expected or unexpected difficulties.
4. *Faster results:* In some situations, fewer units take significantly less time to measure.
5. *Greater repertoire:* For those situations where a census is impractical, the choice is between obtaining the information through

sampling or not at all. If there is a nonresponse problem, it might be easier to handle for a sample than for a census.

DoE = DoS + Manipulation of causal effects

DoS Versus DoE: Both apply randomization to collect representative data, which can be leveraged for estimation. At the aggressive end of both techniques, they require involvement and then delegation to an expert leader or a quant specialist (sub-subject matter expert) with that particular training. At the advanced level, executing DoS or DoE requires specialized training within the specialized training of statistics.

The difference between these two data collection techniques is that DoE facilitates influencing the information collected. Sampling techniques measure a representative subset of observations in order to estimate characteristics of the whole population. Experimentation measures a set of observations under what-if scenarios created by manipulating some explanatory variables—called factors. By observing the corresponding effects due to these manipulations, we can infer cause-and-effect relationships.

DoS randomly selects sampling units (SUs) to measure a multidimensional landscape as it naturally appears. DoE is a Rubik's cube twist beyond observation alone. That twist is viewing possible landscapes created by intervention; we assign treatments to experimental units (EUs). Here each treatment level has a potentially different effect on the response and each articulates one possible landscape. DoS is like DoE with only a control group.

While the terminology[8] differs, there are several parallels between DoS and DoE:

Table 10.1 Mirror of the Data Collection Tools

DoS	DoE
Objective: Measure population	Objective: Measure effects
SUs (sampling units)	EUs (experimental units)
Control Only	TRTs (treatments, includes a control group)
Randomly select SUs to observe	Randomly assign treatments to EUs and observe response
Strata (homogeneous groups)	Blocks (homogeneous groups)
Panels (a set of reusable SUs)	Platforms (a set of somewhat reusable EUs)
Stratify for known distinct subpopulations and adequately represent each	Block for known factors in order to neutralize their effect on the TRTs

Observational Versus DoE: Observational data lack a design to control what we observe. Experimental data are collected in a manner that ensures repeatable results up to some point. In business, models tend to be built on observational data. The modeling process must sort through patterns in the data to find those that are likely to repeat in the future. The whole point of designing experiments is to control for what we randomly observe—the design forces some degree of self-validation. Both observational data and results from DoE rely upon separate Statistical Diagnostics to measure performance. For observational data, there is a greater degree of creativity involved. For DoE, these techniques are almost built in. For many applications, the advantages of DoE require training to discern.

Randomization

Randomization protects us from subjective biases. Randomization self-validates the data. However, it can be thwarted by missing observations.

For DoS, randomization consists of randomly selecting observations from a population. This facilitates better estimation by allowing all elements in a population to have some probability of being selected into the sample. For DoE, randomization consists of randomly assigning treatments to the elements in a population. For simulation, randomization incorporates the out-of-control "what ifs." Randomization balances out unknown underlying factors.[9] Randomization makes it possible for a sample to represent a population and for an experiment on factor manipulations to infer causal relationships.

For DoE, subjective bias is thwarted by randomly assigning treatments to experimental units. For DoS this is accomplished by assigning probabilities to the elements in the population and mechanically selecting the sample. In anecdotal sampling, there is no protection, no randomization.

Randomization is the key ingredient that defines representative means of extracting information.

Interval Estimation = Point Estimation + Parametric Assumption(s) + Variance Estimation(s)

Interval and Point Estimation

One objective of collecting information is to estimate parameters (population characteristics, such as the mean). On a regular basis, corporations make two mistakes in estimation. First, they overvalue estimates based on anecdotal data, and second, they use a point estimate when an interval estimate is wanted. The root causes for these mistakes are an unwillingness to delegate and a lack of training.

An interval estimate answers more questions than a point estimate. To illustrate, consider one commonly understood prediction: an election for public office. Suppose that the commentator on TV claims that the incumbent will receive 51% of the vote. The trained statisticians say that the incumbent is ahead of the challenger 51% to 48% with a bound of $\pm 3\%$. These are remarkably different answers. After about the second retelling, the former answer becomes "the incumbent has won." While the latter answer will become "the incumbent is leading, yet the result is uncertain."

There are numerous trade-offs between a lone point estimate and one with an interval estimate wrapped around it:

1. There is some expectation that an estimate should be "close" to the true value, which we might later observe. In the fullness of time, we may lose credibility when point estimates repeatedly "fail" to be close enough. There is the risk in misunderstanding that the most likely value, which might be represented by a point estimate, is not necessarily likely.
2. There is greater finality with an interval estimate. A point estimate might appease some business need without solving it. We often return for another point estimate because the first one failed to keep the problem solved.
3. Multiple decisions: Suppose we want to choose between competing choices or to track choices over time. Interval estimates allow fuller comparisons.
4. The width of the interval is excellent for comparing estimates and visualizing the information.
5. For advanced business problems, we will combine estimators into equations or base them conditionally upon one another. For those applications, confidence intervals are extremely helpful for simplifying the results—just not the calculations.

There is something extreme about the need to always know the exact answer. This can be taken to the pathological point of self-deception. Interval estimation accepts and quantifies the incompleteness of our information.

Return on Data Investment

Acquiring new data is a traditional stumbling block for corporations. There is some difficulty in forecasting the future value of the data. While resistance has lessened over the years, there is still some reluctance to delegate to or at least involve the quant specialists, who usually want more data. Their background in data analysis will offer certain advantages:

1. They are in a better position to estimate the potential of the data.
2. They will set a reasonable burden on "proving" that the data will be a good investment.
3. They can better ascertain the requisite time horizon in collecting the data and delivering a return.
4. Should the data collection involve statistical sampling or experimentation, then they know how to leverage training in DoS and DoE to lower costs.
5. They will place less emphasis on the charm of the old ways.

Even with expertise, the data acquisition question can be an informed guess. If the cost is reasonable, sometimes the right answer is to acquire the data and play with it. People work hard and they will find unanticipated ways to leverage new data—the serendipity of statistics. If the cost is unreasonable, then statistical technique might be able to lower the cost for a sample large enough to make comparisons.

Measuring Information

Data are measurements on observations. As such they are the product of measurement devices, such as a yardstick or a thermometer. The accuracy of the measurements is relative to the measurement device and the data storage.[10] Hence, continuous data are already rounded to the maximum precision that the measuring device and data storage can support. This is not a problem as long as we can meet our accuracy needs.

There are several types of measurement devices including: questionnaires,[11] direct observation, yardsticks, thermometers, machines monitoring an assembly line, and so on. Sometimes people are a functional part of the measurement devices, and other times data entry software plays this role. Every functional part of measurement merits scrutiny. There was a large litigation between two major corporations that went badly for the plaintiff because the data entry software restricted the precision of the information. Hence, the plaintiff's data could not connect the defendant's product to particular failures. In understanding the measurement device, we must reflect upon the business context. In practice, we are aggressive about pursuing the business contextual information. Missing values can represent a failure to measure, and other times they really are the measurements. For example, if amount of loan loss is missing, it could be because the loss amount was not entered into the computer or because the loan never defaulted. In the latter case, the value can be thought of as either zero or as "does not apply," whichever is more appropriate for pursuing the business objective.

Measurement Errer[12]

Another source of poor decisions is from numbers measured with error, which have not been adjusted for the measurement error. Measurement error is created by the imprecision of the measurement device and/or the storage device. This problem is routine in occurrence and sometimes only noticeable by the trained professionals looking for the problem. **Measurement error cannot be fixed by increasing the sample size.**

Consider the following yardstick example. Suppose that we need to infer which of two "identical" buildings is the taller. An extremely accurate, laser-sighted device for measuring the heights of buildings is not available. Instead, we are handed a yardstick and led to a window-washer basket.

If the buildings are very tall and extremely close in height, then the yardstick probably lacks the necessary precision to get the answer right on a single attempt. Each tumble of the yardstick could be off by the width of a pencil line. This is a simplistic example of the measurement error problem, which illustrates how decisions are exposed.

The best way to thwart the measurement error problem is to recognize it before the data is wrongly collected. The best way to recognize this problem is to have an expert looking for it. Once the problem is recognized, we can fix the measurement and/or storage devices—if it is not too late. Otherwise, there are options for adjusting the estimation, yet there are few options for repairing the data.

The coming sections are more detailed discussions of four basic data collection paradigms.

Section 10.1 Observational and Censual Data (No Design)

Most data is observational and censual in nature. This data will always play important roles in business analytics. Often this data just appears as a consequence of regular business operations. This data might be less expensive on the front end because less planning is required, no design, no quant specialist.

Now we will discuss when to be wary of observational and censual data. We need to look for costs on the back end due to measurement error, to the data not being representative of the population, to using the wrong data just because it is there, and to collecting too much data when it is expensive. If the data are atypical of the population or collected with measurement error, then every subsequent analysis has this problem.

Using data that is not representative of the population of interest can lend credibility to an anomaly, which is actually a mere coincidence. All of these "fooled by coincidence" problems should be addressed with Statistical Diagnostics or a better design for collecting the data. These can help us to avoid or correct biased estimates.

We should not avoid planned data collection when it is appropriate. Observational and censual data has become a crutch in some settings, keeping us from designing better ways to collect the data. Even with these concerns, observational and censual data are rich sources of often inexpensive information.

Section 10.2 Methodology for Anecdotal Sampling

Anecdotal samples are actively collected without the benefit of a statistical design. There is no randomization; some elements in the population have a zero probability of selection into an anecdotal sample. The results are not intended to be "directional" or representative of the parent population. They provide insight into the possible rather than the probable. While this method is often misused, there are many valid situations that merit collecting anecdotal data, and there are techniques for obtaining the best anecdote.

To obtain the best anecdotal sample, there are two common selection paradigms: expert choice and quota samples. Expert choice leverages judgment to try to find a desired distribution and quota sampling seeks a distribution that matches certain quotas. Both can be used for selecting focus groups. Such "samples" are not representative of the overall population because they do not provide every element in the population with an appropriate probability of being selected into the anecdotal sample.

Expert Choice

This method relies upon an expert to select what is important. It is excellent for finding interesting elements. Sometimes when experts try to pick an anecdotal sample to represent the whole population, they recognize and avoid selection patterns that appear "nonrandom." Instead, they select "representative" subsets based on a pattern-less veneer. Randomization is blind to patterns. An expert might select a sample that has a "random" pattern such as the one in Figure 10.1.

Behold, Figure 10.2 exhibits a possible random sample of six observations, which is unlikely to be selected by an expert because it does not "look" random.

With regard to representing the shape of the parent population, expert choice is an attempt to randomly select without randomization. It is more

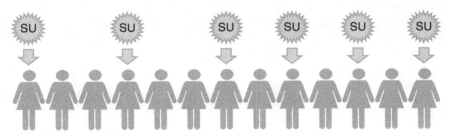

Figure 10.1 Sampling paper dolls—evenly dispersed

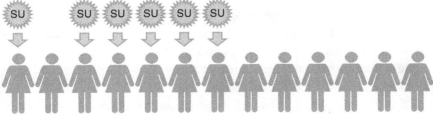

Figure 10.2 Sampling paper dolls—not so evenly dispersed

appropriate for representing a population, when a random sample is not possible.

Quota Samples

Quota sampling consists of assigning quotas to subgroups of elements in the population. Elements are nonrandomly selected into each group until the quotas are filled.[13] Quota samples are not representative, and this leads to mayhem when we want to make estimates. Consider the case of "Dewey Defeats Truman" explained below.

Dewey Defeats Truman

In 1948, the Crossley, Gallup, and Roper pre-election polls for the office of U.S. president were all based on quota sampling. They selected quotas of potential voters from demographic segments. For example, they might have selected a quota of 55 potential voters from the segment, say, Hispanic middle-income females between 30 and 40 years old, and asked them for whom they will vote. This approach is usually better than expert choice for predicting elections. In 1948, all three quota samples "fit" the six-variable (et al.) shape of the population very well, but unknown to the pollsters, one political party was over-represented in the quota samples. That same year the Washington State Public Opinion Laboratory conducted two of their own polls prior to the election: a probability sample and a quota sample. Out of the five estimates (Washington State probability sample, and Washington State, Crossley, Gallup, and Roper quota samples), only the probability sample predicted the correct outcome. Without this definitive result, pollsters might still employ quota sampling today.

Focus Groups[14]

Focus groups are selected using expert choice or quota sampling. They consist of a group of people who are asked their perceptions of a product or service in a group forum. That is, they can influence each other's responses. It is part of their charm to get people to discuss the issues.

Focus groups can generate great insights into the consumers' thinking. They are notable for screening and/or refining new product concepts. While extremely helpful,[15] results from focus groups are not intended to be representative of the entire population.

If we randomly select people for a group and do not let them influence each other's responses, then we have a panel. Panels generate representative results. We reserve the term panel for statistical sampling, and we will discuss panels later.[16]

Corporations make the mistake of treating anecdotal samples as the "accuracy peers" of statistical samples. When leveraged to make population estimates, anecdotal samples require a large additional assumption. While anecdotal samples can provide insight into the possible, they are not designed for point or interval estimation. Estimates merit representative samples. This fact is generally misunderstood, and this is the scene of many tragic mishaps. Local custom is one common wrong reason for using anecdotal sampling. Another is that anecdotal sampling is often what we do when we do not know how to take a statistical sample.

⚑ ⚑ ⚑

Section 10.3 DoS (Design of Samples)

"However, the advantages of statistical sampling do not outweigh the primary disadvantages, which include the need for additional training in statistics and the use of formal techniques to determine sample size, to select the sample and to evaluate the results. Therefore, a properly executed application of non-statistical audit sampling will generally be the preferable approach."[17]

—From an audit guidance manual

There exists a great deal of ignorance about how easy and how important it is to design the sample. In many situations, there is a misperceived impediment to applying statistical sampling. A quant specialist has the training to design samples around many restrictions in a manner that accommodates the way in which the data is collected.

There exists a great deal of ignorance about how easy and how important it is to apply statistical sampling. A quant specialist has the training to design samples around many restrictions in the manner in which the data is collected.

> **Concept Box**
>
> *Sampling unit (SU)*—A sampling unit comprises one or more elements from a population; SUs are the items of selection into a sample. For advanced designs, SUs can be inside larger SUs. Hence, we can sample from within an SU. Typical Sampling Units include households, business units, customers, payments, charges, et al.

Representative samples generate representative interval estimates—our preferred objective. We want to design samples that provide accurate, striving for unbiased, inferences about a population. The basic idea is to randomly select sampling units (SUs) in ways that are effective, efficient, and yet representative.

> **Concept Box**
>
> *Sampling frame*—A unique indexing of SUs, no dupes and no omissions, please. Usually, this indexing consists of a formal list of the SUs. A sampling frame might be a mailing list, a list of registered users, a list of households on a continent, and so on.

For difficult business problems, one underutilized approach is to lead a DoS with a pilot test. The pilot test collects the information needed for building an effective sample design.

Quant Specialist's Role

After delegation, the first phase for the quant specialist is to tackle six inter-related questions:

1. What is the business need?
2. What is the population?
3. What do we want to estimate? Typically, we want an interval estimate for a mean, total, or proportion of some population.
4. What is it worth?
5. How are we going to measure the sampling units?
6. Can we build a sampling frame for this population?

Usually this first phase of questions is either straightforward or already completed. If not, then there is the need for a kickoff meeting and some investigative work. However, the quant specialist should avoid the mistake of taking anything for granted.

For the quant specialist, we propose the following considerations for the process of taking a sample:

1. Kickoff meeting:
   Statement of objectives
   Population definition
   Measurement device
2. Sampling frame
3. Sample design
4. Training for those involved

5. Pilot test
6. Data collection
7. Data management
8. Data analysis
9. Presentation—business and/or technical
10. Analytics-based business decision

Sample Design

The purpose of a sample design is usually to estimate an interval around some population value. Within our cost and capabilities restrictions, accuracy (bias) and precision (variance) of the interval estimate are the driving reasons for choosing the design. More often than not, estimating the variance is the primary driver of the sample-design decisions.

The two basic sample designs are SRS (simple random sampling) and Sys (systematic sampling). More advanced techniques tend to be built on top of these two underlying basics. The key difference is that SRS leverages a formal sampling frame comprising a list of SUs and Sys leverages an implied sampling frame based upon the relative positions of the SUs.

Simple Random Sampling

The most basic, most popular, and most wildly overused sample design is simple random sampling alone. Each element in a population of size, N, has an equal probability of selection (n/N),[18] where "n" is the sample size. This approach requires a sampling frame in the form of a list of sampling units. Each SU comprises one or more elements from the population.

One approach is to:

1. Obtain or construct a sampling frame.
2. Calculate the sample size needed for the desired accuracy.[19]
3. Obtain the sample by randomly selecting n SUs from the sampling frame (without replacement).
4. Adjust for any difficulties, such as nonresponse—discussed later.
5. Estimate the confidence interval.
6. Leverage the information to take action, such as an analytics-based business decision.
7. Redesign the sample for the next business objective.

SRS always produces more representative information than anecdotal sampling. The shortcoming with SRS, relative to more advanced designs, is that it makes no attempt to reduce cost or otherwise seize an advantage.

Recall that there exists a little confusion regarding the appearance of simple random samples. Random samples do not necessarily look random. There is no requirement that the SUs be uniformly distributed in some "representative" shape.

Systematic Sampling

A systematic sample, on the other hand, consists of a set of regularly spaced sampling units. The usual approach is to randomly select one element from the first k elements and every k-th element thereafter. Systematic sampling is popular for QC (quality control) problems; it is oft employed for assembly lines because the elements cannot be listed in the type of sampling frame SRS requires. For QC, the data arrives in sequence and the sampling frame is a function of this arrival. **Systematic Sampling is a solution for certain Big Data problems, allowing us to sample the data as it arrives.**

Advanced Sample Designs

More advanced designs can go far beyond SRS and Sys in extracting information. We can select SUs at different rates from different subpopulations (stratification); select heterogeneous groups of SUs (clustering); select SUs with probabilities relative to some characteristics (probabilities proportional to size); select SUs within SUs within SUs, and so on hierarchically (multi-stage designs); et al.

Advanced sample designs can be more efficient in collecting data. Greater efficiency means lower cost for the same information, **and suddenly some additional business problems can now be solved affordably.** The basic theme of sampling is that every observation needs to have a probability of selection to be represented by the sample. Hence, the nonresponse problem is a genuine impediment in accurately representing the population.

The Nonresponse Problem

Nonresponse is the sampling term denoting missing data. The nonresponse problem is one major impediment for a sample to be representative of the

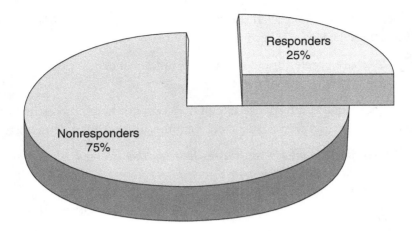

Figure 10.3 Pie chart for population

population. This problem is particularly expensive in the business world because it is overlooked and this results in questionable findings. It cannot be solved by increasing the sample size.

To clarify the matter, suppose we are interested in a population, where 25% of the elements will respond (1's) and 75% of the elements will respond (0's), as in Figure 10.3.

Now if we draw a sample, all of the observations will come from the smaller quarter of the population. Our sample represents only those customers who will respond. Suppose that we ask the sample of customers whether they prefer Brand A over other brands. The best case is that responders will have the same preferences on average as the 'unsampled' 75% of the population (the nonresponders). The worst case is that responders will have vastly different preferences from these nonreponders.

Suppose that of the responders 80% of them prefer Brand A. If we assume that responder preferences are identical to those of nonresponders, then a 95% CI (confidence interval) might look like:

80% ± 8% or {72%, 88%} prefer Brand A based upon a 25% response rate.

Alternatively, a "more" unassuming 95% CI is that:

{18%, 22%}[20] prefer Brand A with 75% unknown or that

{18%, 97%} prefer Brand A. The last interval incorporates the fact that we do not know the preferences of the nonresponders. All or none of them might prefer Brand A.

For the same 80% preference, had the nonresponse been 90% instead of 75%, then the 95% CIs become:

{7.2%, 8.8%} prefer Brand A with 90% unknown or
{7.2%, 98.8%} prefer Brand A.

In the example, a response rate of 10% was not helpful in estimating brand preference. However, statistical solutions do have their detractors:

"When participants in my classes first see this example, they are astounded at the low response rate. However, I tell them that a 10 percent response rate is quite good."

—Other author

We too are astounded. While a 10% response might signify the most information we can collect, the overarching objective is to support an informed decision. We might be producing misinformation. This quote typifies a common break from statistical technique. It is a call for DoS decisions to be overseen by a quant specialist. If we do not believe that the 10% responding are similar to the 90% not responding, then the quant specialist should pursue a combination of the following six remedies for thwarting nonresponse:

1. Prior to taking the sample, we stratify the sample based on likelihood to respond—if we know it.
2. Prior to taking the sample, we reserve some budget for the remedies below.
3. Prior to taking the sample, we make certain that we oversample in anticipation of nonresponse. This protects us from having too small of a sample size. Oversampling helps follow-up techniques like post-stratification or weighting-class adjustments. Also, it is useful if we are stuck assuming that the nonreponse is random or that the bias is negligible.
4. After sampling, post-stratify on the nonresponse and conduct a second round of sampling on the nonresponders.
5. After sampling, explore the relationships between responders and nonresponders.
6. After sampling, apply a weighting class adjustment—if applicable.

Post-Stratifying on Nonresponse

Post-stratifying on nonresponse is one of the few remedies for the nonresponse problem. After post-stratifying, we select a second sample from the nonresponders and follow-up more aggressively. This can cost much more per sampling unit so we plan for a smaller second sample.

There is an implicit assumption that the nonresponders are different from the responders. That is, that the nonresponse did not occur at random.

In the customer preference example above, suppose that a more aggressive follow-up on the nonresponders will obtain a reasonable second sample from the 75% not responding the first time. We observe that their Brand A preference is 60% instead of the 80% preference among responders. We can make more informed assumptions about the remaining nonresponders. This approach facilitates more informed assumptions about the remaining nonresponders and it can dramatically improve our estimation.

Panels, Not to Be Confused with Focus Groups

A panel is the statistical analogue to a focus group. The U.S. government successfully employs panels to provide much of the high-quality economic information leveraged in the business world, such as the Consumer Price medical expenditures panel survey (MEPS), etc. A panel comprises a randomly selected set of individuals, who are not allowed to influence each other. Panels are excellent at collecting information longitudinally over time. Panels offer protection from mixing (confounding) trends over time with sample-to-sample variability.

Section 10.4 DoE (Design of Experiments)

"Until there are experiments, I take no notice of anything that's done."
—William Stephenson

"...[Designed experiments are]... experience planned in advance."
—Ronald A. Fisher

During the course of running a business, we generate a plethora of great ideas worth pursuing, as well as challenging problems requiring great solutions. DoE is the primary tool for inferring[21] cause-and-effect relationships. It can corroborate previously held opinions and exploit new ideas to maximum effect. This powerful tool enables us to test adjustments to our business model without bringing the business to a halt, exhausting precious resources, or risking our income stream. Alternatively, corporations often try out an idea by expensively changing the entire business model—no pilot test (or mini-experiment). It can take years to realize, or rather to admit, that the new idea, while brilliant in conception, is bleeding the company dry.

Experiments facilitate our planning for the future in order to avoid flying by the seat of our pants. We can design them to test numerous ideas in one batch. At the same time, we can quantify how confident we are that the results will apply after the experiment is over.

For difficult business problems, one underutilized approach is to employ a pilot test as the leading edge of a DoE. The pilot test collects the information needed for building the remainder of the DoE. Pilot tests facilitate taking the business to where it has never been before.

Four common failings plague business experiments: (1) an unwillingness to make a long-term investment when warranted, (2) prematurely terminating the experiment ahead of schedule, (3) changing one factor at a time[22] instead of running them all at once, and (4) failing to leverage a quant specialist to avoid the above shortcomings, and many others.

Quant Specialist's Role

Upon delegation, the first phase for the quant specialist is to tackle six interrelated questions:

1. What is the business need?
2. What is the population?
3. What do we want to estimate? Typically, we want an interval estimate for a treatment effect.
4. What is it worth?
5. How are we going to measure the experimental units?
6. What effects do we need to consider?

As with DoS, the first phase is usually straightforward or already completed. Again, this will, at most, require a kick-off meeting and some investigative work. However, the quant specialist should avoid the mistake of taking anything for granted.

For the quant specialist, we propose the following considerations:

1. Kickoff meeting:
   Statement of objectives
   Population definition
   Measurement device
2. Experimental design
3. Training for those involved
4. Pilot test
5. Data collection
6. Data management
7. Data analysis
8. Presentation—Business and/or technical
9. Analytics-based business decision

Experimental Design

DoE provides an opportunity to be aggressive in estimating the relationship between factors that we can control and a response. The response is the dependent variable, which measures performance. For this discussion, we will refer to the independent variables

> **Concept Box**
>
> *Response (dependent variable)—*
> The primary measure of performance. E.g., sales amount, attrition, response to product offering, etc.

as known factors. These known factors in an experiment consist of treatments and blocks. The treatments are independent variables of interest that we can control. The blocks are independent variables that we can usually manipulate, but are not directly interesting. In addition to the factors that we can observe and usually exert some control over, there are unobserved and often unknown factors.

All experimental designs comprise three parts: (1) the treatment structure, (2) the design or EU structure (blocks), and (3) the error structure (unobserved factors).

1. The set of treatments are randomly assigned to EUs. There are often restrictions on this randomization, which can be confusing to the uninitiated. However, this randomization is important protection from bias.

Concept Box

Treatments—Factors (variables) of interest that we can manipulate—randomly assign to EUs. Eg., price, color, and material composition of a product can be treatments. Treatments and other variables have levels. These factors are often changes to a product, process, or to the business model. We regard a control group as one of the treatments—treatment zero.

Blocks—Known extraneous factors (variables) for which we have no direct interest, but we can usually manipulate by grouping similar EUs in order to cancel out their bothersome effects. Eg., store region, month of year, type of customer, et al. can be blocks.

Unknown factors—Unknown extraneous factors (variables), which we cannot assign to EUs. Instead, we employ randomization to cancel out their effects on the response.

---

2. The design structure consists of grouping EUs into homogeneous blocks to facilitate balanced treatment assignments. By grouping similar EUs into blocks, we can force the blocking variable to be balanced across the treatments. This cancels out the mixing, or confounding, of the effects so that we can untangle them. The treatment effects are said to be "confounded" with other treatments and blocks, when we cannot separate their effect from those of other factors.

3. The error structure is a result of the design structure. We "balance" the unknown factors through randomization. Randomization protects us from "confounding" unknown or hidden factors, which we will not measure directly.

Concept Box

Experimental units (EUs)—The smallest units upon which we assign treatments and observe the response. EUs are analogous to SUs. E.g., EUs might be customers, households, businesses, etc. The population of EUs does not have to exist yet—unborn customers.

Concept Box

Confounding—The problem of having the effects of factors inextricably mixed. This occurs when factors change mostly in sync with each other. In such a situation, we cannot attribute an effect on the response with a change in one factor alone.

The purpose of DoE is to more precisely estimate treatment effects on the response by accounting for effects from other factors. To be successful, we need to (1) collect the appropriate data, and (2) strive for efficiency. DoE employs an inductive approach for estimating causal relationships between treatments and the response variable.

The design often implies the analysis and the analysis is self-validating up to a point. The Statistical Diagnostics are integral to the experimental design. The purpose of any design is to measure how much EUs vary with the treatments. This is simple if everything is somehow held constant. The Completely Randomized Design accounts for differences in unknown factors only. The Randomized Block Design accounts for both known (blocks) and unknown factors. Next we discuss these two common designs.

Completely Randomized Design

The first design and most basic design assumes that there are no block effects. It balances treatments to cancel out effects from unknown factors only. That is, EUs are homogeneous except for unknown factors. The first step is to randomly select EUs from the population. Next, we randomly assign treatments (TRTs) to EUs. The randomization balances the underlying unknown factors.

For example, we could randomly assign one of four possible marketing promotions to a sample of customers.

Randomized Block Design

This design accounts for known extraneous factors—blocks, in addition to treatments and unknown factors. When we randomly select EUs, we place them into homogeneous groups or "blocks." Next, we treat each block separately; randomly assigning different treatments to EUs within the block. This imposes treatment balance within each block—canceling out block effects. Hence, we can more accurately estimate the relationship between the response and the treatment without interference from block effects.

This approach constitutes a "restriction on the randomization," which has been a source of confusion. Even with this restriction, the treatments are still randomly assigned to EUs and this protects us from unknown factors.

For example, we could segment our customers into high, medium, and low purchasing behavior and then randomly assign one of four possible marketing promotions to a sample of customers in each segment.

Advanced Experimental Designs

There are numerous advanced designs, built for all manner of needs. Advanced designs leverage additional information; pursue different objectives; and navigate barriers.

Situations that merit advanced designs include screening a large number of factors to identify those with stronger relationships with the response (Factorial Designs); reducing EU effects (Repeated Measures); handling different EU sizes (Split-Plot); searching for optimal factor combinations (Response Surface Models); neutralizing EU differences (Crossover Designs); adjusting for EUs nested within EUs (Nested Designs); among others.

We wish to cover one last situation. If there are too few EUs, then randomization no longer makes sense. A quant specialist should purposefully assign treatments to EUs in a balanced insightful manner, thus "blocking" them. Purposeful selection should only be applied by those competent enough to design a DoE.[23] We are mentioning this as a form of sabotage for those not involving a quant specialist.

Experimental Platforms

Most corporations need an ongoing experimental platform to address their continuing needs, such as:

1. Monitoring the effects of new products and promotions in the market place/estimate ROIs;
2. Testing new product offerings.

We need to monitor more than the overall market statistics. We need to monitor how our corporate strategy is working in the marketplace. An experimental platform needs to be nimble enough to test new business practices and measure ongoing practices.

For example, we might need a control group of customers who are not receiving our primary marketing messages, and so on. This enables us to estimate the overall benefits of our promotional efforts. This approach is more realistic in today's digital economy.

Notes

1. A data analysis infrastructure should address a variety of techniques.
2. This requires a mastery of the tactical details underneath the infrastructure.

3. This is pronounced DEE-OH-ESS. Ironically, a great deal of DoS was developed at the U.S. Census Bureau.

4. A nonzero probability of selection.

5. This is pronounced DEE-OH-EE. A great deal of DoE was developed during the agricultural revolution of the twentieth century.

6. The egg came first. We think a non-chicken can lay a chicken egg.

7. Once they realized that their computers could not handle all of the data, they gave up. This is one of the early failures in addressing today's Big Data collected from the internet.

8. Statistics has a terminology problem. It is as if statistical tools are developed in different disciplines that do not communicate with each other. Imagine that.

9. The known factors need to be balanced out by the design.

10. Accuracy is limited by both the fineness of the units of measurement from the measurement device and the capability of the storage device—computer memory, clipboard, and so on—to preserve this degree of accuracy.

11. It is fitting that a species, so stuck on itself, should spend a large portion of its sampling effort sampling itself.

12. Just joking.

13. Had the selection been random (SRS—Simple Random Sampling) within each group, then this would be stratified random sampling.

14. We wish to distinguish focus groups as lacking randomization and panels as based on randomization—that is, representative.

15. Except when they fail and sometimes in a very bad way. The idea of New Coke was the product of a focus group. The New Coke mistake could only be avoided by employing a panel in a very cleverly planned pilot test and then … maybe.

16. We regret getting retentive with terminology. The alternative is to breed confusion.

17. This passage implies that the shortcoming with applying statistical sampling is that you need to understand statistical sampling. Another problem with using statistical sampling in accounting is that improving our technology opens us up to "malpractice" litigation. That is, we might need to explain why we have not been using readily available tools for audits performed over the past decades.

18. Also, each possible sample of size n has an equal probability of selection— fancy that.

19. After we take the sample, hardly anyone compares the sample variance to the variance estimate that we used to calculate sample size. We heartily recommend trying this.

20. That is, $\{(72\%) \times 0.25, (88\%) \times 0.25\}$.

21. The mechanism of action at play here is inference and not deduction.

22. Who has time for that? Changing one variable, then checking the result; changing the same variable a bit more, then checking the result; and changing it again, etc. This often takes us in a circle that does not intersect with a solution.

23. This concern is not an excuse for avoiding DoE.

11

Data Software

"Data analysis is about creating bits of information from bytes of data."

"It used to be that you were anointed in alphas[1] and now you are anointed in software."

—H. T. David

The electronic digital computer was conceived to solve systems of linear equations. Figure 11.1 illustrates the crude beginnings of a multi-billion-dollar industry that has dramatically influenced business and society. Shortly after their birth, computers, now the size of a room, became programmable, a phenomenon that spawned an evolution in analytics software.[2] After their introduction in the late 1970s, the ascendancy of personal computers further promoted the software revolution. More recently, the internet and electronic devices are generating huge bodies of data, which are collected and managed by software.

There are five main purposes fulfilled by analytics software: collecting data, processing data, monitoring values, analyzing data, and presenting results. Software continues to evolve for all five purposes.

For analyzing data, there are four basic types of statistical tools: programming languages with numerous callable statistical procedures (such as R), procedural programming software packages (such as traditional SAS, SPSS, Minitab, BMDP, Systat, and Stata),[3] menu-driven software packages (such as Statgraphics, Statistica, and many others), and graphical user interface (GUI)-based packages (such as SAS Enterprise Guide, JMP,

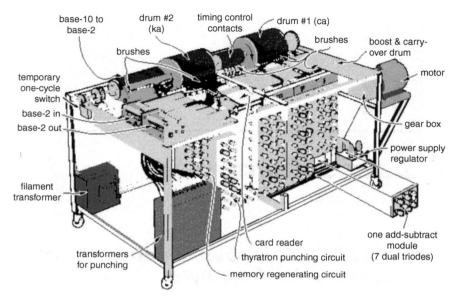

Figure 11.1 The Atanasoff-Berry Computer (1937–1941)
Source: Image courtesy of Iowa State University Library, Ames, Iowa

IBM Modeler, and Statistica). In addition, many packages include a data mining component, such as SAS Enterprise Miner, IBM Modeler's data mining add-in, and Statistica Data Miner. These packages focus on finding patterns in data, without statistical assumptions. Many of the software choices have morphed to combine the best features of the other types. In the hands of a master, all of these are fast and safe.

Some simple statistical procedures can be done in spreadsheets, especially by users who are adept with pivot tables and macros. Summary statistics, contingency table analyses (seeing how cross-tabulations reveal patterns in data), and multiple linear regressions are all readily available. Doing these tasks in spreadsheets opens the way for people without training in statistical software. However, statistical routines, once debugged, are much more readily repeatable than spreadsheet procedures, and the assumptions used in the analysis are easier for readers and reviewers to discern.

One advantage of the procedural programming and menu-driven software packages is that they often keep us closer to the underlying assumptions. That is, we know what statistical model we are using and the assumptions that come with it. Procedural programming software packages are easy to review and have been vetted by many users in the past. There are many practitioners of procedural programming languages available for hire, making it easy to build a team to work on projects. The downside of using procedural programming packages is that it takes a relatively long time to write new programs, and that the code generation process is error-prone by its very nature.

Menu-driven software is more interactive, which is great for EDA (exploratory data analysis). This software is relatively user-friendly. Many menu-driven software packages can build programming code that can leverage high-speed macros. This approach minimizes procedural errors that may creep into procedural programs.

Programming languages provide flexibility and great execution speeds. They can usually handle the most data. The challenge tends be in building and maintaining a comfortable environment.

Instead of picking options from a series of embedded menus, GUI-based packages allow the users to build processing flows (sometimes called streams) that reflect the way that people think about generating a processing operation. Major types of general processing operations are assigned icons in a toolbar. The icons are pasted onto a modeling pane of the display and connected with arrow figures to represent a data flow through a sequence of data processing operations.

This approach to data analysis permits the user to reflect in graphical pictures the conceptual flow of programming logic, similar to the way humans think. The modern graphical programming interfaces of industry-standard data tools incorporate the best features of the procedural programming languages to produce expression and macro languages and thereby create powerful and flexible tools for data integration (e.g., IBM DataStage and Informatica), data quality analysis (SAS DataFlux), and data mining (SAS Enterprise Miner, IBM Modeler, and Statistica Data Miner).

Data mining packages offer numerous well-tested methods to detect clustering or anomalies in data, without statistical assumptions. They have the advantage of making it easy to do such detections. Data mining and other forms of pattern recognition can be conducted either in "supervised" mode, which means the program starts with a target pattern and looks for sets of points in the data that match that pattern, or "unsupervised," which means the program simply looks for clumps of similar sets of points or for sets of points notably different from all the others. The disadvantage, especially for unsupervised analyses, is that it may be quite challenging to determine whether the patterns and anomalies thus identified actually mean anything.

The recent growth in capabilities is most notable in areas like data mining/predictive analytics, text analytics, and Big Data. Smaller-market specialized software tools have also emerged in great numbers.

Software tools for Big Data focus on more efficient methods of collecting data, storing the data in some more or less structured form, and efficiently retrieving elements of the data as needed. Current methods are moving away from the approach of simply warehousing all the data and then searching for it, toward methods that tag and index data as part of the input process.

Many of today's software products have come with powerful data processing and analytics capabilities, which have been combined into analytics "tool boxes" for supporting programming languages. These analytics tool boxes have evolved further into modern data mining "workbenches." This facilitates a generation of highly sophisticated custom code with considerable statistical content. They contain the latest innovative ideas,[4] and many of these are supercharged by parallelism to run extremely fast. **These workbenches can generate stored sequences of analyses, which are a valuable form of intellectual property.**

The corresponding evolution of data software has numerous business implications:

1. Broader capabilities
2. Gains in productivity
3. Greater software fidelity
4. One flood of statistical malfeasance

1. *Broader capabilities:* Data processing software has developed to handle larger volumes of data and to collect data from more input sources, including paper. All data contains information, and expanded data processing capabilities have greatly increased the abilities of corporations to know their customers and their business. The breadth and depth of statistical tools available has vastly increased and matured.

A broader tool set provides greater coverage for even more obscure and computationally intensive needs. The frontiers of what we can analyze have expanded considerably. It is now less common to have to compromise between how we want to solve a statistical problem and the choices available.

2. *Gains in productivity:* Analytics software has improved in a number of ways, providing us with:

- Increased capabilities to handle large datasets,
- Faster processing,
- More choices for handling unstructured data,
- Improved automation (Section 11.2), and
- Better integration with the business.

Data processing and statistical tools have grown immensely in their processing speeds and abilities to handle huge volumes of data. A significant contributor to this phenomenon is faster hardware and larger internal memories. One major benefit of these developments is that we can process even larger datasets in their entirety, rather than analyzing them in pieces. Years ago, analyzing photos, video, and audio were the subject of dissertations or odd one-off projects. These types of unstructured data are heading toward mainstream applications. Another benefit is that, today, a small group of *well-trained, well-led, and well-resourced* business quants can execute enough statistical analyses to meet the advanced analytics needs of a large corporation.

3. *Greater software fidelity:* When we need accurate numbers, we need reliable software. Statistical tools have greatly improved in the reliability of their results. Statistical software packages are already vetted through testing and years of successful applications. Many of the statistical workbenches for programming languages are relatively mature, having progressed through several iterations of customer feedback and design improvements. The availability of these mature tools avoids certain types of errors (calculation errors, round-off errors, and errors of scale[5]) and saves an incredible amount of review time. Custom code, while invaluable, is more susceptible to programming mistakes. It should be employed with care and reviewed by experts.

4. *One flood of statistical malfeasance:* Statistical software has become more user-friendly than ever. This represents a shift away from requirements for software programming expertise. This trend points to the fact that almost

anyone can enter data into a computer, press the button on the GUI, and generate statistical results. And herein lies the danger.

In the past, software capabilities were difficult to use and interpret without adequate training in statistical software. Although this difficulty created additional work on the front end, it protected companies on the back end by forcing them to involve and rely upon well-trained and competent business analysts and business quants. The effect was to reduce errors of negligence and counterfeit analysis. In this way, **previous, less user-friendly, statistical software served to some extent as a surrogate for certification in statistical analysis!**

Even with the barrier created by user-unfriendly software, the issue of enabling people to do inept analysis has been around for a long time. In the early days of the major packages, there was serious discussion of requiring users to pass an online test of basic statistical skills before being able to run the software.

Now the advent of push-button data analysis has facilitated a flood of statistical malfeasance. In some places, we are awash with misinformation. The resulting credibility void encourages decision making based upon fixed beliefs and "tribal rituals." An afternoon of "flash training,"[6] as discussed in Chapter 7, is unlikely to stem this tide.

Section 11.1 discusses the criteria that we should consider in designing a suite of statistical software tools. In Section 11.2, we will discuss automation, which could be better utilized inside the corporation.

Section 11.1 Criteria

Each corporation must plan, build, and maintain a software infrastructure to meet its needs. The cost of software is an investment intended to increase productivity. A firm should select a suite of software tools with the following characteristics:

1. Broad functional and technical capabilities
2. Relatively low maintenance
3. Relatively high fidelity
4. Relatively high efficiency
5. Relatively high flexibility
6. Relatively high user-friendliness of the interface

Functional and Technical Capabilities

A productive analytics core will require a number of software tools to meet all of their standard and exotic needs. A suitable suite of software tools will enable the collection, integration, data quality assessment, manipulation, analysis, and presentation of information derived from the data. The breadth in analysis techniques is immense, and one statistical software tool is probably not enough. The most powerful solution is a combination of software tools,[7] which supplies the best features and addresses the unanticipated. A blend of nimble and flexible programming capabilities with vetted low-maintenance "canned" tools is extremely powerful. For example, extracting data from relational databases in data warehouses for use in analytics processes is a very complicated and exacting operation. These operations are performed at a most basic level by many analytics tools, but more complex extraction, denormalization, and data integration operations are best performed by industry-standard ETL (Extraction-Transformation-Loading) tools. The integrated outputs from ETL tools can be fed directly into analytics tools for further processing. Complicated data quality assessments and integration operations like reconciling multiple versions of the same customer name with different spellings are handled best by data quality tools with fuzzy matching capabilities.

The struggle for corporations is to have enough analytics software breadth. The purchasing decisions can be improved by involving those who have an understanding of statistical principles and a mastery of statistical software. Those who are not indoctrinated in analytics do not and, indeed, cannot understand how analytics applications relate to all of their business operations. The misapplication of software contributes to the flood of statistical malfeasance.

A final and often neglected consideration in selecting statistical software is the skill set of the business analysts and business quants. There is a synergism between the user and the software, based upon their training and the way they think about business problems. Though it is difficult to quantify the value of this synergism, it is easy to see the impact when it is absent. Importantly, an efficient business quant needs to master more than one software solution.

One common foible for corporations is to skimp on software, or to choose simple software and relatively inexperienced analysts. Managers who do this strive to save pennies by cutting what they do not understand. The trouble is that analysts' time is also expensive, so the extra labor effort required to produce results exceeds the savings from acquiring less suitable software or analysts who struggle to use the software available. When key deliverables are delayed substantially, the entire organization incurs a cost as well, often the largest cost of all.

Maintenance

We maintain software in order to reuse it for future planned or unplanned needs. This is usually, but not always, less expensive than rewriting the code for solving similar problems. Maintaining the integrity of the code requires focused documentation and code governance. Documentation establishes and preserves a record of how the code works, the underlying assumptions, and areas needing attention. We maintain a log of the alterations. We correct software errors, keep the software organized, and address other concerns regarding the execution of the code. We alter the code to accommodate different, often newer, hardware or software environments.

Maintenance is a major investment in keeping reusable code reliable. It can be relatively straightforward for programming languages and code generated from menu-driven packages.

Just as the clock does not stop when the crew changes the tires in an automobile race, maintenance should be included in considering the speed of software operations. High-maintenance software runs slower than its low-maintenance equivalent, thus explaining why the ubiquitous spreadsheet is naturally overused.[8]

"The most expensive sex is free sex."[9]

—Woody Allen

Governance and Misapplication

Code governance protects the integrity of the code. Often we need the results to be reproducible or for the software to perform as expected.

Perhaps the greatest governance problem is with the misapplication of software—when we do not have the correct tool, we use the tools available. To better illustrate this problem, we need look no further than the ubiquitous spreadsheet.[10] Spreadsheets come in two types: regular and augmented by "crazy powerful" software.

Unfortunately, spreadsheets are inappropriately employed in the place of statistical software and with great financial loss. Some studies have shown that corporations that rely too much on spreadsheets do not perform as well as those applying statistical software. The expense resides in the labor, the time, the risk, and the opportunity cost. The cost of re-creating capabilities already available and vetted in statistical software can be greater than that incurred in just purchasing them. For one-off solutions already available in statistical software, the labor cost is hard to justify. For repetitive applications, the maintenance cost is an important concern.

We think that regular spreadsheets belong in a category separate from statistical tools. Numerous references suggest that spreadsheets are inappropriate for certain applications.[11] In the main, spreadsheets are designed for deductive calculations on complete data and for generic mathematics problems. They are practical for reporting, analyzing what-if scenarios, and so on. Spreadsheets are not the best choice for dealing with uncertainty and are thus less effective for inductive statistical estimation based upon imperfect or incomplete data. This is primarily the domain of statistical software.

By employing spreadsheets in place of statistical software, we tend to limit ourselves to solutions that are easy for a spreadsheet. We end up further removed from our implicit underlying assumptions. Statistical software facilitates solving new problems and spreading analytics in the corporation. Regular, unenhanced spreadsheets can be used as reporting tools or number crunchers. They can support statistical tools, but they cannot really perform statistics.[12]

Spreadsheets augmented by powerful software are a different matter. Enhancements, like Visual Basic for Applications (VBA), provide additional capabilities to regular spreadsheets. In the hands of a master, spreadsheets are, indeed, performing great feats. Augmented spreadsheets are in the vein of programming languages with a spreadsheet attached to hold and monitor the data.

Fidelity

Fidelity consists of the reliability of the software to produce trustworthy results. We consider two factors:

1. *The degree to which the user possesses mastery of that software tool.* As mentioned, there is a synergy between qualified practitioners and their software. This synergy can provide greater fidelity.

2. *The degree to which the software is vetted.* We are content to pay for a statistical software tool when it is vetted for some applications.[13] This vetting ensures the integrity of the algorithms. In all cases, we must review the applications of the code being employed.

Spreadsheet validation is a must. Spreadsheets tend to have fidelity problems in general and for statistics in particular. In addition to a lengthy history of failures of some spreadsheet programs, these are not vetted for statistical fidelity, and it can become a nightmare to validate any complex analyses performed by them. Even when vetted, it remains important that the software is relevant to the business problem. Some machinations of their failures are troubling, including turning missing cells into zeros for the purposes of calculating summary statistics and not including a y-axis label as a default for graphs.[14]

Efficiency and Flexibility

Analytics execution time comprises three parts: the time it takes to build the software for the first time, usually programming and debugging time; the time it takes for the software to finish running, usually data crunching time; and maintence, which we previously discussed. Sometimes, we pay too much attention to the second part because it can be repetitive.

A very important part of efficiency is user-friendliness. We want software that is user-friendly in that a qualified individual can master it quickly and use it adroitly. This comes at a terrible expense for those without statistical training. For them, the software is overly friendly, setting them up to go beyond their expertise.

We need software that works well with other software. We want a suite of software tools that is malleable enough to address the unexpected needs and the individuality of business analysts and business quants. Practitioners are hardly interchangeable parts.

Another critical feature of good software is upward compatibility. The code we developed under version 3.2 of a software package needs to work without modification in version 5.0. The vendor should also have a good record of offering continuing support for old versions for some time after introducing new ones.

Section 11.2 Automation

"It's all in the algorithm."

—Dr. Rodney McKay, Stargate Universe

Automation is not only about increased speed; it is about increased capabilities and increased fidelity. Software should handle redundant tasks and simplify complex ones. We discuss some areas where software automation can drive productivity gains: data management, data analysis, presenting findings, monitoring results, and decision making.

Data Management

Effective data preparation requires a great deal of work when performed by hand. Hence, to keep pace with demand, this process needs to be semi-automated using software.[15] The benefits of software automation increase with the extent to which the data is dirty or partially missing and the extent to which our computer system is well organized.

There are two promising endeavors for data management: improving the data and generating data to describe the data—so-called metadata. Typical applications include cleaning the data, flagging data concerns, creating new variables, categorizing variables, identifying missing data patterns, and running simple tests on data quality. As we will discuss in Chapter 12, automated software is ideal for keeping electronic data dictionaries up-to-date.

Data Analysis

Automation can improve anything that is redundant in data analysis. For example, one of the most valuable areas of application is CRM (customer relationship management), where we want to mass-produce predictive models for numerous customer types and situations. For modeling, the benefits of automation grow geometrically with the numbers of predictors and observations. Model building is an iterative process.

Presenting Findings

Automated and semi-automated reports[16] have been successful for years in placing findings into standard reports and dashboard formats. Corporate score cards are often built on top of them. Automation can further reduce a mound of reports to notable highlights. Applying quality control tools can simplify the manual reviewing of the numbers.

Monitoring Results

Monitoring results provides a shield against expected and unexpected events. In banking, billions of credit card transactions are monitored daily for fraud. In manufacturing, monitoring software has implemented quality control and process control over the course of several decades. Monitoring capabilities such as these are already commonplace and have been expanding further into more industries.

As the size of datasets increase, and automation increases accordingly, it becomes more and more important to test processes and logic carefully. Tracking down possible errors by hand is tedious and time-consuming even in small datasets. In extremely large datasets, verification by hand is impossible.

Decision Making

As mentioned in Chapter 3, we can delegate large numbers of decisions based upon analytics findings. Software can execute "delegated" or "prewired" decisions in the form of static business rules. More sophisticated software is evolving toward better decision making in the vein of artificial intelligence. This software can start with a set of business rules and evolve based upon exterior feedback.

Here again, as the number of automated decisions increases, trustworthiness of processes becomes more important. Having teams of humans and computers diligently following sets of rules that are poorly suited to the variety of challenges the organization faces will produce results ranging from farcical to tragic. It is critical to have procedures to identify and escalate problems and to provide appropriate decision makers with the ability to implement corrections.

Notes

1. Alpha represents the probability of making a particular type of decision mistake or error.
2. In a sense, data software began before the invention of the computer, which occurred in the late 1930s. Analysts developed complex algorithms that needed to be solved by hand.

3. Sometimes called fourth generation languages (4GL).

4. Sometimes a thorough investigation reveals that these innovative new solutions are very similar to innovative old ideas.

5. These result from adding many very small numbers to generate very large numbers.

6. A consultant comes in for a day of calculating t-tests and such.

7. It is difficult for one software tool to outperform a combination of itself and another tool.

8. When applied improperly, spreadsheets can be very expensive to maintain and can result in maintenance failures.

9. Maintenance, governance, and fidelity problems render some free software to be ... not so free.

10. We are often fitting a spreadsheet into a round hole.

11. See "Spreadsheets And The Financial Collapse" by Grenville J. Croll for insight and several related references.

12. Not yet.

13. Most software tools are vetted against baseline data to check to how many digits the results are accurate.

14. Coincidentally, my spell checker performs about as well.

15. Thus, growing the productivity to perform more analysis, which will entreat more automation.

16. The optimal mix of automation and the human element does vary.

12

Data Management

"A data warehouse is an information system like any other. If analysts cannot use its full potential, we're already taking a value loss."
—Gert H.N. Laursen & Jesper Thorlund[1]

One building block for competing on analytics is a well-organized customer-centric database. Hence, database management is crucial for properly handling and supplying the data. This is even more important for corporations facing the volume, velocity, or variety of Big Data. This chapter focuses on the needs of data consumers. It is written from the analytics practitioner's perspective. We recognize that there are other perspectives to database management.[2]

Corporations have a continuum of data needs, including tracking, reporting, regular analytics, and advanced analytics. These needs dictate the desired quality and structure of the data. Naturally, the quality of the data and analyses affects the quality of the business decisions.

Complex data and more advanced statistical analyses require better data organization. Big Data or not, a few tenets of data management include the following:

1. Support efficient access to data.
2. Ensure data integrity.
3. Ensure data security.
4. Provide efficient storage—including data classification.
5. Assist with anticipating future data investments.

Within these tenets, two oft-neglected services are managing the data pipeline from beginning to end and building database enhancements. A well-managed data pipeline facilitates greater efficiencies, enables better data integrity, and supports taking the initiative in data collection. Management of the data extends from acquisition to application.

Information Strategy

There must be an information strategy that coordinates the needs of the business with the data warehouse. This ensures that the data warehouse does not take on a life of its own, generating irrelevant data. Two objectives of the information strategy are to assess the utility and the accessibility of the information.

Each corporation should have an information strategy or data plan. We need to better manage our current assets and anticipate what information will enable us to compete in the marketplace. This requires an understanding of how data supports risk, marketing, sales, and profitability considerations. We need to map the corporation's data to its information needs. At the same time, we need to consider how our competitors will leverage their data. We must anticipate advances in their ability to improve data quality and decision making.

We want to be judicious in collecting affordable data that meets the business needs. It can be difficult to anticipate for what purpose the data will be used or what data we will need.[3] Strategy is likely to involve maintaining and possibly raising the quality of the data.

> *"I am often bewildered by the degree to which some decision makers trust information obtained from a competitor above the contradictory numbers provided by their own staffs."*
>
> —Thomas Redman

Data Sources

There are two sources for corporations to acquire data: internal and external. These two sources *tend* to possess different characteristics. It is instructive to note the *typical* differences in the value proposition.

Internal Sources

Usually, internal sources provide more transparency regarding the data collection process and greater potential for competitive advantage. That is, when all of the competing corporations have the same data, only the data analysis and how we leverage the results can provide an advantage. Typically, we are more familiar with the foibles of our own internal data. There are some proprietary datasets that should not be handled by external sources.

External Sources

The usual reasons for choosing external suppliers are convenience, cost, and service. External sources are more convenient for consumers who lack the infrastructure, expertise, or determination to collect the data. Advantages in cost and service occur more frequently when there is competition to sell the same data. The proprietary nature of external data can make it more difficult to judge data quality.

In deciding between internal and external data, it is difficult to evaluate the relative value proposition.[4] In practice, corporations sometimes collect data internally or purchase it externally when the opposite would better suit their needs. Quality is often the deciding factor, and it varies a great deal. To compare the quality of alternative sources, we can perform analysis on the data and we can review the collection and processing of the data—the data pipeline. The qualifications of those managing the data and the data collection techniques employed (discussed in Chapter 10) are important considerations.

Regardless of the source, proper incentives encourage better quality, cost, service, and convenience—as always. We want to align the incentives of internal and external suppliers with those of data consumers.

Security

In addition to protecting ourselves from data problems, we have two security issues. These are the twin responsibilities of concealing proprietary information and protecting other people's private information. This might require restricted access to the data or, preferably, we can de-identify the data, which is usually easy.

Section 12.1 Customer-Centric Data Management

Customer-centric data management adds more value to the business than just delivering numbers. This involves engaging the customer and understanding their needs. This is challenging. Those providing data (data providers) and those consuming it (data consumers) often speak different languages and belong to different corporate subcultures. Our experience suggests that those who find a way to partner with their customers earn a better grasp of:

1. The business objectives the data serves
2. How the data needs to be cleaned and otherwise maintained
3. How the data pipeline should be monitored
4. The value of data enhancements

Customer Needs

Beyond storing the raw information, valuable datasets merit ongoing rapport between those that manage the data and those that leverage it. It is necessary to keep up with changing needs and to proactively seek ways to add value. Suppliers armed with experience analyzing data are better able to comprehend customer needs and to anticipate them. Not all of the burden is on the suppliers. Data consumers must help them to succeed.

Most corporations place data managers and data consumers into separate silos—isolated from each other. This is an additional challenge to customer-centricity. The corresponding disconnect is a source of festering bureaucracy with stale meetings. Both sides need to recognize this potential communications gap and foster better connectivity.

Data Quality—That "Garbage In, Garbage Out" Thing

We are awash in dirty data; warehouses of not entirely trustworthy terabytes, petabytes, or more. Data are often missing, incorrect, inaccurate, misunderstood, obsolete, or just somehow lacking. We must protect the data during collection and in storage. Also, we need to follow up by inspecting the data, repairing problems, measuring data quality, and providing reassurance as to the quality. Data quality is often a strategic journey and not solely within the scope of those analyzing the data. As Thomas Redman, "The Data Doc," puts it, data quality is a moving target.[5]

Inspection

To efficiently inspect the accuracy of the data entering the database, we can design software to semi-automatically check its integrity. We can

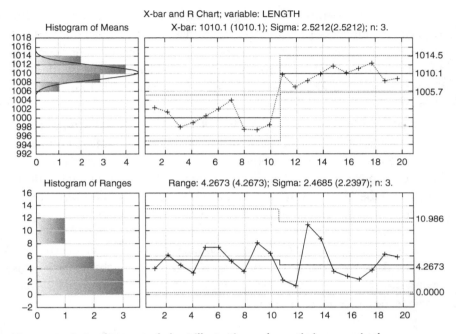

Figure 12.1 Quality control chart illustrating a dramatic increase in the mean

build summary statistics, data ranges, etc. into the data dictionary to serve as benchmarks. Automatic software can perform sanity checks against these summary statistics. We are looking for missing values, outliers, and data mismatches. Statistical tools are particularly valuable for detecting problems with continuously arriving data. Part of due diligence is to employ these independent checks and to regularly audit the integrity of the data. Figure 12.1 illustrates how QC charts can monitor data as it is collected.

Data Repair

The tools of inspection often prevent or catch errors in the moment. In addition to this, we need to take a hard look at the soundness of the data. This second step is to repair traceable problems and chronicle our handiwork in the data dictionary. Many of the problems occur at the point of collection or data entry and get past our preventative countermeasures. Data is not always entered in keeping with business purposes. It is common for numbers to be mis-typed, mis-entered, and missed completely.[6] The data can be unnecessarily rounded[7] or dramatically altered so that it is not so easily re-engineered. Data entry software often over- or under-controls the inputs. The initial effort to repair these problems should reside with those closest to the source—ideally those collecting the data or monitoring data entry.

When we detect errors in the data, the objective is to make repairs that assume the least. Poor data repair will result in lost or damaged information.[8] We need to think about the source of the data and what the numbers really mean. We emphasize repairing the data in ways that address business issues, leveraging background information. It is important that data collectors collaborate with the data consumers in order to take appropriate care.

During this initial repair, we restrict ourselves to "explainable" problems with the data. We defer other concerns with the data to the analysis. This includes purposeful imputation, capping and flooring, and others. Data repair segues to data preparation.[9]

Section 12.2 Database Enhancements

We regard a business's data portfolio as an asset to be managed like any other. We deem database enhancements as profitable investments for the data portfolio.[10] The benefits of database enhancements are efficiency[11] and effectiveness. Database enhancements are obvious to those struggling to use the data—data consumers. However, there is an unfortunate disconnect between those in a better position to provide some of these enhancements (data suppliers) and those in a better position to leverage them (data consumers). Warehouses of useless data[12] are at the expensive end of this disconnect.

In this section, we discuss the most valuable data enhancements: data encyclopedias, data dictionaries, and variable organization. The first two are physical assets containing metadata, which is data describing the data. Variable organization is a journey toward greater efficiency. They all three support planning and move the data toward an analyzable form.

Database Encyclopedia

A database encyclopedia is a "table of contents" listing the company's current dataset inventory and obtainable datasets that can be built or purchased. It provides a foundation for better managing resources. It is essential for those with the vision to contemplate "the possible." A useful data encyclopedia will contain some or all of the following:

1. Purpose(s) of the dataset, including the downstream reports and analyses leveraging the data. Also, this can identify any of the dataset's key measures of business performance.
2. Source(s), including billing, audit, primary research, and others. This is especially important for internally collected data.
3. Schematics. Complex structures merit a diagram illustrating the connections between tables or outlining the data pipeline.
4. Time window, or the time period for which the data is relevant (e.g., medical prescriptions written between March 2008 and January 2011).
5. Cost. The cost of obtaining the data, including purchasing price, when relevant.
6. Availability of the data, when this concern is relevant.
7. Collection techniques. Observation, anecdotal sampling, DoS (statistical sampling), census, DoE (designed experimentation), simulation, focus groups, statistical panels, etc.
8. Collection tools. CAPI, CATI, e-survey, Web, customer generated, machine/device generated, and others.
9. Quality. Relate problems, concerns, and solutions.
10. Completeness. Relate any patterns of missing-ness.

Maintaining a data encyclopedia should be inexpensive. As datasets are built, maintained, or purchased, the relevant information should be collected. This intellectual property is even more important for large companies with high turnover. Figure 12.2 illustrates a set of data linkages.

Data Dictionaries

A data dictionary is essential for higher-end data applications like complex analyses or more meticulous data cleaning. This includes variable names, variable descriptions, numbers of observations, variable classifications, summary statistics, and others. Each dataset should have a data dictionary

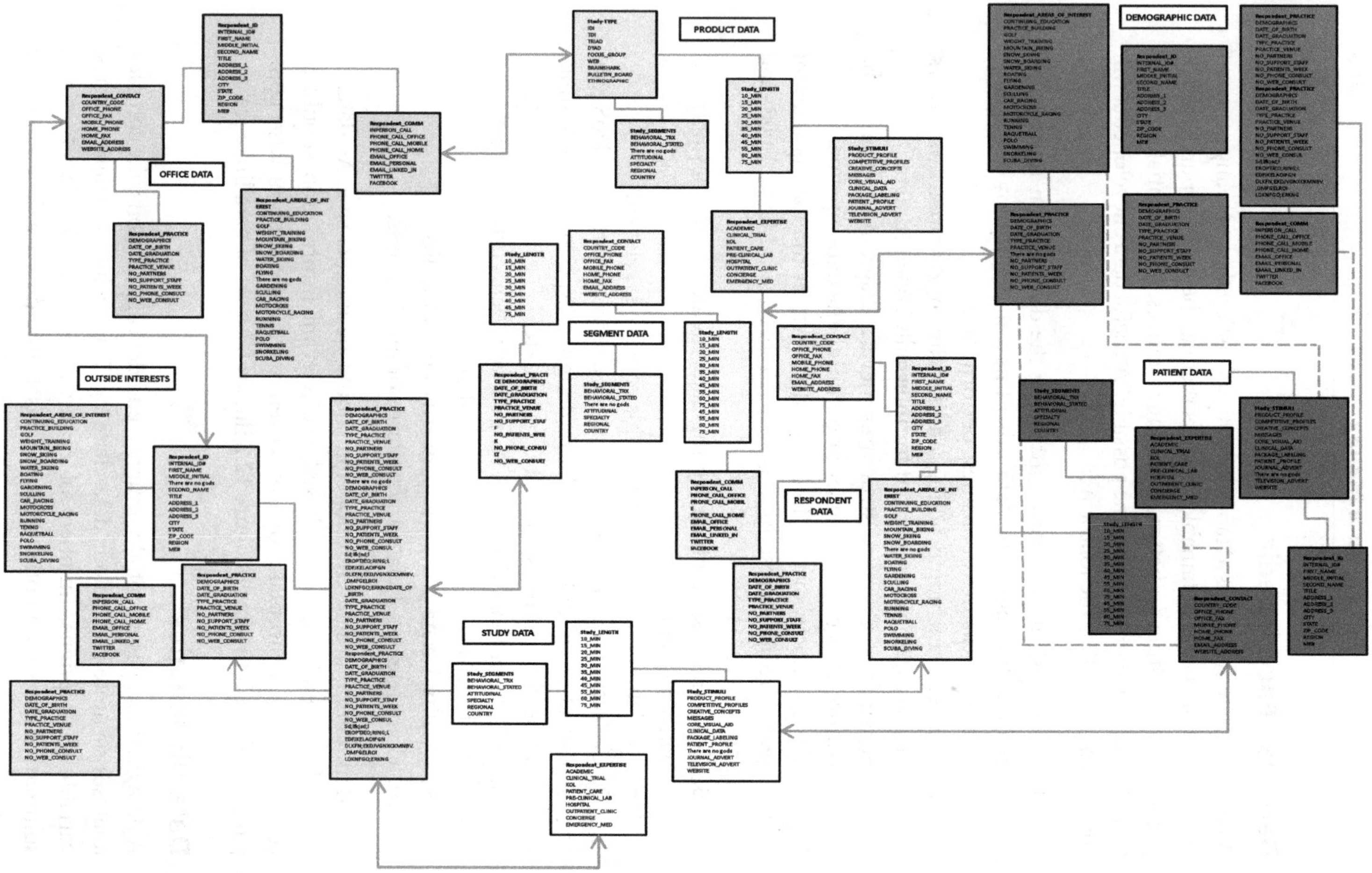

Figure 12.2 Database connections

describing its contents. This is intellectual property that attaches meanings to the numbers. In practice, organizing the dataset around a formal data dictionary[13] has tremendous business advantages over certain alternatives:

1. Letting the data be its own dictionary
2. Relying on employees to be the de facto dictionary
3. Shepherding a neglected collection of documents[14] describing the various data elements in less than full detail

A data dictionary preserves and shares the intellectual property. This fosters greater productivity, and it provides a home where the information can build upon itself. Data dictionaries can collect findings from monitoring data quality, organizing the variables, and cleaning the data. These efforts contribute to a more effective data dictionary, which should contain some of the following information:

1. Variable definitions and classifications.
2. Mapping of the most critical variables to their applications in the business.
3. Summary statistics, data ranges, graphs, and others necessary to monitor the data as it is collected or received.
4. Background information on how the data was collected, nonresponse rates or missing data patterns, which information is self-reported, projection factors, and which information contains measurement error or has similar problems.
5. Explanations of adjustments to the data, such as the projection factors or adjustments needed to handle measurement error.[15]

Data dictionaries have moved from paper to electronic form. Automated software can efficiently write to and read from an electronic data dictionary—variable classifications, summary statistics, and so forth. See Figure 12.3 for an example of a data dictionary, which even includes histograms of the data.

Variable Organization

Variable organization is especially important for advanced analytics. Most or all variable organization can be performed by automated software. The variables need to be classified, ordered, grouped, and meaningfully named. We will discuss variable classifications at greater length. In particular, important variables should be classified by their statistical structure. Within these

prostate
18 Variables   502 Observations

patno : Patient Number

	n	missing	unique	Mean	.05	.10	.25	.50	.75	.90	.95
	502	0	502	251.7	26.05	51.10	126.25	251.50	376.75	451.90	479.95

lowest :   1   2   3   4   5, highest: 502 503 504 505 506

stage : Stage

	n	missing	unique	Mean
	502	0	2	3.424

3 (289, 58%), 4 (213, 42%)

rx : Treatment

	n	missing	unique
	502	0	4

placebo (127, 25%), 0.2 mg estrogen (124, 25%)
1.0 mg estrogen (126, 25%), 5.0 mg estrogen (125, 25%)

dtime : Months of Followup

	n	missing	unique	Mean	.05	.10	.25	.50	.75	.90	.95
	502	0	76	36.13	1.05	5.00	14.25	34.00	57.75	67.00	71.00

lowest :   0   1   2   3   4, highest: 72 73 74 75 76

status : Followup Status

	n	missing	unique
	502	0	10

alive (148, 29%), dead - prostatic ca (130, 26%)
dead - heart or vascular (96, 19%), dead - cerebrovascular (31, 6%)
dead - pulmonary embolus (14, 3%), dead - other ca (25, 5%)
dead - respiratory disease (16, 3%)
dead - other specific non-ca (28, 6%), dead - unspecified non-ca (7, 1%)
dead - unknown cause (7, 1%)

age : Age in Years

	n	missing	unique	Mean	.05	.10	.25	.50	.75	.90	.95
	501	1	41	71.46	56	60	70	73	76	78	80

lowest : 48 49 50 51 52, highest: 84 85 87 88 89

wt : Weight Index = wt(kg)-ht(cm)+200

	n	missing	unique	Mean	.05	.10	.25	.50	.75	.90	.95
	500	2	67	99.03	77.95	82.90	90.00	98.00	107.00	116.00	123.00

lowest : 69 71 72 73 74, highest: 136 142 145 150 152

pf : Performance Rating

	n	missing	unique
	502	0	4

normal activity (450, 90%), in bed < 50% daytime (37, 7%)
in bed > 50% daytime (13, 3%), confined to bed (2, 0%)

hx : History of Cardiovascular Disease

	n	missing	unique	Sum	Mean
	502	0	2	213	0.4243

Figure 12.3 Data dictionary[16]

classifications, we might order the variables by frequency of use or value. Variables can be grouped based upon source, business logic, purpose, and others. Groupings promote efficiency and help detect patterns. For some software, we put the response and major variables at the beginning of the file and the least viable variables at the end. Variable naming conventions are helpful; names such as P4C970[17] should be phased out.

Variable Classifications

Variables play different roles in analysis, and these roles are based in part on their structure. The implications influence transforming the variables to an analyzable form and the underlying assumptions. We will define one

Table 12.1 Typical Variable Classifications Based Upon Structure

Variable Classification	Data Structure
Continuous	Measured as finely as the measurement device and computer storage allow. The data dictionary should include mean, min, max, standard deviation, etc.
Semi-Continuous	Measured in increments of some arbitrary unit such as half inches. The data dictionary should mention this arbitrary unit of measure, and the mean, min, max, standard deviation, etc.
Ratio/Proportion	A special case of a continuous or semi-continuous variable. A ratio might or might not be bound. We often employ the term "proportion" when discussing ratios that are bound by [0, 1].
Integers/Counts	Discrete values comprising some integer measurement.
Categorical: Relative Magnitudes (Ordinal)	Categorical values that are relative to each other in order and magnitude.
Categorical: Ranks (Ordinal)	Categorical values, mostly integers, that are relative to each other in order and *not* magnitude.
Categorical: Nominal	Categorical values which are *not* relative to each other in order or magnitude. We can replace the numbers with random letters without loss of information.
Mixed	A combination of the above. The more continuous aspects of the structure tend to dominate how we leverage the data.

The first three classifications can be regarded as interval data.

type of variable classifications in Table 12.1 and leave the implications for the interested reader.[18]

Notes

1. See *Business Analytics for Managers: Taking Business Intelligence Beyond Reporting.*
2. The best database administrators are dataphiles.

3. The same is true for anticipating all the ways in which we will apply the results of an analysis—the serendipity of statistics.

4. Also, many corporations lack the infrastructure to accurately appraise the value proposition of quality versus price. Instead, their perceptions loom large.

5. See *Data Driven: Profiting from Your Most Important Business Asset* by Thomas Redman (2008).

6. Missing numbers are often meant to be zeros and vice versa.

7. We call this "discretizing the data." The problem is that this introduces unnecessary measurement error.

8. It might be wise to preserve the original data.

9. Most data preparation is the purview of the business analysts and business quants. They need to transform the data into an "analyzable form" that is friendly to the business problem and the statistical software.

10. Even though it is difficult to estimate the ROI for these investments.

11. Alternatively, a mediocre infrastructure will "manufacture" unnecessary busy work.

12. Without this disconnect, there might be enough disk space for the data.

13. Datasets are more reliable with a data dictionary as a rudder.

14. Including notes scribbled on the backs of envelopes and in the margins of old projects.

15. Just what proportion of the variability is due to measurement error anyway?

16. Excerpt from *Regression Modeling Strategies with Applications to Linear Models, Logistic Regression, and Survival Analysis* by Frank Harrell (2002).

17. "Under no circumstances go to P4C970"—Col. Jack O'Neill. The gate address for the home of the Aschen on *Stargate: SG1* episode (2010). This is difficult to keep straight; and that is a concern for data analysis and for traveling to other planets.

18. Academic speak for "we are too lazy to think it through."

Concluding Remarks

"An investment in knowledge pays the best interest."
—Benjamin Franklin

"By failing to prepare, you are preparing to fail."
—Benjamin Franklin

Business is becoming more complicated and corporations are struggling to adapt. One way to deal with business analytics problems is to close our eyes or to chase our tail in a circle.[1] Instead, it is our ambition to help you to better integrate business analytics into the decision-making process, and brandish it to compete in the marketplace. Business analytics facilitates rapid reaction in a dynamic industry and offers new ways to approach the business problem.

Winning in analytics is all about infrastructure. The most important adaptation is to expand and sharpen the team of analytics professionals—analytics-based decision makers, senior leadership advocating analytics, and those leading and providing data analysis. As we build our business analytics team, we need to provide them with the tools of the trade. In Chapter 1, we couched Best Statistical Practice in terms of Timeliness, Client Expectation, Accuracy, Reliability, and Cost. In Part I of this book, we discussed how to update the corporate infrastructure so that we can fully leverage business analytics. In Part II, we supplied three pillars for supporting Best Statistical Practice: Statistical Qualifications (Chapter 7), Statistical Diagnostics (Chapter 8), and Statistical Review (Chapter 9)—or what we have termed collectively as Statistical QDR. We finished with Part III's discussion of three building blocks for supporting analytics: Data Collection, Data Software, and Data Management—or Data CSM. Employ this book in your heated discussions about how to fully leverage business analytics.[2]

In writing this book, we wanted to remember a generation or two who built the first sophisticated analytics capabilities. At worst, this book will be a note in a bottle,[3] from a time that future readers may have difficulty believing or comprehending—the time before business analytics was integrated into corporate strategy.

Notes

1. Wait, those are two ways and they are both for cats and dogs.
2. We triple dog dare you.
3. Or the last surviving "paper" book decorating your shelf. As printed books disappear, we hope this will be one of your last dog-eared books, with scribbling, Post-it notes, and pages of analytics articles hanging out. If, on the other hand, you have the electronic version, then we hope this will be one of your first dog-eared e-books, with electronic highlights, annotations, bookmarks, and links to pages of analytics articles.

Appendix

Exalted Contributors: Analytics Professionals

Contributors	Review	Material Contributions
Isaac "Boom Boom" Abiola, Ph.D.	Ch. 1, 2, 9, 12	
Cynthia "Wei" Huang Bartlett, M.D.		Graphics
Sigvard Bore	Ch. 1	
Bertrum Carroll	Ch. 12	
H. T. David, Ph.D.	Ch. 1, 7, 9	Mentor
Karen Fender		Graphics
Les Fraley	Ch. 1–8	
Hakan Gogtas, Ph.D.	Ch. 10	Chapter 2: Predicting Fraud In Accounting: What Analytics-Based Accounting Has Brought to "Bare"
James W. Hardin, Ph.D.	Ch. 7, 8, 10	Chapter 8: Standard Errors for Model-Based Group Differences: Bootstrapping to the Rescue
Anand Madhaven	Ch. 1	
Girish Malik	Ch. 1, 3, 5–9, 11	
Gaurav Mishra	Ch. 4	
Robert A. Nisbet, Ph.D.	Ch. 11	

Contributors	Review	Material Contributions
Sivaramakrishnan Rajagopalan	Ch. 9	
Jennifer Thompson		Graphics
Doug Samuelson	Ch. 11	
Tom "T.J." Scott.	Ch. 1–6	Chapter 2: The Great Pharmaceutical Sales-Force Arms Race
Prateek Sharma	Ch. 9	
Charlotte Sibley	Ch. 1-12	Mentor, Chapter 5: On-Topic Leadership
W. Robert Stephenson, Ph.D.	Ch. 7	
Ronald L. Wasserstein, Ph.D.		Chapter 7: The PSTAT (Professional Statistician)—ASA's New Accreditation
Brian Wynne		Chapter 2: Inside the Statistical Underground—Adjustment Factors for the Pharmaceuticals Arms Race
David Young		Chapter 5: Management Types

Others deserving mention include John L. Eltinge, Ph.D. (MS Advisor), Michael T. Longnecker, Ph.D. (Ph.D. Advisor), Jennifer Ashkenazy (Acquisitions Editor), Joanne Slike (Copy Editor).

References

Ayres, Ian. 2007. *Super Crunchers: Why Thinking-by-Numbers Is the New Way to Be Smart.* New York: Bantam Books.

Bakan, Joel (Writer), Mark Achbar. (Director), and Jennifer Abbott (Director). 2003. *The Corporation.* (Film). Big Picture Media Corporation.

Bennis, Warren. 2009. *On Becoming a Leader.* 4th ed. New York: Basic Books.

Brealey, Richard A., and Stewart C. Myers. 1996. *Principles of Corporation Finance.* 5th ed. New York: McGraw-Hill.

Brown, S. R., and L. E. Melamed. 1990. *Experimental Design and Analysis.* Thousand Oaks, CA: Sage Publications.

Burkitt, D. 1971. "Epidemiology of Cancer of the Colon and Rectum." *Cancer* 28: 3–13.

Burns, Ken (Director). 2000. *Mark Twain: A Film Directed by Ken Burns.* (Film). PBS.

Cohan, William D. 2010. *House of Cards: A Tale of Hubris and Wretched Excess on Wall Street.* New York: Anchor.

Croll, Grenville J. 2009. "Spreadsheets and the Financial Collapse." Proc. European Spreadsheet Risks Int. Grp. (EuSpRIG).

Crouhy, Michel, Dan Galai, and Robert Mark. 2001. *Risk Management.* New York: McGraw-Hill.

Davenport, Thomas H., and Jeanne G. Harris. 2007. *Competing on Analytics: The New Science of Winning.* Boston: Harvard Business School Press.

Davenport, Thomas H., Jeanne G. Harris, and Robert Morison. 2010. *Analytics at Work: Smarter Decisions, Better Results.* Boston: Harvard Business School Press.

Deming, W. Edwards. 1982. *Out of the Crisis.* Cambridge, MA: MIT.

Ferguson, Charles (Writer/Director), Chad Beck, and Adam Bolt. 2010. *Inside Job.* (Film). Representational Pictures/Sony Pictures Classics.

Fernandez, E., et al. 2000. *Preventative Medicine* 31: 11–4

Gibney, Alex (Writer), Christopher Hitchens (Writer), Eugene Jarecki (Director). 2003. *The Trials of Henry Kissinger.* (Film). British Broadcasting Corporation (BBC), Diverse Productions, History Television, Jigsaw Educational Productions

Inc., SBS Television, TV2 Danmark, Think Tank Films, ZETA Productions, and arte France Cinéma.

Gibney, Alex (Writer/Director), Peter Elkind (Writer), and Bethany McLean (Writer). 2005. *Enron: The Smartest Guys in the Room.* (Film). Jigsaw Productions, 2929 Productions, HDNet Films.

Gonick, Larry, and Woolcott Smith. 1993. *The Cartoon Guide to Statistics.* New York: Collins Reference.

Good, Phillip I., and James W. Hardin, Ph.D. 2009. *Common Errors in Statistics (and How to Avoid Them).* Hoboken, NJ: John Wiley & Sons.

Hardin, James. 1999. Personal communication.

Harrell, Frank E. 2002. *Regression Modeling Strategies with Applications to Linear Models, Logistic Regression, and Survival Analysis.* New York: Springer-Verlag.

Kirk, Michael (Writer/Director). 2009. *Frontline: Breaking the Bank.* (Film). WGBH-TV (PBS Member Station).

Kirk, Michael (Writer/Director). 2009. *Frontline: Inside the Meltdown.* (Film). WGBH-TV (PBS Member Station).

Kirk, Michael (Writer/Director). 2009. *Frontline: The Warning.* (Film). WGBH-TV (PBS Member Station).

Kruger, Justin, and David Dunning. (1999). "Unskilled and Unaware of It: How Difficulties in Recognizing One's Own Incompetence Lead to Inflated Self-Assessments." *Journal of Personality and Social Psychology* 77 (6): 1121–34. doi:10.1037/0022–3514.77.6.1121. PMID 10626367.

Kutner, Michael H., Christopher J. Nachtsheim, John Neter, and William Li. 2005. *Applied Linear Statistical Models.* 5th ed. New York: McGraw-Hill/Irwin.

Laney, Douglas. 2001. "3D Data Management: Controlling Data Volume, Velocity and Variety." Gartner. February 6.

Laney, Douglas. 2012. "The Importance of 'Big Data': A Definition." Gartner. June 21.

Laursen, Gert H. N., and Jesper Thorlund. 2010. *Business Analytics for Managers: Taking Business Intelligence Beyond Reporting.* Hoboken, NJ: John Wiley & Sons.

Lewis, Michael. 2009. "The Man Who Crashed the World." *Vanity Fair.* August.

Lewis, Michael. 2011. *The Big Short: Inside the Doomsday Machine.* New York: W. W. Norton & Company.

Long, Tom "T.J." Scott, and Jeremy Freese. 2005. *Regression Models for Categorical Dependent Variables Using Stata.* 2nd ed. College Station, TX: Stata Press.

Macdonald, Kevin (Director), and Joe Simpson (Author of book). 2003. *Touching the Void.* (Film). FilmFour, UK Film Council, Darlow Smithson Productions, Channel 4, PBS, and UK Film C.

Markopolos, Harry. 2010. *No One Would Listen: A True Financial Thriller.* Hoboken, NJ: John Wiley & Sons.

McDonald, Lawrence G., and Patrick Robinson. 2009. *A Colossal Failure in Common Sense: The Inside Story of the Collapse of Lehman Brothers.* New York: Crown Business/Random House.

Milliken, George A., and Dallas E. Johnson. 1984. *Analysis of Messy Data, Volume I: Designed Experiments.* Belmont, CA: Lifetime Learning Publications.

Mollenhoff, Clark R. 1988. *Atanasoff: Forgotten Father of The Computer.* Ames, IA: Iowa State University Press.

Ott, Lyman R., and Michael T. Longnecker. 2008. *An Introduction to Statistical Methods and Data Analysis.* Pacific Grove, CA: Duxbury Press.

Phillips, Kevin P. 2008. *Bad Money: Reckless Finance, Failed Politics, and the Global Crisis of American Capitalism.* New York: Viking.

Pyzdek, Thomas. 2003. *The Six Sigma Handbook.* Revised and expanded. New York: McGraw-Hill.

Read, Campbell B., N. Balakrishnan, Brani Vidakovic, and Samuel Kotz. 2005. *Encyclopedia of Statistical Sciences.* 2nd ed. Hoboken, NJ: Wiley-Interscience.

Redman, Thomas. 2008. *Data Driven: Profiting from Your Most Important Business Asset.* Boston: HBSP.

Rosenberger, Larry, and John Nash. 2009. *The Deciding Factor.* San Francisco: Jossey-Bass.

Sahrmann, Herman F., Gregory F. Piepel, and John A. Cornell. 1987. "In Search of the Optimum Harvey Wallbanger via Mixture Experiment Techniques." *The American Statistician.* August: 190–194.

Salkind, Neil. 2010. *Encyclopedia of Research Design.* Thousand Oaks, CA: Sage Publications.

Samuelson, Doug. 2006. "The Dance of the Fruit Flies," *ORacle, OR/MS Today,* October.

Scheaffer, Richard L., William Mendenhall, R. Lyman Ott, and Kenneth G. Gerow. 2011. *Elementary Survey Sampling.* 7th ed. Pacific Grove, CA: Duxbury.

Shenk, David. 2007. *The Immortal Game: A History of Chess.* New York: Anchor.

Smith, Martin (Director), and Marcela Gaviria (Director). 2009. *Frontline: The Madoff Affair.* (Film). WGBH-TV (PBS Member Station).

Snedecor, George W., and William G. Cochran. 1989. *Statistical Methods.* 8th ed. Ames, IA: Iowa State University Press.

Sombart, Werner. 1913. *Krieg und Kapitalismus* ("War and Capitalism"). Toronto: University of Toronto Libraries.

Strassler, Robert B. (Editor). 1998. *The Landmark Thucydides: A Comprehensive Guide to the Peloponnesian War.* Trans. Richard Crawley. New York: Free Press.

Weisberg, Sanford. 1985. *Applied Linear Regression.* 2nd ed. New York: John Wiley & Sons.

Wells, Joseph T. 2011. *Corporate Fraud Handbook: Prevention and Detection.* 3rd ed. Hoboken, NJ: John Wiley & Sons.

Zyman, Sergio. 1999. *The End of Marketing as We Know It.* New York: HarperCollins.

Γ Γ Γ

Index

A

ABET (Accreditation Board for Engineering and Technology), 154n.22
Academic training, 146–149
Accelerating analytics capabilities, 133–135
Accounting:
  analytics-based, 46
  unleveraged data in, 73
Accounting fraud, 43–46
Accounting restrictions, 186
Accreditation, 151
Accreditation Board for Engineering and Technology (ABET), 154n.22
Accuracy, 123–124
  balancing reliability and, 196
  for BSP, 8, 9
  of continuous data, 204
  limits on, 221n.10
  measuring, 190
Advocates, 19–21, 84, 86-76. (*See also* Enterprise-Wide Advocates and Mid-Level Advocates)
AIG, 6, 28, 46, 47n.26
AIG Financial Products, 29
Algorithms, 8
Aligned Incentive structures, 18
Allen, Woody, 230
Alpert, Herb, 88
Alpha, 234n.1
American Statistical Association (ASA), 147, 151
Analytics champions (*see* On-topic business analytics leaders (analytics champions))
Analytics phobia, 72
Analytics power users, 85, 89
Analytics practitioners, 84–88 (*See also* Analytics team)
Analytics professionals, 68
  bilingual, 141
  hiring, 134
  reviewing qualifications of, 185–186
  (*See also individual types of professionals*)
Analytics software, 223–234
  for automation, 233–234
  business impact of, 226–228
  efficiency and flexibility of, 232
  fidelity of, 231–232
  functional and technical capabilities of, 229–230
  governance of, 230–231
  maintenance of, 230
  misapplication of, 230–231
  purposes fulfilled by, 223
  review of, 187
  selection criteria for, 228–232
  types of, 223–224

Analytics sponsors, 7
Analytics team, 6–7, 83–112
  analytics power users, 89
  Analytics Professionals, 84–88
  business analysts, 89
  business quants, 88–89
  hiring in a group, 134
  infrastructure for, 90–94
  knowledge workers, 89–90
  leadership for, 95–106
  locations of, 106–112
Analytics training, 77, 141–149
Analytics-based accounting, 46
Analytics-based decision makers:
  in organizational evolution of BA, 87
  role and background of, 85
  training for, 141–144
Analytics-based decision making, 6,
    55–59
  market pressure for, 150
  retrospective on, 115
  speed of, 132
  Statistical Review of, 185–192
Analytics-driven culture, 67–79
  balance in, 76–78
  environments facilitating, 70–74
  evaluating progress toward, 127
  and industry knowledge, 74–79
  and left brain–right brain clash,
    68–69
  myths impeding, 78–79
  plagiarism in, 70
  planning for, 70
Anecdotal sampling, 199, 200,
    206–209
Apple Inc., 59, 60
Applied statistics, 147, 148
Aristophanes, 70
ASA (American Statistical
    Association), 147, 151
The Associates, 41–43, 177

Assumptions:
  in analytics software, 224–225
  parametric, 193n.15
  in testing, 166
  underlying methodologies, 188–189
Atanasoff-Berry Computer, 224
Autocracy, 95, 96
Automation software, 233–234
Ayres, Ian, 62, 63, 75

B

BA (*see* Business analytics)
Baggerly, Keith, 180
Balance, in analytics-driven culture,
    76–78
Banks, 27–34, 72, 73
Banks, Russell, 131
Barrett, Craig, 146
Bartlett's Test, 166
Bear Stearns, 6, 26, 29, 46
Bennis, Warren, 95
Best Statistical Practice (BSP), 8–10,
    137–138
  evaluating execution of, 128, 130
  pillars of, 42
  (*See also individual tools* e.g.,
    Timeliness, Client Expectation,
    Accuracy, Reliability, and Cost)
Bias:
  subjective, 202
  survivorship, 61
Big Bank launches, 63–64
Big Data, 1–2, 4
  and database management, 237
  software tools for, 226
Bilingual analytics professionals, 141
Bilingual leaders, 101, 104
Bilingual teams, 79
Blind Man's Russian Roulette Bluff, 138
Blockbuster, 59
Blocks:

defined, 218
in experiments, 217
Bootstrapping, 162–164
BSP (*see* Best Statistical Practice)
Buffett, Warren, 40, 46n.5
Buñuel, Luis, 157
Business analysts, 10, 89
  on BA team, 7
  on-topic leaders for, 105
  in organizational evolution of BA,
    86, 88
  role and background of, 85
Business analytics (BA), 3–7
  acclimating to use of, 133–135
  combining industry knowledge and,
    52–54, 74–79
  complete business analytics team, 6–7
  defined, 4
  discerning IT and, 5
  evaluating support for, 130–131
  failures due to practices in, 27–40
  focus of, 5
  identifying gaps in, 116
  inefficient use of, 4
  organizational evolution of, 86
  redefining/expanding role of, 18
  skill set for, 5
  strategy needed for, 5–6
  triumphs of, 40–46
Business Analytics Capability chart,
    52–54
Business Analytics leaders, 22–23 (*See
    also* On-topic business analytics
    leaders (analytics champions))
Business Analytics Maturity Model, 131
Business analytics team (*see* Analytics
    team)
Business assumptions tests, 166
Business information needs (*see*
    Information needs)
Business intelligence, 4

Business problems:
  and analytics capabilities, 128–130
  data addressing, 186
  dimensions of, 76
  restrictions on solutions for, 186
  and rigor of analytics, 124, 125
  (*See also* Problem knowledge)
Business quants, 10, 88–89
  on BA team, 7
  certification for, 23, 151
  defined, 88
  in Design of Experiments, 216–217
  in Design of Samples, 210–211
  functional relationship of decision
    makers and, 191
  on-topic leaders for, 105
  in organizational evolution of BA,
    87, 88
  role and background of, 85
  and statistical reviews, 179
  training for, 144–149
Business savvy, 97, 120
Business strategy, for competitive
    advantage, 115

C

CAP (Certified Analytics Professional),
    151
Capabilities, 126–131
  accelerating, 133–135
  in acculturating analytics, 127
  of data software, 226–227
  in decision making, 127
  in executing BSP, 128, 130
  in leading and organizing, 126–127
  in support for analytics, 130–131
  in technical coverage, 127–130
Catalysts for culture change, 71–72
Causality, inferring, 61, 199, 201, 202,
    and 219
Census taking, 198–201, 206

Centralized analytics function, 109–111
Certifications, 150–153
Certified Analytics Professional (CAP), 151
Change, for competitive advantage, 131–135
Chief information officer (CIO), 111
Citibank, 30
Citigroup, 6, 41, 177
C-level leaders, 110–111
Client Expectation (BSP), 8, 9
Communication skills, 97–98, 140–141
Competing on Analytics (Thomas H. Davenport and Jeanne G. Harris), 23, 83, 88
Competitive advantage, 115–135
  assessing business needs, 117–125
  business strategy for, 116
  evaluating capabilities, 126–131
  identifying gaps in analytics, 116
  innovation and change for, 131–135
  intellectual property protection, 116
  internal data sources for, 238–239
Competitive intelligence, 121
Completely randomized design, 219
Composite models, 174n.10
Computers, 223, 224
Confidence intervals, 167, 189
Confirmatory factor analysis, 171
Confounding, 218
Consultants, leveraging, 107–108
Continual improvement, 65n.20, 132–133, 136n.15
Control groups, 143–144
Coombes, Kevin, 180
Corporate culture, 67 (*See also* Analytics-driven culture)
Corporate Fraud Handbook (Joseph T. Wells), 44
Corporations, 17–46
  Delegation in, 24–26
  failures due to poor analytics

  practices in, 27–40
  Fannie Mae's failure, 29–34
  and financial meltdown of 2007-2008, 27–29
  Hierarchical Management Offense in, 18–26
  Incentives in, 26
  Leadership in, 19–23
  pharmaceutical sales, 35–40
  Specialization in, 23
  triumphs of analytics in, 40–46
Cost (BSP), 8, 9
Countrywide Bank, 28–29
Creative destruction, 74, 134
Crisis, as catalyst for culture change, 71
Critical thinking, 55
CRM (Customer Relationship Management), 113n.17, 136n.3
Cross-industry experience, 79, 121
Crossley polls, 208
Cross-validation (*see* Data Splitting)
Cultural imbalance, 76–78
Customer flow, mapping analytics needs and, 117–120, 184–185
Customer needs, 240
Customer Relationship Management (CRM), 113n.17, 136n.3
Customer-centric data management, 239–242

D

Darwin, Charles, 81n.26
Data:
  Big Data, 1–2, 4
  defined, 198
  dirty, 4
  return on investment in, 204
  review of, 186
  types of, 198–202
Data analysis, 5, 6
  assessing appropriateness of methodology for, 187–189

automation of, 233
autopsies on, 9
executing, 57
primary concern in, 77
quality of, 10
reasonable implementation of, 189–190
(*See also* Business analytics [BA])
Data collection, 4, 5, 197–220
anecdotal sampling methodology, 206–209
Design of Experiments, 215–220
Design of Samples, 209–215
expertise in, 120
interval and point estimation, 202–203
measurement error, 205
measuring information, 204–205
observational and censual data, 206
pitfalls with, 197
randomization, 202
return on data investment, 204
review of, 186
Data dictionaries, 243, 245, 246
Data entry software, 242
Data integrity, 186, 240–241
Data management, 237–247
automation of, 233
customer-centric, 239–242
data sources, 238–239
database enhancements, 242–247
information strategy, 238
security, 239
Data mining, 224–226
Data quality, 51, 239, 240
Data quality checks, 165
Data repair, 241–242
Data software (*see* Analytics software)
Data sources, 238–239
Data Splitting, 162, 169–173
Data warehouses, 18, 237, 242
Data warehousing, 2, 4–5, 226
Database encyclopedia, 243, 244

Database enhancements, 242–247
Davenport, Thomas H., 23, 83, 88
David, H. T., 223
De facto data splitting, 171
Decision impairments, 142
Decision makers:
analytics-based, 85
on BA team, 7
building, 51
functional relationship of business quants and, 191
ordinary, 84
in organizational evolution of BA, 86, 87
selecting, 50–51
sophistication of, 72
Decision making, 5, 49–64
analytics-based, 6, 55–59, 141–144
automation of, 234
autopsies on, 9
business analytics team in, 6–7
Delegation of, 24–26
evaluating capabilities for, 127
fact-based, 50–55
impairments in, 59–64
incorporating BA into, 87–88
pace of, 115
quality of, 10
training in, 141–144
Decisive Circle, 103, 113n.20
Delegation, 24–26, 102
Deming, W. Edwards, 61, 102, 107, 110, 114n.34, 131, 136n.16, 157, 177
Densham, Pen, 18
Design of Experiments (DoE), 73, 168, 199, 215–220
Design of Samples vs., 201
experimental designs, 217–220
experimental platforms, 220
observational data vs., 202
quant specialist's role in, 216–217
randomization for, 202

Design of Samples (DoS), 73, 167, 199, 209–215
  anecdotal sampling vs., 200
  census taking vs., 200–201
  Design of Experiments vs., 201
  nonresponse problem in, 212–214
  panels, 215
  post-stratifying on nonresponse, 214–215
  quant specialist's role in, 210–211
  randomization for, 202
  sample design, 211–212
Deterministic Thinking, 61
Diagnostic families, 158, 159
Diagnostics (*see* Statistical Diagnostics)
Directors of advanced analytics:
  skill set for, 95–106
  strengths of, 95
Directors of analytics:
  on BA team, 7
  directors of advanced analytics vs., 95
  on-topic business analytics leaders as, 104
  rigor expected by, 124
Discretizing data, 186
Dispersed analytics teams, 108–109
Distribution-free tests, 166
Documentation:
  reviewing, 191
  software, 230
DoE (*see* Design of Experiments)
DoS (*see* Design of Samples)
Dot-com bubble, 30
Doug Samuelson's Theorem, 158

E

Economic Capital group, 33–34
EDA (exploratory data analysis), 165, 225
Eisenhower, Dwight D., 115

Element, 198
ELs (*see* Expert leaders)
Enron, 43
Enterprise-Wide Advocates, 19–20
  in organizational evolution of BA, 87
  role and background of, 84
Enterprise-wide analytics groups, 109–111
Environments, for analytics-driven cultures, 70–74
ETL (Extraction-Transformation-Loading) tools, 229
EUs (experimental units), 218, 219
Evans, Nathan, 19
Experimental units (EUs), 218, 219
Experimentation (*see* Design of Experiments (DoE))
Expert choice method, 207–208
Expert Leaders (ELs), 19–23, 100–101
  involvement of, 101–102
  on-topic leaders for, 105
  in organizational evolution of BA, 88
  role and background of, 85
  training from, 149
Expertise, in data collection, 120
Exploratory data analysis (EDA), 165, 225
External data sources, 239
External numbers, checking values and results by, 159–160
Extraction-Transformation-Loading (ETL) tools, 229

F

Fact-based decision making, 50–55
Factor analysis, 171
Fair Isaac, 116
Fannie Mae, 6, 29–34, 46

Financial meltdown of 2007-2008, 27–34
Fisher, Ronald A., 215
Fitch Ratings, 6, 28
Focus groups, 208–209
Ford, Henry, 17
Framing business problems, 56–57
Franklin, Benjamin, 249
Fraud, 43–46
Freddie Mac, 6, 29–34, 46
Fuchida, Mitsuo, 67, 74
Functional forms, 187–189

G

Gallup polls, 208
Gaps in analytics, identifying, 115
Gemini myths, 78–79
General Electric, 71
Glass-Steagall Act of 1933, 27–28
Gogtas, Hakan, 43–46
Golden West, 28–29
Graphical user interface (GUI)-based packages, 223–225
The Great Applied Statistics Simulation, 8
Greenspan, Alan, 65n.14
GUI (graphical user interface)-based packages, 223–225

H

Hansen, Morris H., 110
Harrell, Frank, 170
Harris, Jeanne, 23, 83, 88, 100
Hartley, H. O. "HOH," 157, 174n.1
Hierarchical Management Offense (HMO), 18–26
    Delegation in, 24–26
    Incentives in, 26
    Leadership in, 19–23
    Specialization in, 23
Hiring, 134

HMO (*see* Hierarchical Management Offense)
Homer, 55
Hood, John Bell, 19
Horizontal approach to analytics, 93
Housing bubble, 27–29
Hybrid analytics team structure, 112

I

Impact, measurable, 71
Incentives:
    in corporations, 26
    for leadership, 26
    as quality guarantee, 152
    for statistical reviewers, 179
    for teams, 26, 94
Industry experience, 89
Industry knowledge, 5
    and analytics-driven culture, 74–79
    collecting/retaining, 77
    combining business analytics and, 52–54, 74–79
    defined, 49
    general, 74–75
    overdependence on, 62
    specific, 75
    and value of analytics, 134
Industry Knowledge Syndrome, 62
Information Age, 18, 102, 133
Information needs:
    assessing, 117–125
    assigning rigor and deducing resources, 123–125
    new killer applications, 120–121
    process mapping of, 117–121
    scrutinizing inventory of, 120–123
    setting reviews to fit, 181–185
Information quality, timeliness and, 51
    (*See also* Data quality)
Information Renaissance, 18

Information strategy, 238
Information technology (IT), 4–5
    in business intelligence, 4
    discerning BA and, 5
    in the Information Age, 18
Information/disinformation
        overload, 59
INFORMS (Institute for Operations
        Research and the Management
        Sciences), 151
Infrastructure, 195–196
    for analytics team, 90–94
    building, 134–135
    for business quants, 89
    to lower cost of rigor, 125
    for winning in analytics, 249
Innovation, for competitive advantage,
        131–135
Institute for Operations Research
        and the Management Sciences
        (INFORMS), 151
Integration synergies, 91
Intellectual property
        protection, 116
Internal data sources, 238–239
Interpreting analytics, 51, 58, 142–143,
        190–191
Interval estimation, 189, 202–203
Intervals, 166–167
Inventory, scrutinizing, 120–123
Investment banks, 27–34
IT (*see* Information technology)

J
Jackknifing, 162
Juxtaposition:
James W. Hardin, Ph.D., 162–164
    categories of, 160–162
    of data types, 200–202
    by Method, 168–169

K
Kelvin, William Thompson, 197
k-fold cross-validation, 171, 172
Killer apps, 70–71, 120–121
Knowledge workers, 89–90
    accredited professionals' work with,
        151
    on BA team, 7
    role and background of, 85
Kodak, 58–59

L
Laursen, Gert, 116, 237
Leaders (*see* Expert leaders (ELs);
        On-topic business analytics
        leaders (analytics champions))
Leadership, 19–23
    for analytics team, 95–106
    in analytics-based decision making,
        18
    for breakthroughs, 95
    Enterprise-Wide Advocates, 19–20
    evaluating capabilities in, 126
    Expert Leaders, 19–23
    incentives for, 26
    management vs., 96
    Mid-Level Advocates, 19–21
    off-topic and on-topic, 24–25
    On-Topic Business Analytics
        Leaders, 19–22
    Ordinary Managers of Analytics,
        19–22
    in organizational evolution of BA, 86
    and Statistical Qualifications,
        140–141
    training in, 141
Leadership skills, 95–97
Left brain–right brain clash, 68–69
Lehman Brothers, 6, 29, 46
Levene's Test, 166

Leveraging analytics, 18
    failures in, 58–59
    infrastructure for, 17
Leveraging consultants, 107–108
Lift charts, 170
Local analytics groups, 108–109
Locations:
    of analytics team, 106–112
    for BA vs. IT, 5

M

Madoff, Bernie, 65n.14
Maintenance plan, reviewing,
    191–192
Management:
    leadership vs., 96
    managing up, 46n.7
    for specializations, 102
    types of, 103–104
Management skills, 95–97
Manager of analytics, ordinary, 85, 87,
    91–92
Mapping:
    process, 117–121
    for Statistical Review, 184–185
Marketing analytics, 79
Marketing research, 79
Mathematics, 8
Measurable impact, 71
Measurement, 50, 204–205
    functional parts of, 204–205
    of local performance, 109
Measurement error, 205
Mencken, H. L., 60, 62
Menu-driven software packages,
    223–225
Merrill Lynch, 6, 46
Metadata, 242
Mid-Level Advocates, 19–21, 84,
    86–87

Mindset, for Statistical Review, 178–179
Model building, automation for, 233
Model building diagnostics,
    165–166
Model overfitting, 158
Monitoring, 174n.2, 234
Moody's, 6, 28
Mortgage market meltdown, 27–34
Mosteller, Frederick, 27
Multitasking, 91, 92

N

Natural resources, 70–71
Non-analytics managers, 103
Non-parametric tests, 166
Nonrepresentative sampling, 199
Nonresponse (in DoS), 212–214

O

Observational control groups,
    143–144
Observational data, 198, 202, 206
Off-optic professionals, 144–145
Okumiya, Masatake, 67, 74
On-site training, 142
On-topic business analytics leaders
    (analytics champions), 19–22
    advantages of, 102–106
    involvement of, 101–102
    in organizational evolution of BA, 88
    rigor expected by, 124, 125
    role and background of, 85
    training and experience of, 98–100
On-topic training:
    for advanced analytics, 144–149
    for business analytics leaders,
        98–100
    for business quants, 144–149
    as catalyst for culture change, 71
    optimal degree of, 96

Ordinary managers of analytics,
19–22, 91–92
in organizational evolution of BA, 87
role and background of, 85
Organization, evaluating
appropriateness of, 126
Out-of-time validation, 170, 171
Outsourcing analytics, 107–108
Overanalysis, 60
Overconfident Fool Syndrome, 63
Overdependence on industry
knowledge, 62
Overload, information/disinformation,
59
Oversimplification, 61

P

Paired statistical models, 169
Panels, 201, 208-209, 215, 221n.14,
221n.15
Parameter estimation, 189
Parametric assumptions, 193n.15
Pattern recognition, 225–226
Peer pressure, as catalyst for culture
change, 71
Performance measurement tools,
165–166
Permutation Tests, 162
Pharmaceutical sales, 35–40
Pilot studies, 63–64
Pilot Test, 210-211, 216-217, 221n.15
Plagiarism, in analytics-driven
culture, 70
Planning:
for analytics-based decision
making, 115
for analytics-driven culture, 70
Point estimation, 202–203
Political paralysis, 72
Population, 198

Post-academic training, 149
Post-stratifying on nonresponse,
214–215
Potential data, knowledge of, 120
Prediction intervals, 167, 189
Predictive modeling, 73
Problem knowledge:
of business quants, 89
defined, 74
mixing advanced analytics training
with, 91
in scrutinizing inventory, 122
Procedural programming software
packages, 223–225
Process mapping, 117–121
Productivity:
gains with analytics software, 227
and infrastructure improvements,
135
Professional certifications, 150–153
Professionalism, 152–153
Profit, traceable, 71
Programming languages, 223, 225
Proprietary information, 116
PSTAT, 151–152

Q

QC (quality control) charts, 73, 241
Qualifications:
of analytics professionals, 185–186
of reviewers, 179
(*See also* Statistical Qualifications)
Quality:
of collaboration, 184
data, 51, 165, 239, 240
of decision making, 10
incentives guaranteeing, 152
Quality control (QC) charts, 73, 241
Quants (*see* Business quants)
Quota samples, 208

R

Randomization 199-202, 206-207, 217-220, 221n.14.
  for Design of Experiments, 202, 218–219
  for Design of Samples, 202
  restriction on, 219
Randomized block design, 219
Recession of 1989-1992, 30
Recommendations for future enhancements, 192
Redman, Thomas, 23, 43, 64n.5, 83, 238, 240
Regions, 166, 167
Regulatory restrictions, 186
Rejoinders, 192
Reliability, 123–124, 143
  balancing accuracy and, 196
  for BSP, 8, 9
  measuring, 190
  and professional certifications, 150
  review of, 186
  of software, 231–232
Repair, data, 241–242
Reporting:
  automation of, 233–234
  BA and IT in, 5
  by business quants, 89
  in HMO, 18
  for local groups, 109
  in organizational evolution of BA, 86
Representative samples, 200
Resources:
  deducing, 123–124
  restrictions on, 186
  for Statistical Review, 178
Response (dependent variable), 217
Restrictions:
  on randomization, 219

on solutions for business problems, 186
Results monitoring, automation of, 234
Retrospective determinism, 61
Return on data investment, 204
Review:
  capability for, 135
  qualifications/roles of reviewers, 179
  training through, 149
  (See also Statistical Review)
Rigor:
  assessing methodologies for, 187
  assigning, 123–124
  desired level of, 122
Ritchey, Don, 144
Roper polls, 208
Rosenker, Mark, 27

S

Sagan, Carl, 49, 177
Sampling frame, 210
Sampling unit (SU), 209
Samuelson, Doug, 158
Satyam Computer Services, 43
Security issues, 239
Self-monitoring skills, 63
Sequential validation, 171–173
Set of models, 174n.10
Sevareid, Eric, 49
Shillington, Richard, 27
Sibley, Charlotte, 98–99
Simple random sampling (SRS), 211–212
Simulations, 51–52, 164–165, 199–200
Six Sigma, 7, 71, 73, 135
Skill sets:
  for advanced analytics leadership, 95–106
  for BA vs. IT, 5
  of software users, 229

Smothers Brothers, 18
Snedecor, George, 154n.23
Snee, Ronald, 147
Software:
    analytics tool boxes with, 226
    automation, 233–234
    for BA vs. IT, 5
    fidelity of, 227
    upward compatibility of, 232
    user-friendly, 227–228, 232
    (*See also* Analytics software)
Sombart, Werner, 134
Sony, 59
Specialists, delegating decision making
        to, 24–26
Specialization(s):
    on analytics team, 91–93
    in corporations, 23
    management limitation on, 102
Speed:
    acquired through training, 145–146
    for competitive advantage, 132–133,
        135
Spreadsheets, 224
    inappropriate use of, 230–231
    validation of, 232
SRS (simple random sampling),
        211–212
Standard & Poor's, 6, 28
Statistical assumptions tests, 166
Statistical Diagnostics, 157–173
    bootstrapping, 162–164
    business assumptions tests, 166
    Data Splitting, 162, 169–173
    Design of Experiments, 168
    Design of Samples, 167
    diagnostic families, 158, 159
    external numbers, 159–160
    intervals, 166–167
    juxtaposition, 160–162, 168–169

and model overfitting, 158
    performance measurement tools,
        165–166
    regions, 167
    resampling techniques, 162
    reviewing, 190–191
    simulation, 164–165
    statistical assumptions tests, 166
    stress testing, 165
    techniques in, 158–168
Statistical errors, 27–40
    Fannie Mae's failure, 29–34
    and financial meltdown of 2007-
        2008, 27–29
    pharmaceutical sales, 35–40
    and software capabilities,
        227–228
Statistical "mythodologies," 143–144
Statistical Qualifications, 139–153
    advanced analytics training, 144–149
    and corporate capabilities, 130
    and decision-making training,
        141–144
    and leadership/communications
        skills, 140–141
    professional certifications,
        150–153
Statistical Qualifications Diagnostics
        Review (Statistical QDR), 27–40
    (*See also individual components,
        e.g.:* Statistical Diagnostics)
Statistical Review, 133, 177–192
    of analytics-based decision making,
        185–192
    context of, 184–185
    and level of training, 146
    in medicine, 179–181
    mindset for, 178–179
    need for, 179–181
    purpose of, 181–182

reviewer qualifications/roles, 179
  scope of, 181–184
Statistical sampling (*see* Design of
  Samples (DoS))
Statistical software (*see* Analytics
  software)
Statistical techniques, repertoire of, 121
Statistical theory, 147–149
Statistics, 8, 70, 77, 95 (*See also*
  On-topic training)
Stephenson, William, 215
Stochastic processes, 73
Stone, Oliver, 40
Strategy:
  for business analytics, 5–6
  for competitive advantage, 116
  in decision making, 51–52
  information, 238
Stress testing, 165
SU (sampling unit), 209
Subject matter expertise, 99
Subjective bias, 202
Subprime mortgages, 27–34
Super Crunchers (Ian Ayres), 62, 63, 75
Support for analytics, 130–131, 195–196
Survivorship bias, 61
Systematic sampling (Sys), 212

T

Teams:
  bilingual, 79
  incentives for, 26, 94
  (*See also* Analytics team)
Teamwork, 93–94
Technical compatibility, 94
Technical connectivity, 91
Technical coverage, evaluating
  capabilities for, 127–130
Thorlund, Jesper, 116, 237
Thucydides, 144

Tigar, Michael, 3
Timeliness:
  for Best Statistical Practices, 8, 9
  and information quality, 51
  in scope of Statistical Reviews, 184
Toastmasters, 141
Tocqueville, Alexis de, 141
Tolerance intervals, 167, 189
Tom "T.J." Scott., 35–37
Toy analyses, 123
Traceable profit, 71
Training, 9
  academic, 146–149
  in advanced analytics, 144–149
  in analytics, 77
  for analytics-based decision makers,
    141–144
  of business analytics leaders, 98–100
  for business quants, 144–149
  as catalyst for culture change, 71
  in leadership and communication,
    141
  post-academic, 149
  in statistics, 121
  through review, 149
  of whole staff, 135
  (*See also* On-topic training)
Treatments, 217, 218
t-test ceremony, 142, 153n.10
Tunnel thinking, 62–63
Twain, Mark, 8, 152

U

Understanding of business, 120 (*See
  also* Industry knowledge)
Unknown factors, 218
Unnecessary analyses, 123
Unused data analyses, 9
User-friendly software, 227–228, 232
Utility functions, 143

V

Validation (*see* Data Splitting)
Value at risk (VaR), 165
Value diagram, 118, 119
Variable organization, 245–247
Vertical approach to analytics, 91–92
Virtuous analytics cycle, 54

W

Wachovia, 29
Washington Mutual (WAMU), 6,
      28–29

Wasserstein, Ron, 150
Weighting structures,
      187–189
Wells, Joseph T., 44
Wells Fargo, 29
Whitehead, Alfred North, 60
WorldCom, 43
Wright, James, 152
Wynne, Brian, 37–40, 166

Y

Young, David, 103–104

About the Author

Randy Bartlett, Ph.D. is among the rising authorities on Business Analytics. He is currently a Senior Principal with Infosys Technologies Limited, where he leads a growing Business Analytics practice. He has 20+ years of experience in delivering BA, several years of leading analytics teams, and nine years of training: Ph.D. & M.S. Department of Statistics, Texas A&M University; B.S. Computer Science & Statistics, Iowa State University. His first-hand experience includes work at Applied Research Associates (ARA), AHQR (Agency for Healthcare Quality and Research), Astra Zeneca, Bell South, BMS, Fannie Mae, Infosys, Inspire/Merck, JDA Software, NHA (National Highway Administration), Pricewaterhouse Coopers, The Associates/Citigroup, UnitedHealthcare, Wells Fargo, etc. He has worked both sides of the desk: consulting and hiring consultants; and he has a great deal of experience reviewing projects and statistical analyses. He has provided a number of novel statistical solutions in business and holds two patents for predictive modeling. He designed *A Practitioner's Guide to Business Analytics* to be the foremost reference on how corporations can compete on business analytics and in this era of Big Data. He previously contributed to the *Encyclopedia For Research Design.*

9 780071 807593